Missed Opportunities

MISSED OPPORTUNITIES

OPPORTUNITIES

RETHINKING CATHOLIC TRADITION

GABRIEL MORAN

MISSED OPPORTUNITIES
RETHINKING CATHOLIC TRADITION

iUniverse books may be ordered through booksellers or by contacting:

iUniverse
1663 Liberty Drive
Bloomington, IN 47403
www.iuniverse.com
1-800-Authors (1-800-288-4677)

Because of the dynamic nature of the Internet, any web addresses or links contained in this book may have changed since publication and may no longer be valid. The views expressed in this work are solely those of the author and do not necessarily reflect the views of the publisher, and the publisher hereby disclaims any responsibility for them.

Any people depicted in stock imagery provided by Thinkstock are models, and such images are being used for illustrative purposes only. Certain stock imagery © Thinkstock.

ISBN: 978-1-4917-8441-9 (sc)
ISBN: 978-1-4917-8442-6 (hc)
ISBN: 978-1-4917-8440-2 (e)

Library of Congress Control Number: 2015921478

Print information available on the last page.

iUniverse rev. date: 02/18/2016

Contents

Introduction 1
Church Language 4
Sources of Church Doctrines. 7
Papal Glasnost and the Synod 12

Chapter 1: Church Reform 17
The Unfinished Work of Vatican II 18
Reforming Tradition 23
Conservative-Liberal Reform of the Roman Catholic Church 25

Chapter 2: What Is Catholic Church Teaching? 31
To Teach 32
Languages of Teaching 35
How the Roman Catholic Church Teaches 38

Chapter 3: Controlling Birth and Death 44
Nature and Artifice 45
Control of Dying 48
Control of Birth 50
Conclusion 55

Chapter 4: Abortion: Can We Talk? 57
The Changing Context 59
The Roman Catholic Church and Abortion 63

Possibility of Compromise? 68
Conclusion 71

Chapter 5: Death Is Natural, but Human Death Is Not 74
Nature and Catholic Tradition 76
The History of Nature. 77
The Christian Attitude toward the Natural World. 81
Conclusion 85

Chapter 6: Suffering, Pain, and Nonviolence 88
Right to Die?. 89
Suffering and Pain. 92
Hastening Death. 95
Allowing Death to Occur 97

Chapter 7: A Healthy Attitude toward Grief and Mourning . . 103
Public Mourning. 106
Personal/Communal Mourning. 110
The Process of Bereavement. 111
Stages of Mourning. 112

Chapter 8: Gays, Lesbians, and Homosexual Orientation 117
Bases of Official Teaching 119
Roman Catholic Church Documents .124
Sex and Same-Sex Marriage 128
The Synod of 2014–15. 134

Chapter 9: Catholic Tradition and Passive Resistance 136
The Bible and Nonviolence 136
Postbiblical Tradition 139
The Twentieth Century. 142
Individual Leaders. 144

Chapter 10: Revelation: Divine, Not Christian 152
Finding the Question 153
Revelation and Faith 156
Divine Speaking, Human Answering 164
Community 167

Chapter 11: Responsibility, Obligations, Rights. 170
Moral Responsibility 171
Responsible to, Responsible For. 172
Responsibility as Personal/Corporate. 179
Responsibility and Time 182

Chapter 12: Human Rights and Catholic Tradition. 186
Human Rights 187
Natural Rights 191
Catholic Tradition. 192
Seventeenth to Twenty-First Centuries 196

Chapter 13: Catholicism and Environmentalism 199
The Environmental Movement 202
Humanly Unique 206
Humans and Their Environment. 208
Ethics for Men, Women, and Their Kin 211

Chapter 14: Missing in Action: Religious Education 214
Religious Education Movement. 216
Ambiguity of *Education*. 220
Two Meanings of *Religion* 222
The Two Parts of Religious Education. 224
Conclusion 230

Notes 233
Bibliography 251
About the Author. 259
Index 261

Introduction

The title of this book, *Missed Opportunities*, refers to things that might have happened in the Roman Catholic Church but did not. In some cases, the church's official teachers have taken a road with a dead end from which it will be difficult to escape. In other cases, where the Roman Catholic Church could be making an important contribution to society but is not, the failure may or may not be the church's fault, but regardless, it lacks an effective voice. There is no presumption in this book that a minority view in matters of ethics is wrong. But if one is going to take a stand against the position of a large majority, it is imperative to listen to their arguments and to draw from the best resources in one's own tradition.

The subtitle of this book, *Rethinking Catholic Tradition*, indicates the main tension of the book between official positions in the present and other possibilities of the tradition that are dormant. The meaning of tradition is explored in the first chapter. Here I only note that tradition does not have good standing with political and religious reformers, especially in the United States. Progressive and traditional are often presumed to be opposites. But it is the nature of tradition to be the source of change as well as resistance to change. The title's *rethinking tradition* applies to elements within church tradition and to the idea of tradition itself.

As for the term *Catholic*, I use it to distinguish throughout these essays between the Roman Catholic Church and a claim to catholicity. Catholic tradition includes the last five centuries of the Roman Catholic Church and the Christian centuries before then. Ultimately, the term

1

catholic implies what is universally human, such as the concept of human rights. One part of the mission of the Roman Catholic Church could be described as aiming to become genuinely catholic. To approach catholicity, the Roman Catholic Church has to examine what is good and bad in its own history and to engage in dialogue with other traditions that also aim at catholicity.

The following chapters criticize some current doctrines of the Roman Catholic Church. The criticism is not based on opposition to the church but instead is mainly drawn from the church's own long and varied tradition. There is no neat separation between the current church and its tradition. But many of the official teachers in the Roman Catholic Church seem to have a stunted view of their own tradition. This book, while containing objections to some doctrines of the Roman Catholic Church, includes a search with the help of Catholic tradition to find a corrective in those areas.

The groups addressed in this book are, first, Roman Catholics who are saddened that the good things they have experienced in their church seem to be lost among scandals and a collapse of authority; second, people who are not Catholic but who recognize that the Roman Catholic Church still has some wonderfully dedicated people who are doing extraordinary work for healing the world's wounds; and third, the many people who have reacted positively to Pope Francis's signs that the Roman Catholic Church could change for the better.

I owe to the reader an indication of where I am located on this map of outlooks. I am more sad than bitter at what has happened to the church that shaped my life. I am a member of a fast-declining group who were witnesses to the US church during and immediately after World War II and to the apparent stability of the church during the 1950s. On the path that led up to the Second Vatican Council, there were some brilliant and courageous men and women who made preparations for a reform of the church. They worked quietly; some of them lived under a cloud of suspicion or condemnation, but they continued to be devoted to the Roman Catholic Church and Catholic tradition.

The Second Vatican Council seemed to promise that there would be a stronger church after some needed reforms. What no one could see in the first years after the council was that the Roman Catholic Church had shattered into two pieces. One segment believed that the reforms were not up to the urgent needs of the present, and the other segment never accepted the need for any serious reform.

The words on paper from the Second Vatican Council did not bring about fundamental changes in church structure. I had thought that the last action of the council should have been to burn all of its documents so that every bishop would have to go back to his diocese and replicate conversations that had begun in Rome. One important result of those conversations would have been to guarantee that the Third Vatican Council would be a truly ecumenical council of men and women. Instead, the documents became a conclusion rather than a beginning of rethinking the whole Catholic tradition in a way that could involve every member of the church.

In recent years, there has been a debate whether the Second Vatican Council was continuous with the past or a radical break with the past. Both sides of that debate tend to misunderstand the nature of tradition. The way that the question is proposed assumes an image of time as a line in which the present is a point in the middle, the past is behind us, and the future is in front of us. The question posed is whether there was a break in the continuity of the line. In the United States, we are constantly told to forget the past and look to the future. Tradition is a resistance to that linear image, a reminder that the past is not wholly past and that the future is not here for the taking.

Tradition's image is a piling up of human practices. Any attempt to make a radical break with the past will be sunk under the weight of the past. But anyone who wishes to engage in the radical transformation of what exists will find tradition to be an indispensable source of content, inspiration, and caution. The proper attitude toward tradition is neither preservation nor rejection but to rethink the whole tradition with the help of present knowledge.

In his first major document, Pope Francis was surprisingly definitive in saying that the ordination of women is "beyond discussion." That pronouncement was understandably disappointing to many people. But perhaps the discussion should start with this question, Why ordain men? The place of priestly and other ministerial activity in a community needs to be part of the discussion. The Roman Catholic Church has a structural problem in a lack of equality for women. Ordaining women into the present structure would not guarantee the kind of change that is needed for recognizing the equality of women in the church. Whether the present pope fully grasps the extent of this problem remains a question.

Serious attempts to restructure the church would have been easier fifty years ago when reform would not have seemed to be an attempt to shore up a collapsing system. Still, the Roman Catholic Church continues to have enough size, loyalty, vitality, and influence to combine the stability and insights of a long tradition with the flexible organization and worldwide communication that are necessary in the twenty-first century. If democracy is understood to mean a system in which policies and beliefs are determined by majority vote, the Roman Catholic Church cannot be a democracy. But if democracy means a respect for each man and woman, as well as the protection of minority views, the Roman Catholic Church is plainly in need of becoming more democratic.

Church Language

Much of the language that is used in the Roman Catholic Church is unintelligible to outsiders. That is hardly surprising; every large institution develops a way of speaking that is the intimate language of the insider. At some points, however, every institution has to explain things to outsiders. In the case of the church, it often intends to influence the nonchurch world and to attract new members. It would be a sign that the church is not communicating well with the outside world if its own members do not understand many of its important rules and beliefs. Not everyone has to know all of the language of the institution. But the most fundamental beliefs and rules of an institution have to be clearly intelligible to all members.

An exploration of what prevents the church from drawing upon its rich tradition requires examining some key terms that are assumed in church discussions. A rethinking of tradition involves tracing the origin and evolution of terms that can obstruct a view of what reforms are possible. In many cases, a term is traditional, but its meaning today has been narrowed down or distorted in ways that prevent even formulating questions of reform.

The question of language is not a matter of defining a few words at the beginning of a discussion. Institutional reform requires a consistent use of language that concretely and clearly names reality, thereby clearing away abstruse terms that either by design or accident have the effect of obstructing significant change. This entire book is a reflection on language with emphasis upon the way the Roman Catholic Church categorizes its own membership and the linguistic assumptions that church officials make.

The most obvious misuse of church language in the Roman Catholic Church is the use of *church* itself. It is not surprising that church officials slip into using the term *church* when they are in fact referring to the offices, officials, and official policies of the church. It is understandable, though not entirely excusable, that the secular press simply reproduces this language. Most Roman Catholics hardly notice what they take to be shorthand. However, church members who are convinced of the need for reform of the church rebel against officials equating the church with themselves.

In one form of rebellion, some Roman Catholics attack the *institutional church*. That phrase was used by some Protestant churches in the nineteenth century, but it was practically unknown in the Roman Catholic Church until after the Second Vatican Council. The phrase *institutional church* is used by some reformers to distance themselves from bishops or church bureaucracy. But it implies that there is a noninstitutional church to which one can belong. Unless there are changes in its institutional pattern and the language that describes the institution, no church reform can be accomplished.

A central obscurantism of the present church is the term *magisterium*, a Latin word that is used as if it were English. The word originally referred to an office of teaching. Thomas Aquinas referred to the bishops and theologians as each having a magisterium. In the nineteenth century, magisterium was narrowed down to episcopal teaching, and later almost exclusively to papal teaching.[1] The bigger distortion of the term was a shift in the meaning of *the Magisterium* to refer to the bishops themselves. The term simply obstructs questions about who are teachers in the Roman Catholic Church, what do they teach, and how do they teach.

The primary division in the church's structure is said to be between *the hierarchy* and *the faithful. Hierarchy* is an ancient term that was used to describe a sacred order of the cosmos; its original image was concentric circles. Starting in the twelfth century, hierarchy was applied to church structure, and unfortunately it became identified with the image of a pyramid. In the nonchurch world today, hierarchy is almost always understood to refer to a pattern of authority, not to a group of people. So long as the bishops are called the hierarchy, it is impossible to examine the hierarchical pattern of the church and the alternatives to its current form.[2] The faithful logically refers to all the members of the church, but in official uses, it usually refers to the nonofficials.

The Roman Catholic Church describes its members as falling into one of three categories: clergy, religious, and lay. It is language that goes back to the Middle Ages and obstructs thinking about how members might participate in the church. Terms such as *ministerial priesthood, women religious,* and *lay ecclesial ministry* are composed of English words, but they are not intelligible English. Not so long ago, there were thousands of idealistic young people who each year entered a seminary or a novitiate; those places are mostly empty now. There are still a great many young people who would be willing to devote some years of their lives to the great missions of the church, but the church is not set up for them. As the religious orders slowly disappear (the average age of the members is well above seventy), some of them are trying to continue their legacy in new forms of volunteer work within communities of men and women. These new and fragile organizations need some recognition and support. But their members do not fit into a medieval way of speaking.

These examples of obfuscating language are not a random collection. When the description of membership in an institution obscures how the institution functions, the resulting language consists of abstractions that do not name the realities of the institution. It is useless for church reformers to argue about the definitions of *the magisterium, institutional church, ministerial priesthood, woman religious,* or *lay ecclesial ministry.* The only effective strategy is to stop using such terms. After the silence, a simpler, clearer language can eventually emerge.

Sources of Church Doctrines

A theme that runs throughout these chapters is that the current Roman Catholic Church is almost right but is tragically wrong on a range of issues central to human well-being. As the basis for its doctrines, especially its moral teachings, church officials invoke two sources: natural law and revelation. Very seldom is there any attempt to explain or justify these two bases of church authority. The attitude seems to be as follows: *here is the basis of our doctrines; the validity of these two sources has long been established.* My claim in this book is that, while these two sources can give Roman Catholic teaching a solid basis in history and philosophy, neither source as currently invoked makes much sense, and that distortion puts the Roman Catholic Church on the wrong side of many issues.

The first source, natural law, is said by church officials to be available to any reasonable person. Why then does not everyone—or at least any reasonable person of good will—accept these laws that are written in nature? The paradox is obvious: by invoking natural law, the Roman Catholic Church seeks to gain wide support for its teachings; however, for a majority of people, the effect is to drive them away from what might be a sensible position on some public policies.

Today's church teaching that invokes natural law is based on a distorted understanding of the church's own tradition. That tradition does not have answers to today's moral and political issues; there are no answers before one listens to what is known today from a range of studies and from personal experiences. When Cardinal Timothy Dolan in his frequent interviews is asked about various issues, such as gay marriage, his standard response is that church doctrine cannot change because it is based on unchanging truths of natural law. It would be fascinating if a reporter were to ask for an explanation of what that means and whether a list of these truths is available.

The Roman Catholic Church may be right in its defending certain principles that it claims to derive from what is natural to a human being, but principles do not of themselves provide answers to questions of practice.[3] This distinction is at the heart of Thomas Aquinas's treatment of natural law.[4] The move from principle to practice may involve either a short or a long trip. When the journey is brief, the church can jump from principle to practical conclusion without the danger of seriously losing its way. When the journey is long, one has to engage in the complexities of history, science, politics, and interpretation.[5]

Consider what it means to defend life. A protest against the state execution of prisoners (euphemistically called the death penalty) has only one step from principle to practice. The Roman Catholic Church is a severe critic of the United States continuing this barbaric and immoral practice that violates the most basic human right. Concerning state executions, the practical conclusion from the principle can be briefly and emphatically stated: stop it.[6]

When Pope Francis addressed the United States Congress, the statement that received the loudest applause was "The Golden Rule also reminds us of our responsibility to protect and defend human life at every stage of development." Most of the audience were undoubtedly expecting the next sentences to be a strong condemnation of abortion. They were shocked that what immediately followed was a condemnation of capital punishment and a call for its worldwide abolition. The state execution of prisoners is an obvious violation of what the pope referred to as "every human person's inalienable dignity."

In contrast, the church's use of the phrase *right to life* as the only relevant concern in the state's policy on abortion does not admit that there is a range of facts to consider and testimonies to be heard and differences within the church's own tradition that need to be explored. Roman Catholic Church officials declare that there is no room for compromise, no possibility of even beginning a discussion of how to move beyond the present stalemate in the United States. That means that so long as abortion exists, the Roman Catholic Church does not contribute to policies that might make abortions early, rare, and safe. The result is a tragedy for the country.[7]

Because its positions are said to be based on natural law, the church is understandably involved in politics, claiming that its positions should be accepted by all political leaders, whatever their religious convictions. If Roman Catholics believe the teaching on abortion to be true, that should lead them to work for change in the political sphere. If you are a Roman Catholic politician, it is not enough that you profess to accept official teaching on abortion; you must take political stands to change the laws that allow abortion. But on policies regarding abortion, as well as some other issues, the invoking of natural law by church officials is not persuasive to many Roman Catholic legislators and is offensive to many intelligent and open-minded people.

If *natural law* is not entirely convincing for Roman Catholics, then appeal to *revealed law* is brought in as the clincher. It seems strange that church officials usually put the natural law argument first and then bring in revealed truths as a backup.[8] That sequence suggests that any proofs from the "revealed word of God" are often vague and shaky. Otherwise, why not just present the eternal and unchanging revelation of God for the Catholic believer to accept. The embarrassing fact is that answers to today's questions—for example, concerning contraception or homosexuality—are not available by quoting a "revealed truth" from the Bible or from an ecumenical council, although the Bible and two thousand years of church history may have something relevant to offer.

When Roman Catholic Church officials appeal to revealed law or revealed truths, they are working from a truncated, sixteenth-century conception of a divine revelation. In that framework, God's truth is available in a *Christian revelation*, which is an addition to what is known from natural law. The idea of a divine revelation that might challenge assumptions that are built into the modern idea of reason is worth exploring, but it is a task that the Roman Catholic Church has barely begun. A divine revelation is not a collection of truths that the Roman Catholic Church possesses; it is an activity requiring interpretation by religious bodies, including the Roman Catholic Church. In a religious use of *revelation*, the word can only function as a verb, not a noun.

The Second Vatican Council's document on revelation was hailed at the time as a great achievement; it was undoubtedly a big improvement over what had been originally proposed.[9] But its first chapter on revelation itself does not even attempt to explore the intelligibility of the idea. If the council document were understood to be a starting point for discussion of revelation itself, instead of the answer to what revelation is, its scriptural phrases and pious sentiments would not be a problem. But because little intellectual inquiry on revelation itself followed the council, the Roman Catholic Church has an underlying crisis in its intellectual foundation. Until the idea of revelation is confronted, the whole structure of official Roman Catholic Church teaching rests on a shaky foundation.

The elaborate system of church doctrine is protected by a study called theology. It is a strange word that was imported into Christianity from philosophical speculation about the gods. Christians, together with Jews and Muslims, insist that the one who is called god cannot be given a proper name or controlled for human purposes. The term *theology*—talking about God—would not seem appropriate. Other religions sometimes use the term *theology*, but it dominates discussions in the Roman Catholic Church.

Theology is taught in Roman Catholic seminaries as the vehicle for church teaching and carries a stamp of orthodoxy. Theology, used as an academic language to explore the nature of the church and its activities, unavoidably runs into conflict with official doctrines. During the last fifty years, church-related universities have tried to open some academic space by talking about religious studies. Theology, however, still hovers in the background as a control of the academic venture. I do not disparage the writings of men and women who work within the rubric of theology. Some of them have produced brilliant systems that stretch the human mind. The writing of theologians, such as Karl Barth or Karl Rahner, can compete in profundity with anything written in the twentieth century. Nevertheless, theology is not a language for dialogue with the secular culture in which the church exists.

I recognize the need for church theologians to elaborate the system of beliefs that flow from the central doctrines about God, Jesus as the Christ, the Holy Spirit, the sacraments, grace, redemption, and more. Roman Catholic theologians do their work of making these doctrines intelligible to church members while working under the close scrutiny of diocesan and Vatican officials. I sympathize with theologians who are trying out new ways of thinking while remaining loyal to the tradition. This book, however, is not theology, Catholic or otherwise. The book addresses questions of history, philosophy, social science, and education, particularly in areas where the Roman Catholic Church intersects with the surrounding world.

A half century ago, some people around the world began trying to develop an academic field of religious education. It would be a field with a diversity of religious languages (which could include Christian theology) situated within education that extends from birth to old age. I still think that the world needs such an approach to religion (see chapter 14), but the United States and the world are nowhere near engaging religion in this way.

The richness of the Catholic tradition is not found in a series of truths. With the help of the Jewish tradition and spurred by reflection on Jesus of Nazareth, the early church provided hope and consolation to millions of people. The Christian movement began with the announcement "He is risen." A belief in resurrection existed in Jewish tradition as a political doctrine about the triumph of a particular people who were to be a stand-in for all people. The great tragedy of Christianity was its sharp repudiation of the Jewish tradition within which it was born. A distinct Christian tradition was not necessarily a bad idea, but the condemnation of Jewish tradition and the persecution of the Jewish people were unconscionable actions.

The early church was hobbled by its anti-Jewish outlook. Fortunately, it never succeeded in cutting all ties to its deep past. Reforms of the church always go back to the Jewish roots of the Christian movement. Jewish influence on the Catholic tradition includes an affirmation of the body, an emphasis on the communal nature of human life, and a passion for justice in a wounded world. These characteristics are as important today as at any time in the past. At its best, the Catholic tradition still produces millions of admirable lives, people who are at the forefront of resisting the destruction of bodies and communities.

Progress in healing the Western split between Protestant and Roman Catholic Churches has been a necessary step in the retrieval of the best of the Christian tradition. That intra-church dialogue has led to the beginning of Jewish-Christian conversation. The world needs these dialogues within the Christian Churches and between Jews and Christians. And the peace of the world depends on bringing the third sibling, Islam, into a conversation.

Catholic tradition has much to offer in the project of a genuine ecumenical discussion, but the current Roman Catholic Church is so preoccupied with its own internal turmoil that it cannot concentrate on the positive role it might play. The great work that many Roman Catholics do in protesting violence and defending the vulnerable can get obscured. I try to show in several of the following essays that the Catholic tradition could make a valuable contribution even in discussions of sexuality, but that is not where the Roman Catholic Church is today. Even the present pope said that there is a danger of the church being obsessed with a narrow range of moral issues.

Papal Glasnost and the Synod

Some people have likened the moves of Pope Francis to Mikhail Gorbachev's glasnost in the 1980s. There are any number of differences that one can point out between the Roman Catholic Church and the Union of Soviet Socialist Republics. The church has a much longer and richer tradition than did the USSR. And whereas there were few fervent believers in the Soviet system when Gorbachev made a bid to reform the system, Roman Catholicism still has hundreds of millions of people who are the faithful. Still, both systems exhibit the apparent stability of powerful organizations which are held together in a hierarchic pattern of authority that may be more fragile than it appears.

Systems of this kind are practically impossible to change by using the official language within the system. And assaults from outside the system usually have little effect. But the man (usually) at the top of the system, someone like Pope John XXIII, can open a window that sets off unexpected changes. Pope Francis has changed the tone of language that is spoken at the top. The significance of his moves has been less in what he has said than in how he has said it. And many of the changes did not require any language at all. That approach is no doubt the way to begin changing a system that prides itself on its unchangeableness. Not even the pope can simply declare that an important doctrine has been erroneous and will now be reversed. The great ecumenist Pierre Duprey said many years ago, "The pope must be left to make gestures and send messages." From within that papal limitation, Duprey concluded, "The gestures will create a familiarity and when that has been done, one day, the formulas will be able to be accepted."[10]

Pope Francis, at the time of his election, was an unknown even to most Roman Catholics. From his first day in office, he has surprised the world with some simple changes in style and gestures. His enigmatic answers to questions about church doctrine fueled the expectation that big changes were going to happen. He cannot produce what many people expect. If a man supposedly has more than a 70 percent approval rating in a job that usually draws severe criticism, he should perhaps be concerned that many people have misunderstood him. The pope seems to be aware of that problem, but he cannot control the world's news media.

The Roman Catholic Church's great strength is that its long tradition contains such variety that it can draw upon a different strand of that tradition when the necessity of change becomes apparent. The church does not deny its past; instead, it emphasizes something from the past that differs from the current picture. The Vatican once described religious freedom as madness, but eventually the value of religious freedom came to be recognized. Similarly, after a long history of condemning interest on loans, the Vatican set up its own bank. Such a strategy for changing the church may seem fraudulent, and sometimes it is. But given the ambiguity of all language and the variety of contexts in which church teaching has existed, a *near* reversal of doctrine can sometimes be defended.

The church likes to move at a pace at which change can be brought about during decades and centuries. Today's world does not allow for that kind of leisurely movement. The window of opportunity for significant changes is open for a short time, not decades and centuries but months and years. Cardinal Walter Kasper, a key voice for reform, said in a 2014 speech that Pope Francis's plans are "a program for a century or more." That is the way a pope should be thinking, but he still needs parts of that program to be taking effect in the immediate future.

One of the first statements of the pope that caught the public's attention was his answer to a question about gay people. "Who am I to judge?" was part of his reply. It was a great first step in a change of attitude for church officials. However, several people, including a few late-night comedians, came back with the comment that judging is precisely what popes do. They were right. There are other things that popes do, but doctrines are about judging. It is not sufficient for the pope or a bishop to say that they do not judge. They judge every time they simply state a church doctrine. Their job in some areas is to correct inaccurate judgments from the past that are still on the books.

The Synod on the Family's session in 2014 received mixed reviews by the media and by some of the participants themselves. Cardinal Reinhard Marx described it as three steps forward and two steps backward. If one judges the two-week meeting by the high expectations that many people had, the results were disappointing. But if one examines the preliminary documents leading up to the synod meeting itself, the results were surprisingly positive in tone, language, and future possibilities.

In preparation for the meeting, the Vatican had sent out a questionnaire with thirty-eight items that included many on contentious moral issues. The survey confirmed what empirical studies had already shown—namely, that church members, especially younger ones, have views on divorce, abortion, homosexuality, extramarital sex, and contraception that are far distant from official teaching.[11] What are bishops to do if, in response to a question on contraception, more than 90 percent of married church members say, "Yes, we use contraceptives; it would be immoral not to do so." Do the bishops simply shout louder, or do they rethink their position? The strategy of avoiding the question is no longer tenable. The recent silence on this central issue of family life and world population (while leaving the teaching unchanged) is quite shocking.

The results of the questionnaire were summarized in a paper that was prepared for the synod. The contents of that paper did not bode well for what the meeting would discuss.[12] On the one hand, the paper was honest in admitting that the bishops' teachings were not persuasive to great numbers of church members. It admitted that "in a vast majority of responses and observations, the concept of natural law today turns out to be … highly problematic, if not incomprehensible." On the other hand, the paper was unclear about what to do. Should the bishops try harder (having first to figure out for themselves what natural law means), or should they simply jettison the idea? Neither approach would do justice to the church's long tradition. The good news is that the synod seems to have put aside this preparatory paper so that the bishops had an unscripted discussion.

After the first week of the synod, an interim report suggested big changes ("pastoral earthquake at the synod"). The news media seized on a few phrases as indicative of a revolution, particularly its referring to "welcoming homosexuals." The final report's three paragraphs on homosexuality were a big letdown for many people. But the most surprising thing is that a synod on the family discussed homosexuality at all. To understand the significance of what the synod said on homosexuality, one has to put it into the context of the last forty years of statements on homosexuality from the Vatican and the US bishops. I will do that in chapter 8.

The other issue at the synod that produced intense discussion was Holy Communion for divorced and remarried Catholics. In back of that question is the Roman Catholic Church's coming to grips with divorce. The route it will take was signaled by a call for a faster annulment process and "an administrative decision of nullity" by a local bishop. This item in the synod report did not receive much attention. But in September 2015, when Pope Francis directed action to bring about this change, it became headline news. The synod meeting in 2015 affirmed the same position.[13] This new process could mean an end to a Vatican bureaucracy that tries to hide the fact of Catholic divorce.

The ideal of marriage's permanence can and should be maintained by the Roman Catholic Church, but church officials have to admit that some marriages do not work, and others eventually fail. The church could help society rethink marriage not as something made permanent by promises in young adulthood but as a series of stages growing toward permanence. Each stage might have a sacramental blessing, and even divorce could sometimes qualify as a positive step. The synod did acknowledge that in many cultures the church's official view of marriage is not the dominant one and that the church must work with people as they are.

The pope spoke at the end of the meeting and made the remarkable statement that "Personally, I would have been very worried and saddened … if everyone had been in agreement or silent in a false and acquiescent peace." The pope also took the unusual step of thanking the journalists for their coverage of the synod.[14]

Pope Francis has to move from changing the tone of church pronouncements to articulating teachings that are both compatible with the church's long tradition and responsive to the present. The changes cannot be seen as the idiosyncrasies of one man. The pope has to get a major part of the present church population on board and perhaps some of the millions of people who have left the church but who are still interested. No one knows the right pattern to follow. The pope has shown good instincts so far. Many contentious struggles lie ahead.

Chapter 1

∞

Church Reform

In the last few years, there has been a spate of books on the Second Vatican Council. Some people attempt to recapture what they think was the spirit of the council; other people argue that the council did not intend to initiate radical changes. For people who are not old enough to have experienced that moment of history, it is difficult to imagine the surprises and the hopes that swept through the Roman Catholic Church. The surprises that have come from the present pope have stirred up a similar feeling, but many people who put their hopes on the Second Vatican Council fifty years ago cannot avoid feeling some skepticism tending toward cynicism.

If one reads the council documents today, it seems clear that the assembled bishops were struggling with big problems that the Roman Catholic Church was finally trying to face up to. But it is also obvious that the language that they had at hand was inadequate to bring about major reforms of the church. Bishops were not the ideal group for discussing these big questions, but the council was saved by the bishops' experts who in many cases had been studying these questions for decades (and as a result living under a cloud of suspicion).

At the beginning of the 1960s, many people, including bishops, wondered what questions there were for an ecumenical council to address. It seemed that the discussion would be about improving the church's delivery system. The Roman Catholic Church was the sturdy institution that was defending eternal truths in a world that had lost its way. That view remains to this day among some church officials. As one disgruntled member of the synod said, "Doctrine does develop, we understand more deeply, but there are no doctrinal backflips in Catholic history."[1] Doctrines may not have done backflips, but doctrines concerning church practice have certainly changed. The doctrines themselves develop, not just our understanding of them. Now, as well as at the time of the council, the question is, what changes are needed for the church to be true to its past while engaging its current situation?

The first sign at the start of the council that some important changes might actually occur was the rejection of the document entitled "Sources of Revelation." There were bishops from northern European countries and bishops from missionary countries who decided—advised by their experts—that repeating what the Council of Trent had said about the sources of revelation was not adequate for today. They were not sure what should be said, but they knew that the document had to be radically redone. The redoing took three years, and the final document, "The Dogmatic Constitution on Divine Revelation," although a big improvement, was still very inadequate in its treatment of revelation.[2] Nevertheless, the decision to reject a mere restatement of Trent and Vatican I liberated the Second Vatican Council to ask big questions about the nature of the church itself.

The Unfinished Work of Vatican II

Despite differing opinions about which council document was the most important, it can confidently be said that for thinking about the reform of the church, the document on the church itself has a central place.[3] In the council discussion of what became "The Dogmatic Constitution on the Church" (Lumen Gentium), there was a moment when it seemed like a shakeup of the whole church was happening. But there is a single sentence in the document that signaled the council's inability to rethink the nature of church membership.

What caused surprise and raised expectations was the decision of the council to begin the discussion of the church with a description of the whole church. To most church members, that procedure seems pretty obvious. But these were bishops. At the start of the council, the presumption was that, Vatican I having been interrupted after describing the papacy, Vatican II would continue on the same track by describing the episcopacy and moving on from there. By a surprising jump of imagination, the bishops (and their advisors) decided that the whole church should be described first before locating the bishops within the church's structure. Their task in describing the church was to recover some ancient terms that had suffered distortions, eliminate a few terms that were unsalvageable, and shape some new language with the aid of appropriate metaphors. They did try, but the task proved to be impossible within the assumptions governing their language.

In the first chapter, the council chose *mystery* as a way to describe the church. *Mystery* is an ancient term with rich connotations in church history. It connects the church to its central narrative of the life-death-resurrection of Jesus. *Mystery* is not a word with much meaning in the contemporary secular world, except for a problem that cannot or has not yet been solved. That meaning of mystery was not new or necessarily a disqualifying of the term for describing the church. Augustine, in his day, struggled to assert a meaning of mystery not as something unintelligible but something that can always be understood further. The church as mystery was a theological starting point, even if to most outsiders the term was only mystifying.

The second chapter of the document continued the approach of describing the church as a whole. This chapter was called "People of God." That was a phrase that quickly gained a footing in church language. It is still regularly used, although most of the time church officials misuse it. The phrase was meant to include all church members, not the people addressed by church officials. The council's intention in using the phrase is clear enough. They were moving from the language of theological mystery to a description of what constitutes the institution. Starting with "the people" was a good idea. But their use of "the people of God" said both too little and too much. It failed to give any indication of what is the organizing basis of this particular people; at the same time, the phrase comes across to outsiders as arrogant. If the Roman Catholic Church's people are the people of God, where does that leave all the other people?[4]

As a description of the church's peoplehood, something more specific is needed than people of God. The following phrases would be actual descriptions of a church, some of them specifically of the Roman Catholic Church: the people of church, the people of the gospel, the people of Jesus, the people of Christ, the people of baptism, the people of Christian faith, the people of Catholic tradition, or the people of a sacramental world. There are other possibilities, but the point is that "the people of God" was inadequate and destined for failure.

The third chapter entitled the "Hierarchical Structure of the Church" may seem to be in conflict with the previous chapter's people of God. It is true that *people of God* connotes no institutional structure, but that is a problem with *people of God*, not *hierarchical structure*. That is, any large institution has a structure; some people have jobs that others do not; individuals or teams of people report to other people. Some jobs are permanent; other jobs are temporary. An institution has a structure by which decisions occur. For an institution to survive, it has to exercise authority over its activities.

A bureaucratic pyramid is a form of hierarchy that is widely criticized today, especially by the people at the bottom of the pyramid, but even by some people at the top.[5] A pyramid is not an efficient form of organization except for repetitive tasks that do not require much thinking or imagination. A hierarchical structure does not have to consist of one class of people giving orders and another class of people obeying. Devising alternate patterns of organization for political, economic, social, or religious purposes is one of the great challenges of the modern era.

The phrase *flat hierarchy*, which was coined a few decades ago, seems to some people self-contradictory, but the problem with the term is that it describes only a first step. The second step would be to devise patterns of interaction in the institution, most effectively an arrangement of small communities in which power in the institution moves to and from the center, not from the top to the bottom. Hierarchy as concentric circles would be closer to the original cosmic meaning of hierarchy than is the image of a pyramid.[6]

The title of this third chapter includes a note that special attention would be given to the place of the episcopacy *within* the hierarchical structure. One might be skeptical about the bishops locating a place for themselves. Having only bishops talk about the role of the bishop has obvious drawbacks. But surprisingly, they had waited until the third chapter and therefore had a context. Unfortunately, mystery and people of God were not strong enough metaphors to situate the episcopacy in an institutional setting. There was no challenge to the nineteenth-century language that makes the bishops *the hierarchy* instead of one element in the pattern of authority called hierarchy.

The result of that failure appears in the first sentence of the fourth chapter entitled "The Laity." This sentence shows that either the bishops did not mean what they said in the previous three chapters or did not understand what they said. In either case, the sentence signaled the end of any chance of church reform at that time and ever since then. The sentence reads, "Having made clear the functions of the hierarchy, the holy Council is pleased to turn its attention to the state of those faithful Christians who are called the laity." That is, we have finished the chapter on *the hierarchy*, and now we will have one on *the laity*. If they believed what they said in the previous chapters, they might have begun this chapter by saying, "Having treated the episcopal office within the church's hierarchy, we now return to examining the lives and practices of all of the members of the church (including bishops)."

This first sentence of chapter four contains two deadening words, faithful and laity. It is true that *faithful* is a beautiful word when appropriately used. It describes a person's loyalty and trustworthiness. *Faithful* can apply to every member of the Christian Church as well as to people beyond the church. Even people who ridicule the idea of religious faith might lay claim to being faithful, for example, to their marriage partner.

The reason why *the faithful* is a deadening term in documents of the Roman Catholic Church is that it is most often used in contrast to the people who give orders.[7] What is most clear about the faithful is that they are to obey. Obey whom or what? Very often it is said "obey the church," but actually the demand is to obey a rule or a formula of belief put forth by church officials. Because bishops are called the hierarchy in contrast to the faithful, the interesting implication is that the officials are faithless. I am not attacking the idea of the faithful, simply arguing for acknowledgment that church officials can be faithful.

Laity has an entirely different status from *faithful*. There is no reason why the term should exist in a description of the church. John Henry Newman famously said that it would be a foolish church without a laity.[8] It is no longer foolish. *Laity* is not a salvageable term for church use. It remains an important word in the secular world for contrasting the professions and the clientele they serve. The laity are people who lack the knowledge and skill that professionals claim to have. The Christian Church is largely responsible for giving the word *laity* to the modern world, but the church does not need the term.

Originally, as it is often noted, laity simply meant people. The council could have called the second chapter of the document on the church "The Laity of God," but no one seriously considered that. Laity has had for many centuries the meaning of people who lack something. The church is the only big institution that keeps trying to find a positive meaning for laity. It should be clear by now that is never going to happen.

The great scholar Yves Congar wrote a monumental study on the place of the laity in the church. He struggled within the limits of current church language to find a positive meaning of laity in relation to clergy. By the end of the council when the second edition of his book was published, he had decided that the question should be reversed: how to define the clergy in relation to the laity.[9] Congar might have come to the logical conclusion that if the offices of the church are defined within the baptized membership of the church, there is no need for a separate word for those members who do not occupy an official position.

If the split between a clerical class and a laity were eliminated, it would raise questions about the fluidity of various forms of ministering by some members to other members. The pope seems to have opened a wide door in saying, "It would be opportune for all roles of service to have a time limit—there are no lifelong leaders in the Church."[10] For example, might it be worth experimenting with temporary priesthood, a man or woman might serve in that capacity for ten years and then stop. He or she would be a church member before, during, and after serving in the priestly role for a community (no need for "reduction to the lay state"). The present pope has given indications that he views his papacy that way: he will do all he can for a few years and then die or retire. His predecessor's great contribution was making retirement from church office a reality.

The Roman Catholic Church is likely due for more chaos and contentiousness before a new structure can emerge. But the church is seriously in danger of losing generations of educated people who will not play laity in a structure that divides into two classes. The solution for *laity* is not a better definition of the term but simply to stop using it. When there is no group of people called *the hierarchy* and no *laity*, a discussion of church reform can begin.

This proposal is hardly a radical demand. It is simply following through on the Second Vatican Council's aborted attempt to say that if baptism establishes one's full membership in the church, then there is no higher class to aspire to in the church. Whatever titles and offices some members (temporarily) hold, all members are called to serve one another and to present to the larger world a community of brothers and sisters who are dedicated to justice for all people.

Reforming Tradition

Is such a radical change in the language and structure of the Roman Catholic Church compatible with its tradition? First, the changes suggested above are mainly linguistic. They do not constitute a reform package for how to restructure the church. Instead, the purpose of these changes of language would be to open a more fruitful discussion of what changes are both needed in the present and compatible with tradition. Second, any human tradition includes differences and therefore debates about how to preserve the essentials of the tradition in the midst of continuous change. What follows in this chapter does involve proposals of structural reform. All such speculation has to be subjected to vigorous debate. No one person, however learned he or she might be, has a blueprint for how the structure should look.

Some people assume that tradition means that one has to conform to a set way of doing things and that, therefore, any kind of change has to be resisted. The French Revolution set the modern language of political choice: right versus left, conservative versus liberal, progressive versus traditional. The world before the revolution was said to be based on tradition; after the revolution was a new world of progress. Conservatives were those people who advocated conformity to the traditional way; liberals were people who advocated the spread of liberty. From today's perspective, it should be clear that there was diversity and change in the world before the revolution and that the spread of individual liberty after the revolution has been a more complicated process than was first imagined. The assumption that tradition is the enemy of progress needs to be examined.

The idea of tradition was a brilliant invention of the Pharisees in ancient Israel.[11] Instead of attacking the priestly interpretation of the sacred texts, the Pharisees proposed to broaden and strengthen authority. They claimed that there was a second source of authority. In addition to the written tablets given to Moses, there were oral truths that Moses received and that were passed down by word of mouth. The adjective oral would have been redundant as a modifier of tradition until such time as the oral source was itself put into writing.

The image captured in the term *tradition* is a handing over. In a preliterate culture, the idea of tradition might be said to encompass everything that has been handed over from the past. The term *tradition*, however, surfaced at an important moment when the authority of the past was in transition. At the same time, tradition was a liberal and liberating force, a reassertion of a fullness of life that can never be captured in writing.

Although traditions could be put in writing, and in fact they were, tradition retained its power as the context for all writing. Put another way, while *tradition* as a verb is the act of handing on both written and unwritten material from the past, *traditions* is a noun referring to what is produced by and remains from the process of tradition. As often happens in the English language, the verb is nearly swallowed by the noun, and we confuse tradition with the residue left by (the act of) tradition. The human race is in a constant process of reinterpreting the past, or rather reinterpreting as much of the past that is remembered. The discovery of more about the past inevitably leads to rethinking the present.

If history were a straight line of progress, then appeals to the past would be unhelpful and even dangerous. For several centuries, in the Western world there was indeed a general belief in history as a straight line of progress. Somewhere in the twentieth century that fervent belief in the future was undermined. The horrendous world wars did not inspire confidence that the world was getting better every day. But abandoning hope for progress would also be a disaster. In confidently moving into the future, the world "must attempt to see with eyes that are thousands of years old."[12]

Conservative-Liberal Reform of the Roman Catholic Church

Given current usage, it is almost inevitable that people will assume that *conservative* and *liberal* are opposites. A division of thinking into liberal versus conservative does damage to almost all institutions but none more so than religious institutions. Some authors raise a passing complaint about the opposition between liberal and conservative, but then with a reluctant sigh they go right ahead and describe the world that way. If one thinks that an opposition between liberal and conservative is not helpful to understanding institutions, then the most effective strategy is not to abandon either term; what has to be changed is their opposition.

For overcoming a split between liberal and conservative, it is important to start with terms that are descriptive adjectives rather than with ideological abstractions. Conservatism and liberalism are by definition opposed to each other. But if one starts from the verbs *to conserve* and *to liberate*, there is no reason why conservative and liberal have to be opposites. In fact, the only way to conserve what is best in the past is to be liberated from elements that are a threat to continuity with the past. Conversely, the only way to be liberated in the present is to draw from the conserved past.

The Roman Catholic Church is an ideal institution for bringing these attitudes together. The reforms of the Second Vatican Council came about because historians and exegetes dug deep into the past so as to clear away some formulas and practices that were a distraction from the center of Christian life. Pope Francis seems to be trying to follow this route. He has said that "the greatest revolution is what goes to the roots, to recognize them and see what these roots have to say to this time."[13] That process requires an education that respects the past and learns from the past while facing up to the radical changes in today's world. The pope cannot immediately make major changes in church doctrines because the pope has to be both liberal and conservative in his approach to reform.

Reform means a change of form, but a profound change of form requires a knowledge of the entire tradition. For church reformers, a patchwork of biblical and patristic statements will not be conservative enough. The great liberal reformers of the Roman Catholic Church, in the years leading up to the Second Vatican Council, were ardent students of the church's past. Writers such as Yves Congar, Henri De Lubac, M. D. Chenu, Josef Jungmann, Jean Daniélou, Romano Guardini, and dozens of other less-heralded individuals were loyal to the tradition even while they were sometimes accused of being less than orthodox. Some of these people were excluded from the council as too radical, but their influence was felt, whether or not they received credit.

The greatest theologian of the era, Karl Rahner, had been under suspicion since the 1930s. Rahner was deeply conservative. He consistently went deep into the tradition for the basis of proposed reforms. Rahner could brilliantly analyze what might have seemed to be a deadening theological doctrine (for example, that the sacraments work *ex operae operato*) and show how the contemporary church might learn from such a formula instead of either preserving it or just dismissing it.

What would the Roman Catholic Church look like if a liberal-conservative reform were to occur? Such a reform would learn from the Protestant Reformation of the sixteenth century and the missed opportunity of reform in the century that preceded the Reformation. It would also have to rebalance elements of the church that were misconfigured in the nineteenth century. The Second Vatican Council began this process of reform, but it was unavoidably limited by the terms that it had at hand. The synod of 2014–15 seemed to reappropriate the council's atmosphere of freewheeling discussion. Every topic was open to debate, guided by the tradition of the church and today's best available knowledge.

A sympathetic but critical-minded student of the Roman Catholic Church would point out that the church has a problem that is obvious to almost everyone. What is taught as the beliefs of the organization differs widely from the practices of the members. The gap between doctrine and practice is a result of a structural gap in the church. This gap, however, is perceived differently by three groups in the church.

For nonofficial members, the main gap is between church officials and themselves. The Roman Catholic Church has a two-class structure constituted by a professional class called the clergy and a class of members called the laity. Priesthood is identified with the clerical class so that the difference between priest and lay person is the unfortunate gap that most members experience. Overcoming this gap would require eliminating the terms *lay* and *laity*. Office in the church does not have to be identified with a separation of classes in the church.

For a priest in the Roman Catholic Church, the big structural gap is between the bishop and the priest. It is understandable that priests wish to have a vote on the selection of bishops. But so long as the bishops are called the hierarchy, there is no possibility of closing the gap between priest and bishop. Bishops are almost forced into ruling from the top instead of being at the center of discussions with their brother (and sister) priests. Having a vote on who joins the hierarchy would have little effect. But a community in a hierarchic institution choosing its own leaders is one of the most important steps of reform.

Finally, what a bishop sees as the big gap in the Roman Catholic Church is the one between bishops and the pope. The bishop is sole ruler in his diocese, but he often feels that he is a mere cog in an institution ruled from the Vatican. At the top of the church, there is not just the pope but a whole institution surrounding him. The power of the pontiff to do good works is inevitably subject to bureaucratic corruption. Since 1870, the pope (or the Vatican) has occupied an outsized role in the governing of the church.

All three perceptions of a structural gap, by laity and priest, priest and bishop, bishop and pope, are accurate. A new language and imagery would have to address all three perceived gaps at the same time. The biggest problem in reforming a large institution is where to begin. The people at the lowest level of a hierarchical pyramid may have the best sense of what is wrong, but they are not likely to know how to bring about major changes. The people at the top are usually blocked from seeing the full extent of the problem. Even when they genuinely wish to bring about reform, their instruments cannot reach most of the people.

The way major change occurs in big institutions is with small experiments that seldom have permission from the top. The experiments are supported by people who have an imaginative language of reform that draws from the institution's own past. If an experiment can produce an alternate form of life in which the values of the large institution flourish, the lack of permission ceases to be a concern. The reforms that started at Vatican II often used biblical and patristic language. Roman Catholic reform has to struggle against sixteenth- and nineteenth-century language that distorts the longer tradition. Church reformers have to use a clear and simple language that resonates with the church's tradition and its people.

At present, the pope occupies a paradoxical position in church reform. The pope has extraordinary power, but it cannot be used directly for structural reform insofar as the pope's outsized power is a major part of what needs reforming. The pope has to move in the direction of de-absolutizing the papacy, but how is a pope to do that? A necessary step is to work at freeing himself from the Vatican bureaucracy that surrounds him and controls him. Only a clever politician who realizes the power of gesture, style, and symbol can liberate himself from the current surroundings of the office and from aides who are there to protect him (from reality).

The pope can change the understanding of the papacy by acting differently in where he lives, the way he dresses, the way he is addressed, where his office is located, how he gets to work in the morning, who his dinner companions are, and other items, each of which may seem inconsequential but together can fashion a straitjacket, or in this case, the trappings of monarchy. The experiments in church structure together with new language will follow from the pope *not* answering questions and *not* trying to redesign the church. The synod's addressing serious issues in an honest way depends on the *nonintervention* of the pope.

Through a long series of gestures by which the pope refuses to act like the pope, he can eventually find his place with his brother bishops in an episcopal college. The bishop of Rome will continue to have a special role, and the title of pope should be retained for continuity with the tradition. Other bishops should retire by age seventy or seventy-five. The pope should perhaps have a *minimum* age of seventy or seventy-five and be appointed for ten years.

The central authority of the church should be vested in the ecumenical council. This change would fulfill the reform started in the fifteenth century when the Council of Florence had to choose among three claimants to the papacy and necessarily acted as the authority of the church.[14] The fear in modern times has been that the pope's authority might be usurped by a council. The Second Vatican Council struggled with how to balance papal and episcopal authority. If one thinks of the pope and the (other) bishops as competing for legislative power, there is probably no answer. But if the pope is one of the legislators and also has an executive role, there is no inherent conflict between papal and episcopal authority. In a parallel to secular politics, the pope should be imagined more as head of state than head of government. The Catholic Church's state is not the Vatican but the worldwide church. Similar to the presidents of countries such as Ireland or Germany, the pope should speak for all the people.

One of Pope Francis's first actions was to appoint a body of eight cardinals to aid him in the governance of the church. He pointed to this new body as "the beginning of a church with an organization that is not just top-down but also horizontal."[15] He seems to be very aware that a restructuring of the church will take more time than he is likely to have. But he correctly senses that what he can directly do is de-absolutize the papacy and begin creating a collegial structure of church organization. A flat hierarchy with concentric circles of all church members would constitute a mystical body that continues the work of the Christ.

A church whose central authority was a council would preside over a church of councils or communities. These communities would choose their own ministers. The community would sometimes be a parish, which is an organizational unit based on locality. However, for many people today, a local community is not the main communal form in their lives. In today's world, people belong to a diversity of communities, none of which is a perfect example of community. A religious community has to take many forms, and the church would have to be where people live, work, and play. Ideally, a liturgical community would provide a sense of coherence and stability in a world of fast-changing communities, but there is no sure way to produce that.

The church's future lies in many experiments, some of them likely to fail, and a slow emergence of something workable for the pope's hundred-year program. Would this still be the Roman Catholic Church? It would certainly be more catholic or universal. It would have a pope closer to his traditional role than the role he has occupied in the government of the church since 1870. The communal basis of membership would be closer to early Christianity than is the division of the church into administrative units. The church could turn its full attention to its mission of being a light to the nations and the incarnated sentiment for humanity.

Chapter 2

What Is Catholic Church Teaching?

The above question may seem to be a simple one to answer: the doctrines of the Roman Catholic Church have been precisely stated and are available in textbooks that are judged to be orthodox presentations of what is taught by the bishops in association with the pope.[1] Individual Roman Catholics might disagree with one or more of these doctrines, but those people cannot claim to represent the official teaching of the church. The alternatives for the Roman Catholic are clear: believe or leave.

The fundamental problem that I explore in this chapter is the equating of teaching with doctrine. It is true that the English word *doctrine* is derived from the word *teaching*. Doctrinal formulas are undeniably a form of teaching, but the verb *to teach* and the object of what is taught are far richer in meaning than what is captured by the term *doctrine*. When discussing the teaching of the Roman Catholic Church, it is important to start at the beginning with the act of teaching rather than with attempts to capture what is taught in spoken or written formulas.

The *act* of teaching obviously precedes something described as *a teaching*. Surprisingly, there is very little literature that tries to answer the question, what does it mean to teach someone something?[2] Modern society suffers from an absence of reflection on the activity of teaching. Teaching is a fundamental act of every human being (and some nonhuman beings).

The Roman Catholic Church, therefore, is not the institution that is mainly at fault here. In fact, the church in its long tradition can point the way to a recovery of the many forms of teaching that are used every day. Unfortunately, on this point the church is too much in conformity with the surrounding world. The church unwisely subscribes to modern meanings of teach, teacher, and teaching rather than affirming the much richer meanings of these terms that are present in Catholic tradition.

To Teach

The secular world's narrow meaning of teaching is traceable in large part to the rise of school systems, starting in the richer parts of the world and spreading almost everywhere. No doubt schools have been a great advance for the human race; individual lives are immeasurably enriched by what school courses can provide. In parts of the world that lack schools, people are understandably desirous of being able to better their lives by school credentials, which are a ticket of entrance to the modern world.

A side effect of the great success of schools has been the identification of teaching with the form of teaching that is done by teachers in schools. The paucity of writing on the meaning of the verb to teach seems to stem from an assumption that everyone knows what teaching is, that it is the activity of people who are school teachers. When *teach* is used in other contexts, it is thought to be a metaphorical extension of *real* teaching done by an adult at the front of a classroom with a group of young students. Even parents, who are obviously the main teachers of their children, are typically referred to within the phrase *parents and teachers*.

The second main source for the narrow meaning of teaching is that philosophers and writers on education have been scandalously neglectful of how infants and young children learn. Philosophers throughout history have not begun with the infant's experience.[3] Modern psychology has produced valuable studies on infant learning, but that material has not been integrated into philosophy or most of educational theory.[4]

On the meaning of *to teach*, the philosophy of education has little to say about infants and young children. A human infant is born with almost unlimited possibilities but almost no instincts or skills. The capacity to take in the whole world is the source of the human's greatest strength and its greatest vulnerability.[5] Everything not given at birth has to be learned, and the infant can only learn if it is taught by other humans, by animals, and by its physical surroundings.[6] The infant's ability to absorb lessons that are taught is fantastic. The teachers for the most part are not aware that they are teaching; they interact with the infant, and they show the tiny creature what is needed to survive in a complex and dangerous world.

Based on the way that *teach* has been used by most people in history, a realistic meaning of the verb to teach is *to show someone how to do something*. Teacher and learner include every human being and many nonhuman beings. Clearly, nonhuman animals teach their own kind as well as provide lessons for humans. In fact, because intention is not a necessary element in teaching, anything in the whole world is a potential teacher. But the someone who is the recipient of teaching has to have a capacity for learning. One can teach a dog, a horse, or a dolphin, but, as far as we can determine, a plant does not learn from being shown how to do something.

Three insights about teaching can be drawn from the teaching-learning of infants. First, teaching is a communal activity; a community demonstrates a way of living. One person or a group can represent the community. Biology establishes that the primary teacher is nearly always the mother. Without a mother or a substitute for the mother, the infant would not survive. However, from the first moments of life, there are other humans and nonhumans who represent a larger community of teachers.

A second insight to be drawn from the teaching of infants is that most teaching is nonverbal. The infant does not learn its lessons by being told things. Teaching starts with physical gestures, such as an affectionate embrace or a bedtime ritual.[7] Adults tend to talk to the infant long before it is capable of speech; that adult instinct is well placed. The adult receives clear signals that the infant is responding to what the adult says. The infant smiles, swings its arms, pushes away food, cries, and otherwise shows its agreement or disagreement with its adult teachers.

Third, when language is introduced, the first words are best used as direct commands. Teaching an infant is mainly showing the child how to perform physical actions; the showing is accompanied by commands. The tone and rhythm of the language are more important than the meaning of the words. At some point, the child does begin to grasp the meaning of a few words—"open your mouth," "hold on," "move your foot"—that are immediately translatable into doing something with the body insofar as the infant can control its bodily movements.

The fact that a young child has to be given precise directions to habituate its actions leads to a common but unwise contrast between *to train* and *to teach*. There is no reason why the word *teaching* should not include training. In fact, nearly all teaching includes training, the mastering of routines. The term *instruction* is used for the precise directions that a small child's training requires. Interestingly, the word *instruction* returns for the most sophisticated teaching when *academic instruction* aims at the precise use of language.

When training and teaching are opposed, teaching becomes a rationalistic activity of trying to convey knowledge by telling people what they should know. And the training of a human being (or an animal) becomes a mindless set of practices instead of including the learner's responses and the teacher responding to the learner's responses.[8]

The great storehouse of wisdom embodied in language slowly opens for a young child as it reacts to whatever language is spoken by the people in its surroundings. The capacity for language is innate, but language has to be spoken by the parents and a wide community of speakers; then the child can respond to phrases that accompany physical activities.

As for the object of teaching, the more particular the object is the more likely successful is the teaching-learning. At the beginning, putting a nipple or a spoon into the mouth can be shown by a simple physical gesture accompanied by the word *open*. With the acquiring of language, teaching-learning can be more complex, but it still needs particularity. If one is learning to get dressed, to use a computer, to cook, to swim, to ski, to drive a car, the learner needs from the teacher a series of executable commands: do this, then do that, do that again, then do this ... [9]

To teach is to show someone how to live. And since living eventually includes dying, then teaching can most comprehensively be described as teaching someone how to live and how to die. Religions have recognized that if someone does not know how to die, then he or she cannot learn how to live. Most ancient and medieval philosophies were aware of this connection, but modern philosophy has tried to avoid the connection between teaching and dying. As a result, teaching is reduced to giving people rational explanations. The modern flight from death is reflected in the flight from teaching.

The great teachers of how to die are dying people.[10] And because everyone is dying, anyone can find himself or herself in the role of being such a teacher. There are instances of young children who are affected by a fatal disease and become stellar teachers of the people in their surroundings. Generally, it is the aged who are the teachers of how to accept life that is inclusive of death. One of the most neglected groups of teachers is grandparents. A young child or a teenager often has a close bond to a grandparent, someone who represents the maturity of human life. The death of a grandparent can be a very traumatic event for a child or a teenager. Being shown how to manage grief at that moment is a big step in a young person coming to grips with what life offers.

Languages of Teaching

At the beginning of life, teaching by means of language is impossible. *Infant* means one who cannot speak. In a matter of months, however, the infant recognizes that there is a mysterious power in the sounds uttered by its caregivers. The small child begins to imitate these sounds before knowing what words mean. The grown-ups do not have to invent some kind of child-speak. The young child is impelled to join the conversation and use whatever phrases are at hand. The child does not begin by learning the meaning of words; the child imitates the sounds associated with physical actions and is able somewhat mysteriously to put the sounds into a structure of language.

I will describe three families of languages for the activity of teaching. Each of these three families includes three languages in its scope. These languages can provide a generalized account of how human beings should act, although the teaching is still tied to particular conditions of location and time, as well as a focus on the particular recipients of the teaching. The first family is called rhetorical; it consists of languages that are used with an object in view toward which teaching is directed.

Storytelling. Human beings have always been storytellers. Every child begins to make sense of the world from the stories heard in the crib. Some of those stories are told in nighttime rituals in which a parent reads from a book or recounts a tale. What the child is learning from these stories is not clear since many of the words are not comprehended by the child, and yet the child pleads for some of these stories to be told over and over. In school, the child learns elaborate stories called science and reads classic stories judged to be literature. Great stories teach people throughout their lives how to be a good human being.

Preaching. The second language in this directive family of languages is preaching. The teacher as preacher uses emotion-laden words to push for action in the lives of the hearers. Despite the bad name that preaching commonly has, it is a practical necessity in many situations. Parents, who before they were parents swore they would never preach, find themselves giving sermons to their misbehaving children. Preaching needs some strict specifications for its exercise to be effective: who the audience is, the basis of the message preached, the length of the sermon, and the tone of voice.

Lecturing. The third language in this family is lecturing, which is the use of a rationally organized set of ideas to convince an audience of the truth of what is said. The lecturer's attitude is not "this is my personal belief, and I urge you to follow me" but instead "this has been established as true, and my aim is to help you to understand it." In practice, any effective lecturer makes use of stories, humor, and occasional brief sermons to keep an audience engaged with the rational content of the lecture.

The second family of teaching languages is called therapeutic. These languages are a necessary complement to the rhetorical languages; their purpose is not to move the hearers to action but to restore the will to act. This family has paired languages because of a mutual relation in which teacher and learner easily switch roles.

Welcome/Thank. The infant begins by welcoming in the universe, and throughout life we are called to open ourselves to what the universe offers. A human being who has a welcoming attitude toward life as a whole is likely to treat kindly and with respect each human being. Especially when human beings are different or have a disability that can set them apart, they need to be welcomed by gesture and word. Welcoming is complemented by an attitude of gratitude, which is expressed in the ritual "thank you."

Confessing/Forgiving. When there has been a disruption in the positive relation of welcome-thank, human beings need a ritual of confessing-forgiving. Forgiving one's enemies is the way to make them no longer enemies. A person or a nation that can confess their faults and ask forgiveness teach the world the need to restore what is broken. The power to forgive is in the hands of the one who has been wronged. Forgiveness does not come easily. It should be the result of bringing the whole self into line with the formula of forgiving.

Mourn/Comfort. The relation mourn/comfort has to be learned early in life and has to accompany us to the very end of life. *To comfort* means to bring strength. When the death of a loved one occurs, no words are adequate. Friends comfort mainly by being there. The roles can sometimes switch; the one who comes to comfort may be in need of comfort. Few teachers are as powerful as a dying person and the realization that we are all members of one another.

The third family of languages, the conversational, draws from the first two but moves to a level just above them. The body is not left behind, but language is the central reality that is drawn upon and reflected upon. The conversation is talk about talk itself.

Dramatic performance. A play can tell a story or a play can be therapeutic, but great drama transcends categories to teach life itself. A play has a written text from which the actors work, but the play only exists as it is performed. Actors feed off the reaction in the audience; each performance therefore differs although the same words might be spoken. Great actors challenge an audience to think about what a play is and what a peculiar experience it is to be the recipient of the actor's passionate production of a world inside a world.

Debate. In a genuine debate, the ambiguities of language become evident, and a listener grasps that the truth is not easily expressed in words. The debaters highlight the fact that while truth has many sides, we can by means of civil discourse move closer to agreement on many points. The problem today is that what is called debate is usually two people (or a string of presidential candidates) arguing for their version of the truth without any interest in learning from their opponent.

Academic Criticism. The form of teaching that is most appropriate for the classroom is a questioning of what the students already know. The student has to come to class with some knowledge of the subject that has been acquired beforehand. The teacher's first task is to listen to the student's words and ask, "What do those words mean?" Then the student's task is to reflect on what the teacher proposes as an improvement of the student's formulation of the truth. This academic procedure may sound suitable only for university courses, but it can be as effective—sometimes more so—in the second or third grade. What is often dismissed as merely academic can transform a person's whole life.

How the Roman Catholic Church Teaches

For the meaning of *church teaching,* a first and crucial distinction is one between teaching that is intended for members of the church and teaching that is for the world at large. If officially appointed church teachers fail to make this elementary distinction, the teaching of church members will lack a needed specificity, and outsiders will at times be offended by church teaching.

The great strength of the Roman Catholic Church is that it has in its tradition all three families of languages—nine languages of teaching— that it can use.[11] But the unfortunate reality is that church officials seem almost completely oblivious of all but one language of teaching— namely, preaching. People do not get converted by preaching; they are converted by other forms of teaching that prepare them to be receptive to preaching.

Most teaching is communal and nonverbal. The main way that the Christian Churches attract members is by the activities of the church in the public sphere and by the example of individual Christian lives. One of Pope Benedict XVI's most insightful comments was that the church ultimately has only two proofs: it has produced great art and great saints. Neither art nor saintly lives have the intention of teaching. Teaching is often more effective when it is not intended. If a local church runs a food pantry that serves poor people, the activity is the teaching. The intention of the work should be to feed people; sermons should not accompany the bread.

Pope Francis has said that "when you want to know *what* the Church teaches, you go to the Magisterium ... but if you want to know *how* the Church teaches, you go to the faithful people."[12] That contrast is a strong vote of confidence in the lives of Christian people as central to the church's teaching. It is usually possible in teaching situations to distinguish between what is taught and how it is taught. Ultimately, however, the what and the how are not separable. If the lives of church members teach, then what they teach is at least as significant to the outside world as what bishops (the Magisterium) say.

Therapeutic Teaching. In a sacramental church, the therapeutic family of languages takes precedence over the rhetorical. The first language of Christian teaching is welcome/thank. A Christian attitude of thanksgiving for all the gifts of creation underlies an attitude of welcome to fellow Christians and to all members of the human community. Not surprisingly the central act of worship for Roman Catholics is called Eucharist, which means thanksgiving. A Eucharistic attitude has to move to and from the liturgical meal of thanksgiving.

Liturgical assemblies should be welcoming bodies that make each participant feel at home. Protestant churches have usually done a better job at conveying a sense of welcomed participation. The congregation is the teacher, and every member is a learner. Liturgical assemblies are designed for believers, and the action cannot be transparently meaningful for anyone else who happens to be there. Nevertheless, what is done and said in the liturgy should be tested by whether it respects any outsiders who are present and does not make them feel like aliens.

A second therapeutic language for church teaching is confessing/forgiving. The Roman Catholic Church has a long history of rituals for its members to confess their sins. Less developed is a practice of the church confessing its faults to the larger world. The Roman Catholic Church has a sacrament of penance that seems to have largely fallen into disuse. That is too bad because there remains a human need to ask forgiveness of those we have harmed by our failures. Some efforts have been made to create a new form for the sacrament of penance, but a radical change in church structure is needed first. It has always been said that confession is to God and that the priest is not the one who forgives; he is the representative of the church. There is no reason why a parent, a friend, or a trained therapist could not play the role of church representative. Some experiments in facilitating confessing/forgiving are needed lest the church lose its historic connection with this universal language.

As for confessing/forgiving directed beyond the church, there is a need for simply acknowledging that in its long history the church has sometimes failed to be a beacon of justice. A triumphal church, a church that claims to be God's work, has a difficult time accepting its faults and asking forgiveness by individuals and groups that have been harmed by actions of the church. An incarnational or sacramental church needs to accept its human side with its human faults. A confessing/forgiving attitude is especially important in interreligious dialogue. Thankfully, the leaders of major religious groups have increasingly spoken for tolerance, respect, and cooperation among religions. Christians and Muslims have plenty of confessing and forgiving to do before they can convince a skeptical secular world that they are agents of peace.

The third therapeutic language of mourning/comforting is an area where the Roman Catholic Church has excelled. For its own members, the church has had an elaborate ritual of death, burial, and bereavement. Some of that ritual may need reform, but what surrounds death does not change much over time. Children still grieve for their parents, even if the children are in their fifties; parents are still devastated by the death of a child of theirs; spouses in a long-term marriage are bereft when the first one dies. An excellent development in the funeral liturgy has been a friend or relative providing the homily (while the priest should keep quiet). None of the other languages of teaching will work unless there is a ritual that gives comfort to the grief-stricken. The church is often the one institution on the scene that can provide fellow mourners who know how to comfort. For example, a parish is a likely setting for a widow/widowers group; a professional may help, but women and men who have experienced the death of a loved one are experts in their own way.

Toward the outside world the Roman Catholic Church could bring to bear on public tragedies its realistic perception of life and death. The Internet and its accompanying social media have been transforming the way that death is publicly acknowledged and the dead are remembered. Despite a long-standing tendency in this country to deny the value of ritual, and to skip a period of bereavement, death does not go away, nor does the need for comfort lessen. The church can be a leader in showing how to mourn and how to comfort.

Rhetorical Teaching. Among the rhetorical languages, storytelling has priority for church teaching. The life of the Catholic is shaped by the example of others, by participation in liturgy, and by immersion into the story that the Bible tells. Historically, there was first a basic story, *good news* about the one who became known as the Christ. In the context of early liturgy, especially the Eucharistic meal, more details were added to the story. It did not take long for questions to arise about the behavior of Jesus's followers. Early written documents, such as the First Letter to the Thessalonians, are examples of a form of teaching that today would be called moral instruction. Paul, the early convert, elaborated the Christian story in fruitful tension with his knowledge of Jewish history.

Eventually the gospel narrative was put into writing. It may seem surprising that the early church did not decide to get its story straight and blend the three synoptic gospels into one consistent narrative. And later the church even added a fourth gospel with a very different tone and content. Of course, if the aim were doctrinal orthodoxy, then only one formula would be acceptable. But if the point of the gospel is to tell a story, then it is quite understandable that there be several versions with a variety of emphases. When the gospel is read in the Sunday liturgy, the point is not that this doctrine has to be believed but here is a great story to be listened to once more.

The second rhetorical language in the church is preaching, which is illustrated by the Sunday sermon. Its place in the Eucharistic service indicates that it should be a reflection—perhaps for about five minutes—on the story that has just been heard. The purpose of preaching in the liturgy and at other times is to draw some practical implications for the hearers. The preacher, whether in politics, religion, or advertising, does not preach beliefs; the preacher's task is to assume the beliefs of the hearers and urge the implied consequences of the beliefs.

For the preaching to church members, there is plenty of material from the Bible and other church sources that can be included. In contrast, the church preaching to the nonchurch world has severely limited possibilities. What universal beliefs can be assumed? The language has to be mainly secular, and the object of the preaching has to be what these days is called human rights violations. The Roman Catholic Church has a right and a duty to denounce the execution of prisoners, the waging of war, environmental destruction, and the starvation of children.

Conversational Teaching. The third family of teaching languages in the church is the conversational. It includes dramatic performance in which all the senses are touched by actors who engage an audience. The Second Vatican Council recommended a "noble simplicity" for the liturgy.[13] The emphasis was rightly on simplicity and getting rid of centuries of dead rituals. Dramatic performance can have a simple and artistic elegance. Internally, well-performed liturgy is a powerful teacher of church members. Externally, the need is for simple gestures of openness to all peoples. For example, the papacy, even with its checkered history, is still without comparison in its possibility of world teaching through symbols and gestures.

Good artistic production links the liturgy to service to the needy. Art transforms the soul and awakens the realization that we are members of a single human community. The liturgy in most parishes does not measure up well relative to its potential. The music, for example, remains depressing or absent in most local churches. That is not surprising if music is thought of as a disposable extra instead of a main teacher of the congregation. The lack of appreciation of artists, including musicians and architects, left the modern church with some bad art. Church members who have some artistic talent have to be encouraged and not be censored when they contribute something controversial. Church leaders, like many politicians, prefer art that is nice, meaning art that is banal and simply an instrument for moralizing.

Academic criticism is the final language in the third family of teaching languages, and it is the language most appropriate for the classroom. The academic question is, what do the words mean? In a classroom, every official doctrine—whether political or religious—should be subjected to questioning. If a group is not willing to question its orthodoxy, it should not be running a school. All orthodoxies are corrupting unless they are challenged by drama, debate, and scholarship.

The purpose of a church history course, whether in elementary school or the university, is not to glorify the institution's past but to discover what is in the past. An open-minded searcher will discover many things worthy of admiration and find inspiration for the future. However, searching for the truth includes an openness to finding what may not be admirable at all. Genuine reform in the present requires understanding the past in its complexity. Church officials need to trust in the value of their own tradition and encourage debate, criticism, and the arts. A variety of teaching is needed to keep healthy and honest a church of orthodox beliefs.

When other forms of teaching besides preaching are neglected, then preaching becomes corrupted. Few educational terms are as negative as indoctrination. People who indoctrinate are usually shocked at being accused of doing so; they deny that they intend to indoctrinate. But if doctrine is the sole object of the teaching and the learner has no way to opt out of the teaching, then that form of teaching is preaching, and that preaching is indoctrination.[14] The way to avoid indoctrination in church practice is to include the rhetorical languages of storytelling and lecturing, the conversational languages of dramatic performance and academic criticism, and the full range of therapeutic languages. If the Roman Catholic Church is to flourish, it has to recover in its tradition all the languages of teaching.

Chapter 3

Controlling Birth and Death

For setting the direction of this book, I compare what the Roman Catholic Church has advocated about the beginning of life to its teaching and practice about the end of life. The answers to today's complicated questions about the use of science and technology for supporting human life cannot be found in documents from many centuries ago. However, if there is a nature that distinguishes humans from other beings, a few principles will still hold true. Despite the absence of accurate scientific knowledge in the past, there may be some insights about human birth and human death that are worth attending to. Catholic tradition would be one source along with many other religious and philosophical traditions.

Other chapters in this book consider birth and death separately. But if there are principles that apply to human life as a whole, then there might be grounds for comparing birth and death. Or, to make a stronger claim, comparing birth and death might be a good way to reveal principles that apply to life as a whole. The following material tilts toward an emphasis on birth, an area where the Roman Catholic Church is accused of being opposed to humane and needed public policies. My argument here is that Roman Catholic Church officials made a tragic mistake about the control of birth. On the basis of its own tradition, the Roman Catholic Church could have taken a different route. A comparison to how it did respond to new situations in the care of the dying suggests the path that might have been taken in relation to birth.

Nature and Artifice

At the center of this chapter and many of the chapters to follow is the meaning of *nature*. In other chapters, I explore the history of the term and how its various meanings might be related. Here I work with a single contrast between nature and artifice (the making of art). The human relation between nature and artifice is terribly confused by the language that we speak. The human is not simply one case of a collection of natures nor one part of a single overarching nature. Human-nature, while not *a part* of nature, also does not exist *apart* from nature. In Catholic tradition there is a fruitful tension between the human and nature; that relation is what constitutes a person. I indicate this tension by consistently writing *human-nature*. This use of a hyphen is not just idiosyncratic; it is an attempt to capture the idea that the person, while not contradicting nature, is not subordinate to nature.

It is the nature of the humans to be makers of art. The human race has always used artifice to make life better or at least less painful. Birth and death are obvious places in human experience that have been in need of artifice. Humans have created artificial helps to exercise some control over birth and dying but always with the risk that intervention in nature's processes can get out of control.

In using its arts, the humans have to be careful not to do violence to their own nature. The artificial is intended to be a help to human beings, and most of the time mechanical things start out that way. They relieve some humans of burdens that no longer need to be carried. Later generations marvel at how earlier people got along without flush toilets, washing machines, airplanes, automobiles, antibiotics, or smart phones. But what might not be noticed is that each invention carries a possible drawback. The flush toilet is an inefficient piece of technology that needs replacement. An airplane makes travel more convenient for some people but at an enormous cost to the physical environment. Preservatives in food can cause health problems. Antibiotics always do collateral damage to the body. An artifice that is destructive of the natural is properly called unnatural, a contradiction of natural processes.

In the Middle Ages, the primary meaning of nature was a particular kind of living being; each living thing was thought to have its own nature, for example, equine, canine, or feline. In the seventeenth century, nature shifted in its primary meaning to the object that confronts human beings and needs to be conquered with the help of scientific and mechanical artifice. As usually happens, the earlier meanings of nature did not disappear, a fact that leads to endless controversies. When people speak today of what is natural, it is often unclear whether they mean natural as opposed to artificial or whether they mean humanly natural, which includes what is artificial.

Confusion about the relation between nature and artifice may seem like an abstruse philosophical problem, but understanding this issue is actually a matter of life and death. Public discussions about contraception, abortion, and birth control are entangled in a terrible confusion of language. Similarly, public discussions about dying—to the extent that there are any discussions at all—are shrouded in bad arguments and secret practices.

The standard dichotomy of pro-life versus pro-choice in discussion of abortion exemplifies the confusion. No one is opposed to all life, but all human beings make distinctions between different kinds of life, including a belief when an individual human life has begun and when a human life has reached its conclusion. No one is against human choice, but all human beings recognize that some choices are good while other choices are bad or likely to have bad side effects. In questions of birth and death, the best ethical guideline is to work out the tension between nature and human-nature in a way that avoids the unnatural, the hallmark of which is violence. If violence is unavoidable, then an ethical person has to act in a way that lessens or minimizes the violence.

My interest here is in tracing the Roman Catholic Church's involvement during the last century in the areas of the beginning and the end of human life. If the church had seen these two areas as similar, it might have gone a different route in its decisions about the beginning of life. In the area of birth, however, the question was not only about life but about sex, an area in which church leaders badly misunderstood the question.

It is regularly said that the church is against "artificial birth control," but that is a redundant phrase. Every human intervention in the birth process is artificial—that is, a human refashioning of a natural process. The moral issue is not artificial birth control but unnatural birth control. Are the means used a violent contradiction of human-nature?

The Roman Catholic Church recognized in the 1930s that control of birth was needed.[1] At the level of world population and in the case of individual family size, it was evident that nature did not automatically provide for the modern needs of human-nature. In their role as responsible guardians of creation, humans are called upon to use their knowledge, skill, and art to regulate birth. Roman Catholic Church officials unfortunately started from a cramped view of human sexuality. At least implicitly, sexual pleasure was still treated as a reward for the willingness to have babies. Not only was sexual activity to be limited to married couples, but even they had to allow that every act of intercourse was open to pregnancy. It is not surprising but is nonetheless tragic that after the 1930s the church's leaders did not pursue effective and nonviolent ways to control pregnancy.

The year 1958 was the crucial moment for rethinking Roman Catholic teaching on both birth and death. That year was the beginning of a positive role for Catholic tradition in the contemporary situation of the dying. At the same time, regarding questions about the beginning of life, there was an opening that was not pursued. Attention to what science and medicine were doing might have led to thinking anew about conception and the control of birth. In the areas of both birth and death, there was a question about the relation between the natural and the artificial. There is room for debate about how they are related in particular cases. The starting point, however, is that the two are not inherently opposed. It is obvious that some artifice has been an improvement in human life; it is just as obvious that some artifice has turned out to have had deleterious effects.

Few people would be aware of two documents published in 1958 by Pope Pius XII. One document spoke about legitimate reasons for removing a respirator from a dying patient, and the other document was about the legitimate use of the pill that came to be called the birth control pill, or simply *the* pill. In both cases, this very conservative pope was ahead of the curve.

In the 1950s, the era of contemporary medicine was only at its beginning.[2] Most people had no idea of technology's ability to prolong a person's dying almost indefinitely. The pope showed remarkable prescience in addressing the issue directly. As for the pill, the pope was two years ahead of the FDA's approval of Enovid as a pill that allowed women to control pregnancy. Pope Pius XII approved its use in 1958 to treat hormonal disorders. He was aware that indirectly it would prevent fertilization and conception. The pope was not endorsing the use of the pill to control conception; it would have taken a leap of imagination to integrate that use of the pill into existing church teaching. Nonetheless, Pope Pius XII had taken a helpful step in the Roman Catholic Church's rethinking of the place of artifice in the human control of life and death.

Control of Dying

On the use of artifice at the end of life, Catholic tradition asserted that a person has a duty and a right to *ordinary* means, in contrast to *extraordinary* means, in the service of life. A distinction between ordinary and extraordinary *things* can be misleading today. Instead of some objects being ordinary and others extraordinary, the important distinction is between actions that humanly make sense in a particular situation and actions that no longer make sense. A Vatican document in 1980 introduced the helpful distinction between proportionate and disproportionate means in the use of medical interventions.[3] Human beings have a right to care from the human community; that right includes provision of air to breathe, food to eat, water to drink, basic medical care, and physical security. Denying a person those needed goods is an attack on human-nature.

Modern medicine has routinely provided many helps that have extended the average life span by several decades. Medicines that would have once seemed miraculous may now be accepted as ordinary. There remain complicated questions about which treatments make sense for a particular patient at a particular time. Questions regularly arise—for example, whether performing a particular surgery makes sense, whether putting a chemical into the body is the right thing to do, and whether using a respirator for a particular patient is an appropriate (proportional) use of technology. These are questions that require decisions by informed patients, or their proxies, and competent health care professionals.

It has become a cliché that death is natural. However, while death is natural, human death is not. Human death is more than natural: it is historical, social, artistic, religious, and artificial. We prolong our lives every day by artificial means. A seat belt in a car is an artificial means; a prescribed drug is an artificial means; washing one's hands is an artificial means. The problem is not the use of artificial means to extend life but a determination of what is an unnatural prolongation of dying. "It is unnatural," Pope Pius XII said, "to prevent death in instances where there is no hope of recovery."

In the hospice movement, the ideal was not natural death. A liberal drug policy is often helpful for a person moving toward death, but hospices generally excluded some technology that interferes with a humane form of death. In hospitals today, the use of artificial means to provide nutrition to the body is a fairly common procedure. But the inability to eat can be a sign that the body is shutting down in preparation for death. If the artificial substitute for eating no longer makes sense and is discontinued, the patient is not starved to death; instead, the body's dying has run its course.

The decision to remove life support mechanisms involves reflecting on the relation between the person's nature and the artifacts of modern medicine The main reasons for removing a respirator are medical, the lack of any hope that a person can recover a place in the human community. Surprisingly, Pope Pius XII included an economic reason. Continuing to pour tens of thousands of dollars into treatment that is not working can ruin a family's chance for a decent life. The pope surely knew the danger of appearing to say that people should be allowed to die if it is too expensive to keep them alive. But the pope was acknowledging that economics is unavoidably involved in decisions about living and dying.

Many secular writers today bundle together euthanasia and abortion, and then they pronounce that the Roman Catholic Church is the main obstacle to humane policies concerning birth and death. The critics are often unaware of church doctrine and the actual practice in the care of the dying. In many of the famous cases in the United States, the Roman Catholic Church has been a participant on the side of humane treatment that allows a person to die.

The church continues to resist the idea of giving over to a physician or anyone else the power to kill. The line between killing and allowing death to occur is sometimes blurred, but in most cases it is clear. When there is doubt about allowing death to occur, then there has to be a consulting in which the patient (if possible), the family or a loved one, and the medical professionals decide on the best route available. When the ethical difference between killing and letting die is dismissed, people are sometimes accused of being murderers after they have tearfully accepted the death of a loved one.[4]

Control of Birth

On the issue of the control of birth, the Roman Catholic Church began to recognize the need when it approved what was called the rhythm method in 1936. From that point onward, the question for the Roman Catholic Church should have been what methods are in accord with human-nature and which methods do violence to human-nature. By acknowledging the need for birth control but refusing to encourage more effective means to such control, the Roman Catholic Church created for itself an impossible situation.

Before the twentieth century, the need was for large families; children were an economic blessing. In addition, almost half of children did not make it beyond infancy. Starting about 1900, world population began growing almost exponentially. There is a desperate need to control the number of births; the need is greatest in the poorer parts of the world, most dramatically in Africa. The big questions are, how is population to be controlled, and by whom?

Similar to death, sex is natural, but human sexuality is not; it is historical, imaginative, artistic, ethical, and religious. The sexual practices of humans are an artificial transformation of animal biology. The human race will be the poorer if all connection between sexual activity and the beginning of human life is ever entirely severed. But the human race discovered at an early stage what every teenager discovers—namely, that sexual activity is a pleasure, an important part of life that needs integration with the rest of life.

When the Roman Catholic Church recognized the need for the control of birth, it looked for a way to protect the integrity of sexual activity. An avoidance of unnatural intrusions into the sexual life of people is an important principle. However, the church accepted that sexual intimacy was a good in itself that could be distinguished from an activity that might lead to pregnancy. The rhythm method included the express intention by a married couple of engaging in sexual intercourse while avoiding pregnancy. The main difference between that method of controlling birth and the use of condoms is that condoms are more effective. But condoms, while they do not do violence to the body, are a primitive technology. They do not aid the expression of love, and they have a significant rate of failure. If Roman Catholic officials had been more imaginative, they could have joined the call for better artifice to regulate pregnancy.

On May 11, 1960, the Federal Drug Administration announced approval of the birth control pill. One of the main persons associated with the project was Dr. John Rock, a devout and conservative Roman Catholic. He was determined to convince church leaders that this pill was their way out of their increasingly indefensible position. Rock insisted that the pill was "an adjunct to nature," that it worked by extending the "safe period," a method recognized by the church. He was wrong about exactly how the pill worked, but he had the right principle that the church could have lived with and worked with.[5]

The church missed the opportunity to rethink its past teaching. Since the church had accepted the need for birth control and the pope had said that the pill did not violate human-nature, the pill would seem to have been acceptable. Of course it is artificial, but that is irrelevant.

If the church's main concern had been violence to the reproductive system of women, it might have been attentive to medical research and supported women's demands for a safer pill for women (or men)—that is, a pill clearly in nonviolent accord with the human body. The Roman Catholic Church could have staked a claim that it was defending life, including the integrity of sexual relations. In the 1970s, there was an explosive reaction against the pill when women found that its side effects had been hidden from them. Fifty percent of women stopped taking the pill during the 1970s. But by that time, the church had removed itself from any debate about improving the means of contraception.

In the church's tradition that was reaffirmed by the papal encyclical in the 1930s, marriage was said to have two ends. The primary end is the procreation and education of children. The secondary end is the expression of love between the partners. The Second Vatican Council altered that teaching by doing away with a hierarchy of ends. That equalizing of the ends of marriage opened the door to further change, but the council was not able to go further in revising official teaching on marriage and sex. That was left to a papal commission.

In 1963, Pope Paul VI appointed a committee to advise him on the issue of birth control. The committee had several meetings that were not publicized, but a decisive meeting in 1966 produced a document that advised the pope on the need for change. Important church figures, such as Cardinal Leo Joseph Suenens, theologian Bernard Häring, and the patriarch of Antioch, Maximos IV Saigh, had recognized the inadequacy of the official teaching on birth control.

Still, when the pope loaded the final commission with fifteen cardinals and bishops who were not likely to challenge any doctrine, no advocacy of a major change seemed likely. But three months of spirited discussion changed minds. The two women on the commission, Colette Potvin from Canada and Patricia Crowley from the United States, brought a needed perspective of married Catholic women.[6] A single document, "Responsible Parenthood," approved by nearly all the members, recognized the need for the church's official teaching to change.

The commission's work, however, was undermined by a group led by Cardinal Alfredo Ottaviani. As a result, Pope Paul VI rejected the committee document and its proposal for change. In his 1968 encyclical, *Humanae Vitae,* the pope tried to incorporate a more personalist kind of philosophy, but a decisive passage declared that "each and every marriage act must remain open to the transmission of life."[7] The principle makes no sense. It is based on a remnant of medieval biology together with an unwillingness to accept sexual activity as a good, even if it is a good that requires discipline in one's life. The principle of open to conception when applied to a married couple in their sixties is obviously a fiction. If sixty-year-olds can choose to express their love sexually without a connection to pregnancy, why cannot thirty-year-olds?

Humanae Vitae was a disaster. One of the few things that liberals and conservatives in the church agree upon is that the encyclical split the church.[8] On one side, there was instantaneous objection by many Roman Catholic theologians, and on the other side, defenders of the encyclical made acceptance of it a chief test of orthodoxy. Millions of Roman Catholics were not interested in fighting; they simply voted with their feet.

Millions of other Roman Catholics maintained that they were loyal members of the church while at the same time they were following their consciences in rejecting the papal teaching. Those Roman Catholics were not what was labeled "cafeteria Catholics," people described as choosing the doctrines that they liked from a menu of offerings. On the contrary, they were claiming that responsibly controlling birth was a more accurate following of Catholic tradition at its best than the pope's distorted vision of human sexuality.

With the intense reaction to *Humanae Vitae,* the bishops and the pope seemed to redraw a line of defense around abortion. That was especially true in the United States after *Roe v. Wade* in 1973. Many bishops and moral theologians in the 1960s had unwisely tied together birth control and abortion. Birth control had to be stopped, it was said, or abortion would be next. It was a terrible premise to assume that birth control and abortion should be condemned on the same basis. In fact, encouraging the use of nonviolent forms of birth control is one of the most effective ways to oppose abortion, which could be called a violent form of birth control.

Whereas the control of birth is a moral necessity, abortion represents moral failure. No one thinks abortion is good; nearly everyone thinks it is bad. Nationwide, three out of ten pregnancies end in abortion; in New York City, four out of ten do. This is a national problem that needs to be addressed. A consensus exists about many of the needed steps to reduce abortions, but not much is being done other than to put obstacles in the path of those women who have decided to have an abortion.

Since the 1970s, there seemed to be a tacit agreement in the Roman Catholic Church not to make a public fuss about "artificial contraception." Roman Catholics decided either to move out or else to stay in the church while quietly following their consciences on sexual matters. There was little inclination to denounce birth control from the pulpit. Suddenly in 2012 it was as if the previous forty years had not happened. The issue of contraception was suddenly in play when Rick Santorum, speaking of contraception like a 1950s Catholic, managed to get his Republican competitors for the presidential nomination to take up the cause.

Then the Obama administration unfortunately unleashed a whole new discussion. A federal rule on insurance coverage for contraceptives exempted churches but not institutions that are church-related. Since similar laws already existed in twenty-eight states, the White House probably gave little thought to possible negative reaction. If at that moment the issue of contraception had not just remerged after forty years of near silence, the reaction might have been limited to the raising of a few questions followed by some quiet adjusting.

Republicans in the House of Representatives and on the campaign trail pounced on this unlikely issue. The question, they claimed, was not just contraceptives but an attack on religious liberty. The claim was that the White House had opened war on the Roman Catholic Church, religion, and the God-given liberty of every American. The Catholic bishops seemed happy to have an issue on which to reassert their authority. Every poll warned them that they had no chance on this issue, especially with the fertile part of the Roman Catholic population.

The Obama administration immediately backed off and offered a compromise that might save face for both the White House and church officials. But at that point, compromise was unacceptable. And so the bishops aligned themselves with the political far right's opposition to extending health care to all citizens. That may qualify as pro-life to some people, but it was not a support of the lives of millions of people who lacked health insurance.

In the US Supreme Court's decision of 2014, *Burwell v. Hobby Lobby*, the court sided with the claim that the religious liberty of the corporation was violated because it had to provide particular means of contraception to its employees. The grounds for the claim was the owners' religious beliefs concerning abortion.[9] The discussion in the news media blurred the difference between contraception and abortion. The US bishops did not seem to mind that confusion. The bishops joined in celebrating the defense of religious liberty, but no one knows where that decision may eventually lead.

Conclusion

On the whole, Catholic tradition has been on the side of protecting human beings against intrusions of technology that are violent. It would be tragic for society to lose that perspective due to the distorted picture of sexuality that is held by many church officials. Eventually, church officials are going to have to come to terms with reality, including the practices of their own members. Those officials had seemed to take a first step by being silent for a while. The next step might have been a few distinctions that acknowledge the acceptability of some contraceptive practices besides the rhythm method. The church could have turned its attention to protesting truly horrendous violations of human-nature. There is no shortage of such cases.

One of Pope Francis's worst slips of the tongue—one that he quickly apologized for—was he said that there is a mistaken idea that "in order to be good Catholics, we have to be like rabbits." In addition to being a crude metaphor, it was especially offensive in referring to Catholics who were following church teaching. Like other popes, Pope

Francis recommended responsible parenting, adding that "God gives you methods to be responsible." The plural of the word *methods* in his statement is puzzling because Roman Catholic Church officials have been unyielding in saying that only one method is allowable, what they call "natural family planning." Millions of Catholic parents have concluded that responsible parenting can include other methods that do no violence to human-nature.

When Pope Francis was asked about the encyclical *Humanae Vitae* and contraception, he replied, "The question is not that of changing the doctrine but of going deeper and making pastoral ministry take into account the situations and that which is possible for people to do."[10] That enigmatic statement perhaps suggests the way that the doctrine will be changed without a Vatican admission of error. The Synod of the Family in 2014 followed the pope's lead in recommending that "we should return to the message of the encyclical, *Humanae Vitae*, which highlights the need to respect the dignity of the person in the moral evaluation of the methods of regulating births."[11] That is quite a creative reading of the encyclical's "highlights." Such an approach to the encyclical might work, but with the glare of today's media, a more forthright admission of a needed correction of the encyclical's highlights might be in order.[12]

Pope Francis's environmental message in *Laudato si* is undermined to some degree by a sidestepping of the birth control issue. The pope says that as a response to poverty and economic inequality, "some can only propose a reduction in the birth rate."[13] There may be a problem in outsiders to Africa trusting in the mass distribution of condoms as a solution to poverty, but a great many people think birth control is an indispensable part of any solution. The pope is on firm ground in condemning consumerism and the waste of food. He also has a strong basis for criticizing the ineffectiveness of national and international bodies to address world poverty and "imbalances in population density." But it is also the case that the Roman Catholic Church has to do a better job than it has so far in getting out of the corner in which it has painted itself by not recognizing the human control of birth as a main challenge of this era.

Chapter 4

∞

Abortion: Can We Talk?

T he first two sentences that anyone uses about abortion will be enough to get him or her classified. The classification is done by the news media and by spokespersons who are not interested in a conversation that might lead somewhere. Questions about abortion deserve a national conversation that would involve debate, acknowledgment of uncertainty, and willingness to compromise. No such conversation has occurred in this country. A US conversation also needs an international context, but, as often happens, the United States is not interested in learning from the experience of other countries, such as Denmark, Germany, France, and Italy.[1]

The strangest aspect of this rigid division into two camps is that it does not reflect the views of the vast majority of the public. Opinion polls for decades have shown that people have a range of views about abortion that do not fit on either side of the classification.[2] Nationwide polls consistently show that people are no more pro-choice than pro-life when asked to choose a label. More detailed questions yield similar results. And women are no more in favor of "abortion rights" than men. "Abortion is not heading in either party's direction," says Andrew Kohut of the Pew Research Center.[3]

It could be that people are just confused and not thinking logically. It seems more likely that people are uncertain about something where uncertainty is called for. Their answers reflect the best compromises that they can come up with, given that they are not getting much help from their political, religious, and scientific leaders.

This chapter is not directly about abortion; it is about the language in which the practice called abortion is discussed. Because people want answers to questions, they are often impatient with questioning the question. But if one cannot ask a useful question, one cannot get a useful answer. The word *useful* here means an answer that will at least advance a conversation.

A first needed comment is about dividing any issue into two sides and assuming that one side is called x and the other side is called y. Wherever there are intense disagreements, the description of the conflict as x versus y is almost certainly a large part of the problem.[4] This deadlock can arise in various ways. It is sometimes the result of a genuine but inaccurate effort to describe a controversy in an unbiased way. Especially in moral matters, any terms that are employed will carry an historic bias. When there is a complaint about the unfairness of either the x or the y in the description, the answer is not likely to be found by simply substituting a synonym to replace x or y.

Sometimes the description of x versus y has been chosen by people who call themselves x. They may say that the description is unbiased, and possibly they believe what they are saying. However, in an area of sharp disagreement, it is almost impossible that one side in the dispute can be trusted with a description of what the dispute is about. When people who call themselves x call other people y, and when y lacks an understanding of what is happening or does not have the power to resist the imposition of terms, y has already lost the dispute. People called y may continue to snipe at x, but the resulting situation cannot be called a debate.

The way out of an intense moral dispute can only come from reconstituting the terms for debate. Who can do that? The immediate inclination is to seek an impartial observer. But on profound issues there may not be anyone who is impartial. Instead, a more promising possibility is to find a bipartisan umpire, someone who can see that neither x nor y is the answer but that both x and y are affirming something valuable in the disputed area. The answer therefore is both x and y.

However, when people say that the answer to a question is not either/or but both/and, they usually just restate the disagreement. The need is to recognize that while people called x and their opponents called y may each be affirming something worthwhile, their language conceals and distorts the truth. They may or may not be conscious of that fact. In intense debates, people tend to think that the meanings of the words they are using are obvious, but any important words in the language are ambiguous in meaning.

The first step in trying to open a real debate is by responding to the question "Are you x or y?" with the answer "w," which means both/neither. Lest that answer seem to be just a captious avoidance of the issue, the task is to show that w is a complex description that accepts neither x nor y as stated but also does not oppose much of what x and y are intending to affirm. That answer will be unsatisfying to many people because it cannot be put into the form of a slogan.

The first point about abortion, one of the main points, is that there can be no useful discussion of abortion so long as the language of pro-life versus pro-choice is used. This assertion would not bother some people because they are not interested in having a useful discussion. They already know what the truth is and what public policy should be. Many people, however, feel uneasy about aspects of this question and are ambivalent about their own views. This chapter is for people who are not absolutely certain of their position.

There may be aspects of abortion that are reducible to two sides, but immediately reducing the whole question to two sides aborts the discussion. As for naming the two sides, the terms *pro-life* and *pro-choice* are misleading names that prove the point about the present absence of conversation. While each group can make its case for *life* or *choice*, the two abstractions hide where they disagree. Is anyone against life? Is anyone against choice? Perhaps somebody somewhere is. But for discussing abortion, the claim to be in favor of life or in favor of choice tells us nothing.

The Changing Context

Until the nineteenth century there was leniency toward a practice that was believed to be morally wrong but could not be entirely eliminated. A major change occurred in the nineteenth century with the emergence of the medical profession. In the United States, the physicians, with the support of evangelical Protestants, passed a series of strict laws outlawing abortion. The Roman Catholic Church was not much heard from. "Nineteenth-century abortion laws were by no means passed in response to Catholic concerns. If anything, they were passed in response to feelings *against* Catholics, in particular their higher fertility rates."[5]

The practice of abortion was not eliminated by the anti-abortion laws. A secret vernacular existed for conveying to women that medicines that were supposedly for other ailments were in fact for causing abortion. A remedy might actually warn that it should not be taken when a woman is pregnant. Names such as Uterine Regulator and Samaritan's Gift for Females were widely and legally available.[6] The law got too far in front of a hoped-for progress in eliminating abortion. So long as abortion is perceived as necessary by millions of people, a law simply declaring abortion to be illegal is not going to stop the practice.

The male physicians who constituted the medical profession asserted that they were the competent authority for the "therapeutic exceptions" to the new laws outlawing abortion.[7] Between 1890 and 1950, physicians performed abortions for a variety of reasons. There was very little public outcry about the discrepancies between the law and medical practice. Women had the choice either of submitting to the physician's judgment or of inventing their own means when they believed abortion was needed. As usual, the rich had access to safe means, and the poor suffered from dangerous home remedies.

In the 1950s, there was a growing uneasiness among physicians who tried to establish boards of review for decisions about abortion. In the 1960s, abortion began to be openly discussed, and there were movements at the state level to decriminalize the practice. As the feminist movement emerged, the political and social significance of abortion became an issue. The invention of the birth control pill and its approval in 1960 changed the dynamics of birth control. The balance of power to control pregnancy and birth shifted from men toward women. Many women felt that for the first time they were in control of their lives. The world of the professions began to be transformed by the presence of large numbers of women.

Improvements in contraceptive devices greatly reduced but did not eliminate unwanted pregnancies. For women whose main work was motherhood, the addition of an unexpected child would very often be manageable although 60 percent of women who have abortions are mothers. For professional women, unwanted pregnancies could be an obstacle to their advancement at work and their sense of personal identity. The attitude toward abortion became a chief marker for how women imagine the nature of womanhood. This split among women that began in the 1960s has continued to the present and shows no sign of going away.

Nearly everyone agrees that a decision by the United States Supreme Court was a key moment in the history of abortion. In the United States, nine people have immense power to decide if something is legal. These nine people are supposed to rise above passing controversies and say what is consistent with previous laws. Several recent decisions have led women to call into question the Supreme Court's impartiality on issues affecting women. Unlike the 1960s, women are now represented on the court, although they often represent a dissenting minority.

The famous case of *Roe v. Wade* was not the court's worst decision; it was just its usual confused mess when it tries to deal with religion or emotionally charged moral issues. In back of the court's decision was the good intention of finally acknowledging abortion as a legal and moral question. But the court could not have said anything that would settle the matter of abortion.

If the court had been candid about its inadequacy to even discuss the problem, it could have said the following: "Abortion has always been practiced and no doubt will continue to be common until the human race gets serious about better ways to control birth. Abortion raises moral issues for which this court is clueless. Legally, there are two main questions: Who decides about having an abortion? What is the best way to carry out abortions?"

The answer to the first question should be obvious: the woman who is pregnant. Ideally, the man who is responsible should be involved in the process of deciding, but that often does not happen. And because the woman usually needs medical advice and medical assistance, the answer to the second question is that abortion should be performed as early and as safely as possible. Facilities and competent people for that purpose have to be readily accessible to both the rich and the poor. Abortion is both a private and a public issue.

In the court's decision, William Douglas was the only justice to give primacy to the woman's right to choose abortion. Justice Harry Blackmun, who did refer to the "woman's decision whether or not to terminate her pregnancy," used as his central premise that "the abortion decision in all its aspects is inherently a medical decision, and basic responsibility for it must rest with the physician." *Roe v. Wade* tried to shore up the authority of the physician but had the effect of undermining it. As the women's movement exerted its power, subsequent court decisions shifted the focus to the right of the woman to decide about abortion.[8] There could have been a helpful discussion about making abortion infrequent, safe, and available. No such conversation has ever occurred.

People who continued to say that all abortions are immoral had a strong case. Abortion, as the term indicates, is negative; it refers to ending a process that has begun within the body. The body itself frequently aborts the process, but a deliberate intervention is morally problematic. The human race should be trying to get rid of the practice of abortion as far as possible; until that is accomplished, it should try to reduce any violence in abortion practices to a minimum. The Supreme Court decision could have been understood as supportive of people who are morally concerned about abortion.

Instead of working to reduce the number of abortions and to make abortions safer, the most vocal moral critics spent their energies uselessly denouncing the Supreme Court, as if a reversal of *Roe v. Wade* would morally improve anything. Evangelical Protestants fought against abortion in the nineteenth century because of their fear that Roman Catholics would soon "possess New England." In the twentieth century, Evangelicals and Roman Catholics became strange bedfellows in opposing abortion.

The Roman Catholic Church and Abortion

It is well known that the Roman Catholic Church is an unyielding opponent of abortion. At least the official doctrine of the church admits of no qualifications or grounds for compromise. The exact number of Catholic women who have had abortions is impossible to determine. The attitude of Catholics toward abortion is different from the general public but not as much as bishops would like.

While people who are not Catholic may be expecting some modification of the church's position by the present pope, he has not suggested any change of doctrine in his direct comments on the issue. At a speech before an Italian anti-abortion group, Pope Francis quoted the Second Vatican Council's words that "abortion and infanticide are unspeakable crimes."

When the pope warned church officials about having too narrow a range of moral concerns, he was not playing down abortion. He wanted only to situate abortion in the context of what Cardinal Joseph Bernardin called a "consistent ethic of life." Many Catholic groups are admirable in their opposition to all forms of violence. A group such as Consistent Life describes itself as part of the "antiviolence community." Its supporters include Sister Helen Prejean, who has written, "I stand morally opposed to killing: war, executions, killing of the old and demented, the killing of children, unborn and born."[9] Much of the anti-abortion movement, however, neglects the factors that contribute to abortion, and many opponents of abortion seem less interested in the destruction of life outside the womb.

In the 1970s, Roman Catholic Church officials emerged as leaders in denouncing abortion. Those officials had recently lost their fight over what were called artificial contraceptives. To this day, some church officials have not accepted that defeat. Impartial observers and most Roman Catholics understand the battle to have ended in 1968 with Pope Paul VI's encyclical, *Humanae Vitae*. Most Roman Catholics either opted out of the church or decided that on this point the bishops simply did not know what they were talking about.[10]

Roman Catholic Church officials, it seems clear, saw abortion as the fallback position on contraception; that was a terrible way to approach the question. They might have made a connection by saying, "We are against abortion as a violent way to control birth; other nonviolent ways of controlling birth should be encouraged as the most direct way to reduce abortions." That is not the way the ideological battle developed. Instead of saying, "We are against violence to living beings, especially to human beings," they announced that they were in favor of life. The question then became, "When does (human) life begin?" which is not the question that was in need of debate.

For many centuries, there was an assumption that women had nothing to contribute to the process of generating a baby, except to provide a place for the man's seed. Some sects considered a man's "spilling his seed," the seed of life, to be equivalent to murder. The Roman Catholic Church did not make that equivalence, but some preachers and schoolteachers came close to that position in their passionate denunciation of masturbation. The Vatican condemnation of homosexual acts in 1975 has an extended discussion of masturbation as "an intrinsically and seriously disordered act." Each act of masturbation can be a mortal sin "because it contradicts the finality of the faculty."[11] The logic of that teaching follows from the assumption that the purpose of sex is the generation of children. Any interruption of the process of the seed of life leading to pregnancy and birth is a serious sin.

Now that everyone recognizes that the woman contributes to the process of giving life, the clearest marker for when new human life begins is the fertilization of the egg. There is little room for debate here; the embryo is not dead, and it is not nonhuman. However, *fertilization* is a biological term that refers to something visible. *Conception* is a philosophical term about a human being. The human race now knows important scientific facts about genetics and that a DNA profile is established at the start of the process. But it is not a scientific question to ask when an individual human being comes into existence; it is a philosophical question, and one that has no agreed-upon answer today, and it is unlikely that there will ever be an agreement.

The interesting development in recent decades is that the opponents of abortion have called upon modern science and technology to support their case. By accepting fertilization and conception as synonymous, church officials cede authority to biology for determining when a human being comes into existence. It is strange that in this case the Roman Catholic Church chooses to accept the judgment of modern science rather than draw upon its own tradition. "Life" is a category in biology ("the science of life"). Many biologists have gladly accepted the role of declaring what life, including human life, means.[12] For them, if you wish to know when a human life begins, you ask someone in the life sciences.

It is also interesting that anti-abortion literature does not say much about the soul. Throughout most of Catholic Church history, a key question was, when does God infuse the soul? Not so long ago, church leaders talked constantly about taking care of one's immortal soul. During the past half century, there has been a shift of emphasis. A greater prominence of scriptural categories has led to a healthier view of personal integrity as the basis of Christian life. There has been less talk about the soul undergoing judgment at the moment of death and more talk about the resurrection and the final judgment.[13]

This shift of emphasis from a soul encased in a body to personal-communal existence in a material world represents a big improvement. But shifting moral discussions from *soul* to *life* is not the same kind of progress. A philosophical category, soul, has been replaced by an abstraction, life. If Roman Catholic Church leaders are not prepared to talk about the soul, then they need to find other categories that retain the idea that it is the human being or the person or a bodily-spiritual individual who is being defended and not only a life process. Do those who say that a human being exists at fertilization believe that the billions of abortions that happen, even without external intervention, result in one-celled human beings that go to heaven and enjoy a vision of God (while awaiting the resurrection of the body)?

The Roman Catholic Church's position is truly tragic. It has a legitimate moral concern in criticizing the widespread practice of abortion. But church officials seem to have lost the power to make distinctions, something that had been a hallmark of Catholic tradition. Perhaps many people who are called conservative do not know the tradition very well. On abortion, there is a distinction that goes back at least to the fourth century that would open the door to compromise on public policy. In a discussion of abortion, there is surely a need to distinguish between the first month and the last month of pregnancy.

The Vatican document, *Declaration on Procured Abortion*, traces a consistent condemnation of abortion from the time of the *Didache* and the writings of Athenagoras and Tertullian.[14] It does mention that "Excellent authors [none is named] allowed for this first period more lenient case solutions than they rejected for following periods." What is vaguely referred to here is a tradition, at least as old as Jerome and Augustine, that acknowledged a difference between the beginning of life and what was called *animatus,* the moment when the soul (*anima*) is infused by God.[15] The *Declaration* insists that "it was never denied that procured abortion even during the first days was objectively a grave fault." That may be true, but what is certain is that early abortion was distinguished from homicide.

The term *animatus* was a philosophical-theological term, not a biological term. The English word *animation* and the later word *quickening* misleadingly suggest that animatus referred to physical movement that can be tested empirically. Instead, there was an assumption that there has to be some development of the living organism before a soul is infused. Thus, abortion, said Jerome, "is not reputed homicide until the scattered elements received their appearance and members." Augustine agreed that for early abortions "the law does not provide that the act pertains to homicide for there cannot yet be said to be a live soul in a body that lacks sensation when it is not formed in flesh and as yet endowed with sense."[16]

The *Declaration* fails to point out that this distinction made by Jerome and Augustine was the main tradition throughout the Middle Ages. Gratian, whose collection of laws became the basis of the Code of Canon Law, said that abortion is homicide only when the fetus is formed. Pope Innocent III agreed.[17] Perhaps most important, Thomas Aquinas had no doubt that the soul could be infused only at some point along the development of embryonic life. Roman Catholic Church officials are usually quick to invoke the authority of Thomas Aquinas, but on the question of abortion, they are often silent on Thomas's opinion or say only what the *Declaration* does: "St. Thomas, the Common Doctor of the church, teaches that abortion is a grave sin against the natural law."[18]

That is simply a refusal to acknowledge Thomas Aquinas's position.[19] Thomas was clear in asserting that a development was needed before there could be the infusion of a soul, forty days for a male and eighty days for a female. That distinction between the sexes is indicative that his views were entangled with a primitive (and antiwoman) biological theory, which he adopted from Aristotle. Thomas did not profess to be a biologist. His reflections on the human soul and the nature of the person are metaphysical in nature. His philosophical principle is not dependent on embryology. It is based on a common-sense understanding that "a speck of matter is a baby" does not parse in any language.

Catholic tradition remained committed to this view of early abortion until at least the seventeenth century. When moral theology took a turn into casuistry and a focus on individual acts of morality, there was no room for allowing any ambiguity about the moment of ensoulment. Since there is no marker later in the process of pregnancy for when the human person is formed, it was thought necessary to assume that ensoulment happened at fertilization.

Even in the nineteenth and twentieth centuries, there continued to be an admission that we do not know when ensoulment occurs. In the *Declaration on Procured Abortion*, a footnote says, "This declaration leaves aside the question of the moment when the spiritual soul is infused. There is not a unanimous tradition on this point and authors are as yet in disagreement."[20] That is an extraordinary admission buried in a footnote. In the anti-abortion movement since the 1970s, there was not a change of opinion about ensoulment; instead there was a change of language to speak about the beginning of life.

In the Middle Ages, there was no agreement on how long it was after the beginning of life that an individual—an ensouled person—came into existence. The suggestion of some authors, including Thomas Aquinas, of forty days was no doubt a symbolic number. But now as well as then no one can say when a person or individual human being comes into existence. Historian John Noonan subtitled his important study of abortion *An Almost Absolute Value in History*. All that is needed for the Roman Catholic Church to begin a conversation on abortion is a recognition that "almost absolute" is not absolute.

Possibility of Compromise?

The US Supreme Court drew a line at the end of the second trimester of pregnancy for the legal acceptance of abortion. As a line that seemed legally enforceable, the court acted reasonably. Groups that are concerned with the moral side of abortion understandably think that the *moral* line should be much earlier and that later abortions should only be performed for very exceptional reasons. And, in fact, an estimated 98 percent of abortions occur before twenty weeks; nine out of ten occur in the first twelve weeks.[21] The people who urge that the Supreme Court's legal line should be moved forward might better concern themselves with changing the conditions that lead to late abortions. Perhaps twenty weeks, as a legal line, would have been a better choice by the court, but the current rash of bills to set a twenty-week limit is not straightforward and worsens the conflict between the two ideological groups.

The proposal of a legal limit of twenty weeks is being used as a distraction from other provisions in these laws that are intended to make abortion facilities less accessible. One does not have to deduce the intent behind these laws; it is openly admitted by advocates of the laws. The twenty-week provision is meant to be a step toward outlawing all abortions. The chances of that happening are approximately zero. Meanwhile, any helpful provisions to lessen the need for abortion and to make safe abortions available to the poor as well as the rich are lost in the ideological battle.

It should be possible to get agreement that an individual human being does exist when the organism is capable of living outside the womb. Despite changes brought about by medical advances, this principle of viability still holds. Most people think that a human being exists before then. One would think that some agreements about late abortions should be possible, but there is such mistrust by opposing groups that no conversation takes place.

The Roman Catholic Church is surely right in insisting that the entire process of pregnancy should be respected. Abortion at any stage of pregnancy is a moral concern. Violent intrusions into the life cycle should if possible be avoided. There should be a good reason for an intrusion. Even if there is some moral fault, the degree of culpability varies according to all the circumstances. The destruction of the human embryo for trivial reasons is surely a wrong. But to accuse people of murder because of an abortion at the earliest stage of pregnancy is not a way to begin a conversation.

Paul Griffiths, who is a thoughtful Roman Catholic writer, wrote an essay in 2004 advocating church acceptance of same-sex marriage. In that essay, he contrasts the acceptance of gay unions with an opposition to abortion: "The current state of U.S. law about abortion makes impossible the legal restriction of the slaughter of more than a million innocent human beings every year."[22] That is a stunning charge based on a counterintuitive belief that is rejected by tens of millions of responsible citizens. To the vast majority of people, the charge makes no sense at all. It is unintelligible to most people to say that an individual—a person, a human being, a baby, a being, a someone, a who—exists at fertilization. Griffiths's language is standard in the anti-abortion movement and makes any kind of compromise impossible.

A thoughtful essay by Peter Steinfels brings a tone of civility to the disagreement and deserves careful consideration.[23] Steinfels is a committed Roman Catholic who is looking for any possible compromise. He begins with what he describes as two "simple statements." His first simple statement is as follows: "Fertilization, a remarkable process involving the union of twenty-three chromosomes from each parent, creates a new, unique, individual member of the human species, a physically dependent but genetically distinct and self-directing organism. This is a scientific fact, not one dependent on faith or religious teaching." A claim that fertilization "creates a new, unique, individual member of the human species" is far from being a scientific fact. If this assertion were scientific fact, wouldn't the secular critics of the church know that fact instead of that fact being obvious only to opponents of abortion?

Steinfels's second *simple statement* is as follows: "The conviction taught by the Catholic Church and shared by many people, religious and nonreligious, is nowhere near as obvious as many of us who hold it suppose." That is a remarkably low-key way into admitting that the conviction is not only not obvious to the majority of citizens but strikes them as wrong.

Steinfels lays out errors and dangers in the way anti-abortion forces have proceeded—for example, being aligned with reactionary political movements that downgrade the rights of women. He finally comes to his proposal: "Catholics and others opposed to abortion should strive for the legal protection of unborn life not from conception but from that point where not one but a whole constellation of converging arguments and intuitions can be brought to bear." That point, he says, is eight weeks of development when there is "an accumulation of evidence that should compel a majority even in a pluralist society."

The proposal does sound reasonable. If we were starting with a clean slate, perhaps there could be an agreement closer to eight weeks than the Supreme Court's twenty-four. But Steinfels is surely aware that there is nowhere near a majority who would agree to anything remotely similar. And his opening statement that a unique human individual exists at fertilization kills any chance of anti-abortionists endorsing a legal approval of murder. Although Steinfels's proposal cannot get far, his willingness to propose a compromise is a good step.

Steinfels criticizes opposition to abortion by drawing an analogy to slavery. The comparison to slavery might be helpful to the cause of restricting late abortions. But for asserting that a fertilized ovum should have the rights of a human being the case of slavery is evidence against the position.

Aristotle thought that some men were born to be slaves; he did not think that slaves were not human beings. When Columbus encountered the Arawak or when Africans were brought in to work the tobacco and cotton fields, any sane person could see that they were human beings. They were thought to be inferior to the white Europeans, who were prejudiced in ways that are obvious today. Slaveholders were acutely aware that they were dealing with human beings, which is why it was important to humiliate the slaves and it was illegal to teach a slave to read. Only on the basis of a powerful ideology could anyone deny what was apparent to the senses and reason, that a slave was a human being. Those who say that in the future a fertilized egg will be recognized as a human being are on the ideological side of rejecting what the senses and reason recognize as a human being.

A recent political strategy has been to get personhood amendments on state ballots, assigning the rights of a person to the fertilized egg. These amendments do not have wide support; most people recognize that a one-celled embryo is not a person. The idea of *person* emerged from early Christian speculation on God and the relation of Jesus to God. It became the way to refer to what is special about the human being, a responsible agent with rights and duties. For Thomas Aquinas, "person signifies what is noblest in the whole of nature."[24] A legal concept of personhood has been extended to a wide range of things. Corporations have long been considered legal persons because they are responsible public actors with rights and duties, but no one mistakes General Motors for a (natural) person.[25] Even if a fertilized egg were assigned personhood, it would still not be a natural person.

We who are persons can usually recognize others of our kind. We do it on the evidence of our senses and what the mind conceives. There are dozens of signs of personhood in what we can see, hear, and touch. At some point in the development of human life during pregnancy, there exists a combination of characteristics and behavior that are identified with persons. No single characteristic, such as conscious awareness or the ability to feel pain, is persuasive to everyone.[26] Exactly when the person exists will never be agreed upon.

Conclusion

In the 2012 political campaign, politicians who said they were against all abortions found themselves cornered when rape and incest were brought up. Most of them said they made exceptions for rape and incest, but that position made no logical sense. One should not kill babies even if they are the result of rape. The painful choice for these politicians was to renounce either logic or their beliefs. A few politicians went all the way with their logic. Todd Akin famously said that in cases of "legitimate" rape, the body would shut down the possibility of pregnancy. The reason for his use of the word *legitimate* is obvious: his argument was that if fertilization and conception do occur, that proves there was no rape. He was simply being consistent.

The ridicule that was heaped on a few politicians is not particularly helpful. An orthodoxy in most of the news media that constantly refers to a "woman's right to choose" and "abortion rights" obstructs any meaningful discussion of how society should encourage ways to regulate abortion, reduce the need for abortions, and eventually eliminate the practice as far as possible.

The phrase *abortion rights* is a relatively recent phrase, but it is now omnipresent. Why the plural? It seems to be used as a synonym for *reproductive rights*. But reproductive rights is a phrase that does not refer only to abortion. The UN Convention on the human rights of women refers four times to reproductive rights; each time, the phrase is used in the context of birth and maternity. The rights of women pertaining to birth control, pregnancy, birth, and childcare should include the possibility of deciding to abort the pregnancy.

Abortion rights is a strange phrase; presumably it means a right to abortion. But does anyone think that abortion is a good that a person has a right to? Katha Pollitt in *Pro: Reclaiming Abortion Rights* does refer to abortion as a positive social good. But I think her point is more precisely stated when she says of abortion, "It is an essential option for women—not just ones in dramatic, terrible, body-and-soul dramatic situations, but all women—and thus benefits society as a whole."[27] The availability of the option is the good, not the abortion. Would there not be agreement that there are better forms of birth control than abortion? Wouldn't it make more sense to talk about abortion as a tragic if sometimes acceptable choice rather than a good that someone has a right to? That attitude seems to be common among women who have an abortion—that is, they emphasize their responsibility more than their rights.[28]

Catholic tradition has a good, though by no means spotless, record of concern for vulnerable human beings. In many ways, it continues to be a voice for the downtrodden. Abortion as routinely practiced today is worthy of the church's concern. But a respect for life surely includes protests against poverty, the state execution of prisoners, and the militarization of the country. Even Pope Francis, as noted above, suggested that an obsession with abortion may prevent church officials from using the resources of Catholic tradition to stand on the side of oppressed people and to speak out against violations of the human body and the destruction of the physical environment.

Chapter 5

Death Is Natural, but Human Death Is Not

One of the central tenets of the death and dying movement is that death is—or ought to be—natural. This principle is not really argued. It is simply the premise of arguments about how to return dying to its proper place as a natural event. Even when there are strong disagreements about other points, writers agree on the desirability of death being natural. Sherwin Nuland in *How We Die* is critical of the direction that Elisabeth Kübler-Ross gave to the death and dying movement.[1] Nuland attempted to provide a more realistic, sometimes stark, picture of the dying process as opposed to a romanticized view of dying that would make it peaceful and pleasant. However, Kübler-Ross and Nuland are agreed on one point—namely, that dying should be natural.

The thesis of this chapter is that death is never simply natural for a human being; it is a personal act in which the natural is reshaped for better or for worse. A person has a human-nature, but he or she is not reducible to that nature. A person's actions bring about a second nature, which is a reshaping of his or her nature. Humans engage in art, religion, science, and technology in ways that other animals do not. Such activities are not opposed to nature, but they also do not conform to a preestablished natural order.

People who say that they want a natural death are usually fearful of being treated in unnatural ways that dehumanize. There are many ways in which that can happen. When someone is murdered, the usual description is that he or she died of unnatural causes. It is also the case that the use of intrusive technology in a hospital can be unnatural in doing violence to the process of human dying. In contrast, to be treated humanely is to receive appropriate help, including medicines, that helpfully serve a person's living and dying.

Elisabeth Kübler-Ross's *On Death and Dying* did not invent the language of natural death; it has been around for a long time.[2] However, the naturalness of dying had not been emphasized in the first part of the twentieth century. Kübler-Ross's book brought back to the fore a theme that had been prominent in the nineteenth century, and this time the idea took hold in the culture. Natural death became not only a popular but a legal concept. It is regularly said in anti-abortion literature that life must be protected from the moment of conception to natural death.

Since California passed a Natural Death Act in 1976, the phrase has shown up constantly in discussions of death. The desire for a natural death often appears in living wills that state a person's wishes about what is to be done and what is not to be done if the person becomes incapable of expressing those wishes. A standard form for a living will in New York State says that "if life-sustaining procedures are serving only to prolong the dying process, then in that event, I direct that the procedures be withheld or withdrawn, and that I be permitted to die naturally."

If someone were unaware of the technology in today's hospitals, he or she would be puzzled by talk about natural death. Why should anyone have to say that he or she wants a natural death? Is anyone in favor of having an unnatural death? It seems certain that no one wants to die an unnatural death; however, the alternative might not be a natural death.

Although the mantra of natural death may seem almost too obvious for saying, the phrase is actually very ambiguous in meaning. Individuals who say "I want to die a natural death" may not realize what they are asking for. Or what they intend to ask for may not be conveyed to the hearer by the phrase natural death. For example, does a natural death exclude morphine if one is in excruciating pain? Is the use of morphine natural? Does the use of morphine cause an unnatural death?

Nature and Catholic Tradition

How did *nature* and *natural* come to connote the meanings that they have today? Has nature become our guide for living, which eventually includes dying? The only way to answer these questions is by tracing the history of nature/natural. That history has had profound links to Catholic tradition.

Roman Catholic Church officials in recent times have regularly claimed support for their moral teachings in "natural law." That phrase is a bad choice that undermines a support for Catholic tradition's concern to protect what is natural from violation. The term *natural law* is not helpful insofar as it suggests that nature manifests a law (or laws) that can be easily known by any reasonable person. If there were a natural law that gives answers to ethical issues, wouldn't one expect that most reasonable people would be able to perceive such a law and laws?

Catholic tradition took root at a time when nature and natural were generally positive in meaning, at least among philosophers. The early Christian movement could not have escaped the influence of that "pagan" world even if it had wished to do so. The actual relation of the early church to the surrounding world was a complex one. The "world" was sometimes what Christians were told to escape from. That attitude was especially obvious in the monastic movement in which the monk renounced the world and "entered religion." But Christians also expressed their belief that the whole world was the work of a loving God. Humans had messed up the world, but now it was redeemed or at least was in the process of being redeemed.

In its struggle to both affirm the world and yet insist that the world needs a transformation, Christianity developed a language of the "supernatural." The natural world, particularly the world of human-nature, was not bad, but it could become bad unless it was transformed.[3] The key principle was that the supernatural (grace) builds on (human) nature. That saying, however, was open to contrasting interpretations, depending on whether the emphasis was given to the incompleteness and disfigurements of nature or to the fact that nature is the foundation of all living beings, including human beings.

The Roman Catholic Church has never resolved the tension between the goodness of the world of nature and the threat that the merely natural offers. But Catholics are not alone. There is also ambiguity in the rest of the world about the goodness of nature and whether nature is our guide for living a good life. Indeed, during most of the modern era, nature was what was to be suppressed or conquered. Nature as inclusive of death was the last enemy. The present era seems to be in strong reaction against the assumption that nature is something to be overcome.

Examining the complexity of the term *nature* might at least be a warning to some people that the issue of nature's goodness is not settled. There seems to be a widespread assumption today that, while in recent centuries nature was misunderstood, the issue has now been put right, at least in theory. The one sure conclusion that should be clear from this chapter is that any simple statement of the relation between the human and the natural will be defective. Only with a paradoxical formulation does one have a chance of comprehending this relation.

The relation between the human and the natural is of significance in almost every field of study and every aspect of existence. *Nature* and *natural* show up in anthropology, sociology, and psychology. The terms are not so prominent in politics, economics, or engineering, but they always hover in the background. The food industry in the United States exploits the now-positive meaning of natural by claiming that all sorts of products are natural, a claim that usually means almost nothing.

The History of Nature

Why does the term *nature* exist at all? The Greek word for nature, *physis*, seems to have emerged at the very beginning of philosophy and science. Reflecting on the diversity and movement in the world, the early Greek thinkers sought to bring things into a unity and to explain change. What most struck them were living things that are born grow, decline, and die. The term *nature* was coined to identify the source of change in living things. A living being has self-movement—that is, a source of change which itself does not change but instead gives stability to the plant or animal over time. Therefore, each living thing has a nature.

The first snapshot of *nature's* history is found in Aristotle's philosophy. Aristotle identified six meanings that the word had acquired by his time.[4] His first meaning of natural is birth or origin; he thought that there was an etymological connection between nature and birth. Although his etymology may have been inaccurate, nature and birth had been associated before Aristotle and continued to be connected by thinkers after him. The connection was solidified for the future by Cicero's choice of *natura* (from *natus* for birth) as the word to translate *physis*. The English word *nature* took its lead from Latin and retained the connection to birth. Natural things are those that are born.

Aristotle says that nature also has the following meanings: what is inherent, what is a source of motion, what things are made of, what the primary being (or essence) of a living thing is, and by extension what the essence of each thing is. From these six meanings, Aristotle concludes that "nature is the primary being of those things that have in them the source of their own movement."[5]

Aristotle seems to be missing the collective meaning of nature that became prominent later. That meaning is sometimes assumed to be the primary meaning—that is, nature as the aggregate of things, a name for the whole world. While there is nothing necessarily wrong with this evolution of the word, it is helpful to remember that the collective meaning was the secondary not the primary meaning. It may still be helpful to start by thinking of nature as the inner principle of living things before it is used as a general name for everything or for everything outside the human.

Nature is not a perceptible reality but a philosophical concept invented as an explanation. The Hebrew Bible, for example, has nothing to say about nature; it lacks the word. It does have plenty to say about plants and animals, as well as the human relation to the world of living things. But in contrast to Greek philosophy, the Hebrew Bible speaks in concrete terms of flesh and blood and breath and earth. Today's commentators have to be careful about reading the concept of nature back into the Hebrew Bible. High-blown generalizations about the biblical attitude toward nature are almost bound to be inaccurate. In the New Testament, St. Paul, because he was writing in Greek, assimilated the term *nature* into his vocabulary, but he used it haphazardly. His unsystematic use of the terms *natural* and *unnatural* has been the source of unfortunate confusion in the history of Christianity and the secular culture that developed from it. No term has been the source of more confusion in every era of history than the term *nature*.

A main question throughout the centuries has been the relation between humans and nature. The two words human and nature suggest that the adjective human merely refers to a part of a larger reality called nature. The term *human-nature* indicates a distinct idea composed of an interaction between the human and the natural. Humans distinguish themselves from other living beings by their nature, a stable but always changing idea. Unfortunately, "human-nature" has been wielded by powerful humans against minority voices. Women, blacks, gays, and numerous other groups have at times attacked the idea of human-nature instead of demanding their admission to an ever-expanding idea of the human.

The fourth century BCE represents one of the first great shifts in the meaning of nature. The speculative systems of Plato and Aristotle gave a new prominence to individual human life and to rational concepts for speculating on the human relation to the cosmos. It was now possible to think of the human being as in some sense an outsider to the natural world of other living beings. Earlier religions had implied this outsider status, but philosophical concepts, such as being, nature, essence, form, matter, and soul, forced some explicit choices.

At his trial, Socrates spoke of a soul that would survive his death, a belief that seems to entail that the real human being is an outsider to earth's cycle of birth, growth, decline, death, and rebirth. Other Platonic dialogues also suggested an eternal, immutable form as real, even more real than the perceived world.

Aristotle, in contrast, was a biologist, keenly attentive to the material world around him. Despite his hints that intellect is separable from matter, Aristotle treated humans as living beings who have a nature. Human-nature acts through powers that can be trained for intellectual and moral excellence. One might say that Aristotle's first interest is neither the noun *nature* nor the adjective *natural* but the adverb *naturally*. Living beings act naturally when their acts flow from what they are and their actions are directed toward their proper good. "The moral virtues, then, are engendered in us neither *by* nor *contrary* to nature; we are constituted by nature to receive them, but their full development in us is due to habit."[6] For Aristotle, humans have a superior position of power and self-reflection, but they are still governed by the laws that govern living things.

A second snapshot of nature's history is from several centuries after Aristotle. A group of writers known to history as the Stoics made a permanent impression on the meaning of nature. Even today, or especially today, a form of Stoicism is evident in discussions of the environment. The Stoics were one of the groups to move *nature* in the direction of becoming coextensive with the cosmos. At the same time, philosophical thinking had become more conscious that the human possession of reason gave humans a perspective different from other earthlings. The world was made for gods and men—those who possess reason—but clearly the men are subordinate to the gods.[7] Nature is all enveloping; if men claim to be independent of nature, they will only increase their suffering, and eventually death will prove who is the stronger.

The Stoics began the recognition of what became the faculty of free will, but they also advocated acceptance of nature as the only wise course for the human will. "Following nature" might be understood today to mean following natural human impulses. For the Stoics, it meant just the opposite. An allegory by the Stoic founder captures the relation of humans to nature: "If a dog is tied, as it were, to a wagon, then if the dog wishes to follow, it will both be pulled and follow, acting by its own choice together with necessity; but if it does not wish to follow, it will in any case be compelled. The same applies to human beings."[8] Thus, human beings, if they wish to be happy, should willingly follow nature. If they do not, nature will show them who the boss is.

The Stoic Marcus Aurelius said of death, "If only it be steadily contemplated, and the fancies we associate with it be mentally dissected, it will soon come to be thought of as no more than a process of nature (and only children are scared by a natural process)—or rather, something more than a mere process, a positive contribution to nature's well-being."[9] Epictetus, a Greek-speaking Roman slave, also found Stoicism to be a comfort. "If you kiss your child or wife, say that you are kissing a human being; for when it dies you will not be upset ... What upsets people is not things themselves but their judgments about things. Just as a target is not set up to be missed, in the same way nothing bad by nature happens in the world."[10]

The Christian Attitude toward the Natural World

Christianity absorbed many Stoic terms and teachings, especially the realm of virtues. However, the language of man confronted by an all-embracing and intractable nature was incompatible with a Christian philosophy. Christianity had the idea of a creator of living beings, and at the center of those beings is the human being as the priest of all creation. The Christian doctrine of creation asserted the goodness of everything, despite human failings from the beginning.

The Christian movement began from belief in the death-resurrection of the Christ. However strange that doctrine seems to outsiders, it initiated a worldwide movement. The first Christian announcement was not "love one another" but "he is risen." That doctrine implied an attitude toward the whole world. Jesus is portrayed as beginning his resurrection from the center of the world and carrying all creation with him. The resurrection of the body (or bodily self) meant that the human being was not a spirit trapped in matter but a bodily being whose whole self was in need of respect and transformation.

The early church developed a system of sacraments that accompanied the believer from the first to the last moments of life. These sacraments emphasized the earthiness of the human being. The words that were used in the administration of each sacrament were commentaries on the gestures and materials that linked the human being to death and rebirth.

The abstract theology that eventually developed was less important to the masses of people than the sacramental or liturgical life. At the center of the practices was the Eucharist, meaning thanksgiving. The Eucharist (or Mass) was a meal of bread and wine that remembered the past, celebrated the present, and looked forward to the future. Unfortunately, the sacraments, including the sacred meal, lent themselves to being treated as magic.

A school known as Neoplatonism shaped much of the theology of the West. Neoplatonic thought, like early Greek philosophy, saw an organic unity to the world. Humans are not apart from the other natures. All natures participate in a world soul, even though human reason is recognized as a power superior to that of other animals. Human reason is a participant in the *world reason*, which itself participates in a greater reality than reason. The source of beings cannot itself be a being. What distinguishes Neoplatonism is a push *beyond being* to the ultimate source called the One. Nature is given a positive place, but it is not ultimate. Nature has to receive an act of being from the source of all beings.

In Christian philosophy, which drew from both Stoicism and Neoplatonism, the human being has a human-nature that determines *what* it is; however, *who* the person is goes beyond *what* a person is. Each person is unique not from its nature but because of its act of being. Human life is not subordinate to a natural law or laws of nature. A human being is responsible for its actions. Responsibility *for* those actions pertaining to one's life and death depends on responsibility *to* oneself and *to* all those people and things that can guide a person's conscience.

In church life, a grand scheme of theology did not guide the practice of most Christians. Millions of converts were brought into the church by baptism and were given a few moral precepts to live by. In the Christian Church, the availability of education never caught up with the need. The healthy disciplining of the natural inclinations, especially sexual desires, was not conveyed by the simple prohibitions that were provided. The popular view of bodily life tended to be negative. With an echo of Stoicism, Christian teaching seemed to suggest that the soul needed to be protected from disorderly inclinations of the body.

Contemporary scholarship traces the beginning of modern science to the eleventh and twelfth centuries when Christian thinkers articulated their distinction between the natural and the supernatural.[11] This language affirmed the intelligibility of natural things and the human ability to exercise control by the use of rational methods. The newly appropriated Aristotelian philosophy, joined with Neoplatonism, might have given support to a Christian tradition of respect for and celebration of bodily life, but that grand unity never emerged. By the end of the Renaissance, there was a conflict between a desiccated Aristotelianism on one side and on the other side a Neoplatonic philosophy, which was often allied with magic.

The common belief that science and religion were at war in the seventeenth century is inaccurate. "The new physicist wanted nothing so much as a philosophy of nature that harmonized with mainstream Christianity, the better to combat the socio-religious threat of magic."[12] The theologians were only too happy to join with the scientists. Both groups were fighting against magic that was partly derived from earlier philosophy in which nature was a force within living things.

In the seventeenth century, *nature* was conceived mainly as an object for human understanding, mastery, and use. The new mathematical sciences laid claim to discovering the laws of nature that applied to all physical objects. Questions about the moral life of the human being were assigned to natural law, an idea that had been around at least since the time of the Stoics. Humans are free, but they should recognize the law that governs all humans. Thus, physics created a strange adaptation of Stoicism: the human mission is to conquer nature. But in the area of moral rules and moral virtues, human beings had to be subservient to nature.

In the Christian tradition, natural law was and still is often conceived to be a set of laws that are a guide for moral human actions. But there is no way to write a set of prescriptions for human action by peering into human-nature.[13] While there may be some obvious ways that a human-nature can be violated or destroyed, a human morality is by no means obvious. In Thomas Aquinas's view, a law called natural is derived from an understanding of human inclinations, but only with insights based on experience do rules for action emerge.

In the Stoic parable mentioned above, a small dog is tied to a large cart and has only the choice of trotting along with the cart or being dragged by the cart. By the seventeenth century, the dog (man) had grown up and now thought it could drag the cart.[14] Of course, one had to avoid the topic of death, which remained the last enemy for the individual human being. However, the individual's death was not an obstacle to the human race proclaiming its triumph over nature.

Francis Bacon was as influential as any one individual in shaping the meaning of nature during the seventeenth to twentieth centuries. Abstract man was set in contrast to abstract nature. The verbs that Bacon used to describe the relation were command and conquer.[15] But far from thinking that the conquest of nature is arrogant, Bacon describes the needed attitude as one of humility. His governing metaphor was a bridal chamber or a nuptial couch for the mind and the universe. Many contemporary feminists are appalled by this metaphor, but, for Bacon, the scientist is a gallant suitor who must use chastity, respect, and restraint. Bacon condemns those who value knowledge in itself because that is to use as a mistress for pleasure what ought to be a spouse for fruit.[16]

For Bacon, man's religious duty is to read the Book of Nature and restore human control over nature. As with many authors since the twelfth century, Bacon posited three stages to history. In the first stage, nature was cooperative with the human. In history's second stage, nature is affected by the insubordination of matter; man and nature are at odds with each other. In the third stage, nature will be molded by art and human ministry so that at the end of time there will be a reconciliation of the natural and the human.[17]

In the nineteenth century and the first half of the twentieth century, the idea that nature is the ultimate explanation of everything coexisted uneasily with the idea that nature is whatever is to be conquered by man. Nature was a loving mother, bestowing natural rights on man, but nature was also an evil stepmother, which justified man's overpowering of nature to produce the marvels of technology. Freud expressed the outlook of his generation in saying, "The principal task of civilization is to defend us against nature."[18]

What at first seems to be a breathtaking change in the dominant meaning of nature began to occur in the middle of the twentieth century and swept the field in the 1970s. It might seem to be a complete reversal in meaning: from nature as the enemy that needs conquering to nature as our ultimate benefactor that should be revered. The change is not as inexplicable as it might seem. Mother Nature never died. The mother of all life emerged from the shadow of the evil stepmother. A passage from a 1948 book by C. S. Lewis brilliantly captures what was about to occur: "Man's conquest of Nature turns out, in the moment of its consummation, to be Nature's conquest of Man. Every victory we seemed to win has led us, step by step, to this conclusion. All Nature's apparent reverses have been tactical withdrawals. We thought we were beating her back when she was leading us on. What looked like hands held high in surrender was really the opening of arms to enfold us forever."[19]

In this quotation, the capitalization of nature and the use of the feminine pronoun for nature are integral to the view of man's relation to nature. Instead of men and women cooperating with the impersonal forces in their environment, man is being led into nature's arms, and she will enfold him forever. This embrace is not entirely benign. We are told to revere nature as the goddess who bestows on us all good things, but to do so we need to block from our minds that in the end nature brings death to each of us. For the last half century, there has been an attempt to glorify natural death, but when most people are confronted with their own or a loved one's death, it does not seem to be part of a loving mother's bounty. However much we are encouraged to love and revere nature, we still have good reason to suspect that nature is out to kill us.

Conclusion

When one moves away from abstract man and abstract nature, then there is no simple way to state the relation between the natural and the human. The natures of both men and women are in question, as well as the natures of each living thing. What needs examining today are the relations between men and men, women and women, men and women, adults and children, humans and nonhuman animals, humans and other living beings, and the ecological systems of living beings. A conversation is needed between peoples of East and West, North and South, a conversation that might be enriched by earlier philosophy and religion as well as today's science. There might be achievable agreements on what not to do to nature(s) even if there is no agreement on a single law or a set of laws called natural.

A test of understanding nature is human sexuality. The human transformation of the biological activity of sex has produced an imaginative range of expression. The human race, amazingly enough, is still exploring the full range of sexual activity.[20] The sexual drive is so powerful that it can become addictive, and sexual practice sometimes borders on violence. Young people need help to integrate sex into a healthy human life. While the Roman Catholic Church had the right principle, it fell badly short in assimilating knowledge of sexuality and accepting the diversity of sexual practices. Sex and death have always had a mysterious partnership. A healthy transforming of human sexuality is indispensable for a healthy view of death.

It would be helpful if the word *unnatural* were saved for those actions that directly violate either a thing's nature or an ecological system. Attaching electrodes to someone's genitals is an unnatural act; it does violence to a human's nature. Some of the ways in which the life of an individual are being extended in today's hospitals may be unnatural— that is, a violent intrusion into the process of dying when there is no realistic hope of the person returning to life in a human community. One can also say that acts such as polluting a river or using some pesticides, which once seemed harmless, should today be called unnatural acts.

A natural being, in contrast to an artificial being, is one that dies. A human individual, shaped by a human-nature, is a natural being that is born, grows, declines, and dies. Human death can be treated as a biological event, but it is not wholly describable in biological terms. Biologists view humans as one more species of animal that can be explained as following the dictates of animal nature. But politics, art, science, and religion are a refusal to accept the biological limits to a personal life. Human dying is personal and communal.

Kübler-Ross's insistence that death is natural is based on too limited a choice. The alternatives, she assumes, are either to accept death as biologically necessary or else to be hooked up to a machine that will not allow death its place. Her choice is between the biological and the technological. But if human-nature includes both the biological and the capacity for the technological, then the choice is not submission to either biology or to technology. The human alternative is a creative and humane use of technology. An ethical use of technology is one that is proportionate to personal situations. There are other and better ways to resist the dehumanizing of death than by saying that death should be natural.

Chapter 6

∞

Suffering, Pain, and Nonviolence

T he modern era of medicine, which can be dated to the invention
of penicillin in the 1940s, has been a blessing for millions of
people. Those who are fortunate enough to have access to
the new knowledge and its applications generally live longer, healthier,
and more enjoyable lives. The average improvements, however, hide a
dark side. In some areas, contemporary medicine is successful only in
creating half solutions. In the confusion and conflict about the end of
life, the half solutions are obvious.

Many people avoid visiting a nursing home because what is there
can be terrifying to healthy forty-year-olds. In the 1960s, nursing homes
were almost uniformly a scandal, an economic scam in which old people
were treated callously or worse. That is not generally true today. At least
there are many nursing homes where the staff try their humanly best
to provide comfort and care. But despite these good efforts, the whole
scene remains frightening. The unavoidable question for a forty-year-old
is whether that is his or her future.

There is a strong push in the country for legalizing assisted suicide.
The push is not coming from nursing homes and hospices but from
middle-aged people who fear what old age will bring. They wish to
have an available option to check out if they decide to do so. Is this
development a sign of moral corruption and cowardice, or is the move

a realistic response by people who understandably do not wish to be one of medicine's half solutions? Should a person asking to die have his or her wish fulfilled? In many cases, the person is no longer capable of expressing a wish. Who then is to judge what should be done, and on what basis does that person judge?

The Roman Catholic Church could play a helpful part in a discussion of sickness and dying, both on the side of the patient and that of the people who care for the sick and dying. Catholic hospitals in the United States play a major role in the country's health care. There is a long Catholic tradition of reflection on suffering and death. While medicine has made amazing advances in the treatment of illness, the meaning of suffering and dying has not changed much over the centuries. There is nothing more certain in life than its end. Every human being eventually has to engage questions about suffering and death. Roman Catholic Church officials have to know their own tradition well so that they can wrestle with today's questions and not just repeat formulas that they were taught in a seminary.

Right to Die?

Ethical questions in the United States are usually viewed from the standpoint of rights. The premise is that the individual is the bearer of rights that must not be violated. That principle creates a peculiar language for discussing issues about dying. A right to die would seem to conflict with the most basic right, the right to live. In most of the world, the phrase *right to die* would be unintelligible. The phrase can be explained, but its peculiarity should give us pause as to whether the right to die overemphasizes one factor or excludes some important considerations. Because rights are correlated with duties, it is almost inevitable that a right to die will lead to calls for a duty to die.[1]

The US citizen is keenly aware of his or her rights. The US Constitution is thought by many people to be a protection of the God-given rights that are stated in the Declaration of Independence: life, liberty, and the pursuit of happiness. Many people are unfamiliar with most of the US Constitution, but they are keenly aware of the Bill of

Rights, or least a few favorite rights that are listed there. For example, the argument is often made that the Second Amendment, which says that Congress should not infringe upon a right to bear arms, does not grant a right but instead forbids the government from taking away a right that is given by God.

Both the French and American declarations of rights in the eighteenth century had roots in a Christian discussion of rights that had gone on since the twelfth century. By the eighteenth century, however, the link to any religious view was clouded. Thomas Jefferson's Declaration of Independence, while paying lip service to "nature's God," pronounced these rights to be "self-evident." The French Declaration of the Rights of Man and of the Citizen invoked only nature as the source of rights. Both declarations viewed the individual (man) as sacred and inviolable.

One interesting note about the medieval discussion of rights is that there was a distinction between rights that were called alienable and other rights called inalienable. Both declarations in the eighteenth century retained that language. An inalienable right was one that could not be taken from an individual by anyone. It followed that an individual could not renounce his own inalienable rights. An inalienable right to life would mean that an individual has a duty to live and that killing oneself is forbidden.

For the last two centuries, autonomy (a law of oneself) as the ground of individual rights has dominated ethics. Autonomy works well on the good days. An individual has a right to decide how to live his or her life. But it is difficult to see how autonomy is the key ethical principle when an infant is three months old or when an old person is a patient in an ICU. The condition of a dying person in today's hospitals, hospices, and nursing homes reveals the inadequacy of autonomy as either the beginning principle or the comprehensive principle to discuss what is ethically right or wrong.[2]

The ethicist Margaret Pabst Battin has described how the paralysis of her husband became a challenge to her philosophy, forcing her to rethink autonomy as the basis of ethical decisions. Out of her experience with her husband's disability, Battin concluded that more than one principle is needed for end-of-life decisions. I find it strange, however, that what she added to autonomy was mercy. Certainly mercy is an admirable quality. But it is difficult to see mercy and autonomy as a pair; most often mercy has been paired with justice. It is clear that Battin wishes to describe the sensitive interplay between the patient who is in pain and the caregiver who wishes to do what is best. I think that autonomy, even when supplemented by mercy, is not an adequate starting point.

There are two paths open for what to do with the concept of autonomy. Either autonomy can be abandoned as a false ideal or else autonomy has to be rethought so that it is a realistic part of the interdependent relations in human life.

In the strangest passage of the essay on Battin's ethical thinking, she says that "she has become aware of a more subtle kind of coercion from a much-loved spouse or partner who wants you to live." It is true that the refusal of a loved one to let go when a patient's dying is imminent can be a problem. But the conclusion that Battin draws from that fact shows the weakness of autonomy: "The very presence of these loved ones undercuts the notion of true autonomy ... Everyone's autonomy abuts someone else's."[3]

A view of the world in which each one's autonomy abuts someone else's is a zero-sum game in which my gain is your loss. I would say, on the contrary, that it is the presence of loved ones that makes autonomy possible. When there is true love, the person's identity and freedom are affirmed by the one who loves. The incalculable grace of love, says Augustine, is summed up by the words *volo ut sis:* I want you to be. The person who coerces and who refuses to accept another person's decisions about living and dying is shown to be acting not out of love but from selfish personal needs.

As the starting principle of ethics, love may be too much to require. *Love* is an overworked term that is too easily confused with romantic feelings. The most obvious candidate to begin a discussion of dying is *care*. That term has a strong, practical meaning for both the dying person and the people who are called caregivers.

Many women writers in recent decades have used care as central to the development of ethics.[4] Its meaning can transcend the interpersonal realm so as to include the political, social, and environmental. The loved one and the competent professional who care for the dying patient will respect the patient's wishes and not act contrary to those wishes. In the complicated world of today's medicine, the patient's choice may come down to the ability to refuse further treatment. Respecting the patient's wishes may mean "there comes a time when physicians, family and friends must cease their efforts to fight death not in order to abandon the patient, but to provide care and only care."[5]

The key moral principle in support of care is *do violence to no one.* Although that principle by itself solves no problems, it is relevant to every complicated situation. In recent decades there have been frequent references to natural death. That phrase could have the helpful meaning that violence should not be done to the biological organism. But it is the nature of the human to reshape the forces of nature, both human and nonhuman. Human intervention in nonviolent ways can lessen the anguish and the pain of dying.

Because violence is already widespread in the world, the best that one can sometimes do is to reduce violence or to choose the lesser of two kinds of violence. The person who tries to live nonviolently will sometimes be caught in a situation where acting for what is humanly good will likely spillover to unintended violence. The great advocates of nonviolence have been acutely aware of that fact. Few human beings can avoid tragic dilemmas.

Suffering and Pain

A key distinction to make in this area is between suffering and pain. Suffering is what human beings regularly do—that is, they suffer the world. Every sentient animal suffers or takes in the world as the way to having an interior life. Suffering is generally good; one cannot be a human being without engaging an environment that includes human beings, other living beings, and the physical universe. Human beings become (very) unique because they are open to the whole universe.

This openness to all experience can produce a spiritual suffering that is specific to human animals. In spiritual suffering, a person finds it difficult to interact with the everyday world that usually provides a range of emotional responses. Spiritual suffering plays a central role in the experiences of dying. When a person becomes aware that he or she is dying, spiritual suffering is an appropriate response. Everything that a person has cherished is falling away. But there comes a time for a dying person when this suffering is no longer a source of anxiety and fear. The experience is one of letting go, knowing that all will be well.

The bad side of suffering is that it often involves pain, something that human beings wish to avoid. But pain cannot be entirely avoided unless one cuts off much of the human suffering of the world. Sometimes that suffering means the feeling of pain in a bodily organ. In this case, pain can be a useful sign that something is wrong in the organism and needs attention. Also, the disciplining of the body can use pain as a guide to where a physical exercise has reached a desirable limit. A little amount of voluntary pain from exercise can prepare the body for when it is struck with unwanted pain. However, the experience of pain itself is not a good. Individuals avoid pain unless they see it as a stepping stone to what they want to reach. They put up with pain, but they are not choosing pain as a good.

In the past, Christianity was sometimes accused of glorifying pain; suffering, it was said by Christians, is redemptive. Jesus suffered and died for our sins; bear your sufferings as you follow the way of the cross. If you are suffering terrible pains, it is part of God's mysterious plan. I would not ridicule a religious belief that has given comfort to millions of people in terrible situations. But the distinction between suffering and pain is important in understanding the Christian story. Christians these days do not often invoke a belief that pain is good for you. Like nearly everyone else, they try to stop the pain with the resources of modern medicine.

There are people who bring to the question of suffering and pain their particular religious beliefs. Similar to the preacher Paneloux in Camus's novel *The Plague,* they praise or at least justify pain on religious grounds. In response to a sermon by Paneloux, the physician Rieux says, "Every country priest who visits his parishioners and has heard a man gasping for breath on his deathbed thinks as I do. He'd try to relieve human suffering before trying to point out its excellence."[6] The problem here is not religion but an interpretation of Christianity that is out of kilter with the best of that tradition. The intrusion of bad religion is not a reason for excluding religion from the discussion but rather for including a wide range of religious believers who can bring an informed attitude to the table.

The narrative of Jesus's life, death, and resurrection has to be placed into a full human context. The adoption of the metaphor of sacrifice in the early church was not a helpful development for understanding the life, death, and resurrection of Jesus. Christians believe that Jesus suffered the whole world, which inevitably involved suffering pain. The redemption consisted in overcoming the slings and arrows of this life through a suffering that led to resurrection. Pain does not redeem; rather, the human reaction to tragedies within the human community is the saving grace of a human life.

Jesus does not recommend pain to his followers even though they have to be ready to bear with pain. In the New Testament, the clearest basis for a final judgment is found in Matthew 25. Jesus does not say, "I was hungry, and you explained to me that hunger is good for the soul." Instead, he says, "I was hungry and you gave me food." The implication throughout the whole passage is "I was in pain, and you did what you could to relieve the pain."

No one succeeds in avoiding all pain. We admire people who bear pain without complaining. From our earliest experience, we know that life involves a certain amount of pain, and the sooner we accept that fact the less whining we will do. Especially as one becomes old, minor aches and pains are unavoidable. In old age, a person can either complain about the weakening of the organism or else can be thankful for an extension of the life span beyond the experience of previous generations. It is not long ago that men typically lived to their sixties, had a heart attack, and soon died. The more typical pattern now is that men and women survive one or more heart attacks, and they die of cancer or heart disease in their eighties. Advances in the treatment of heart disease have been astounding, but humans are still mortal animals.

What is startling is how unfair life is in doling out the pain. Some people seem to glide through life with only the slightest physical pain;

other people seem to be in the hands of a merciless demon of pain. Contemporary medicine is a blessing for people who would otherwise suffer from relentless physical pain.

Untreated pain is disabling for older people and can hasten death. And yet up to 60 percent of older people living at home and 80 percent of people in nursing homes experience considerable pain. "Older people cope better with pain but the bad news is that they cope by decreasing function and accepting pain as a consequence of aging."[7] There are usually safe and effective ways to reduce pain.

Many people are under-medicated for pain because of a fear that they will become addicted to drugs. If a person does not wish to have drugs clouding his or her mind, that decision should be respected. But there is no reason why drugs should not be liberally used for a dying person so as to eliminate pain as far as possible. Hospices have generally known this, but many hospitals have not.

The Roman Catholic Church's teaching in this area is more flexible and realistic than in many other aspects of morality. The *Catechism of the Catholic Church* says that "the use of pain killers to alleviate the sufferings of the dying, even at the risk of shortening their days, can be morally in conformity with human dignity if death is not willed as either an end or a means, but only foreseen and tolerated as inevitable."[8] If the relief of pain will shorten a person's life, then some responsible person has to make a judgment about the manner and amount of pain killers that are administered. Cutting ten years from a person's life would be wrong; but the probability of shortening the life of a person who has only months or weeks to live should not be an issue if relief from pain is obviously needed. A key question here is how to interpret "hastening death."

Hastening Death

I think the phrase hastening death has to be interpreted very flexibly and expansively. To kill a person, including oneself, is almost always wrong. Intending to kill a person and using the means to do so go counter to our deepest moral sense. Exceptions have always been made, such as if one is defending someone who is being attacked and the defense results in the death of the attacker. But exceptions should not be casually made. The justifications of war and the state execution of prisoners seem to me outrageous and immoral.

Doing nothing to prevent a person's death, when clearly one could do so, can be equivalent to killing a person. However, there is a conceptual difference between the deliberate killing of a human being and the case of allowing the process of dying to be completed, even though an intervention might keep the person alive for a while. There have always been cases where the line is blurred between those two concepts. There are new questions that have to be asked in many situations today. What does the process of dying mean? What kinds of interventions do and do not make sense in a particular case? What does living for a while longer mean? Today's medicine has made more common the cases of a blurred line.

What does it mean to be dying? "Birth is the messenger of death," says the Talmud. One could say that we are always in the process of dying. We do not usually think that way because it could be paralyzing if we always had before our mind the thought, *I am dying, so what is the point of doing anything?* Living in denial of death is what most people do most of the time. We usually act as if we are never going to die, which can be a positive attitude. The healthiest way to live is with an occasional but not obsessive consideration of our mortality.

Every day in numerous ways we either hasten or postpone our moment of dying. Since we seldom know how any particular action factors into our dying, we calculate the odds, usually subconsciously. Some things are known on the average to shorten life, but it is impossible to know if one of them will shorten *my* life. Crossing the street every day could shorten my life, but the risk is a practical necessity. Everyone knows that cigarette smoking kills; no one knows if my smoking will kill me. Many people play the not-so-great odds with cigarettes. Some jobs have an exceptionally high mortality rate, but there are people who think that the odds are worth taking. Police officers, fire fighters, and reporters in war zones think that the work is worth doing despite the dangers. The rest of us benefit from people who risk shortening their lives in doing dangerous but necessary work.

Teenagers very often do dangerous things because they have a feeling of immortality; time will teach them otherwise. But a middle-aged man who is conscious of mortality and who smokes, drinks excessively, and has an unhealthy diet appears to be trying to kill himself. Karl Menninger called this pattern of life "chronic suicide."[9] The eventual death will not go into the books as suicide, but the middle-aged man has begun the quickening of his life's end. In most such cases, there is some kind of spiritual suffering, which can have a variety of causes. In the obvious cases of suicide, the great majority of the people are clinically depressed, which is one way that our culture talks about spiritual suffering. Hastening of death in such cases needs to be resisted with medicine, psychology, or spiritual counseling.

Allowing Death to Occur

There is a quite different wish to hasten one's death that probably deserves another name than suicide.[10] There are tens of thousands of people in nursing homes and hospitals who believe that their lives are now complete. They have lived for a longer time than the vast majority of human beings. They have accomplished everything in life that they have thought important. Their friends have died. One or more family members may occasionally visit, but the old person does not function as a family member. It is a puzzle to them that they are alive. If the person is religious, he or she is likely to ask, "Why doesn't God take me?" They are not in despair; they just think it is time to go.

There are thousands of other people who are in a worse physical condition, which makes it impossible for them to express a similar conclusion. A person in a coma cannot decide about treatment. He or she may have left written instructions; most people have not. Usually, an advanced directive still needs interpretation. If a person suffers from dementia, one has to try to interpret his or her wishes. Until the very end of life, dementia patients may be capable of stating their own wishes, including a wish to die.

Should people be allowed, with help if needed, to end their lives? Here is where the principle of do no violence comes in. What is morally desirable is that one live nonviolently, which includes the way we die. If someone clearly wishes to die, then there are ways to hasten the death either by the way actions are taken in the care of the patient or by simply not doing things to postpone death. Whatever is the process, it should be the least violent way possible. A nonviolent means is a sign that a caregiver is helping along the process of dying instead of deliberately killing. Violence is a sign of an impatient intrusion into the process of dying.

In the extraordinary movie *Amour,* the man caring for his wife who is afflicted with dementia may seem a model of good ethical practice. But as the world closes in on the couple, one has to wonder whether he should have reached out for help. He had taken on a task that was beyond his human endurance. The woman is ready to die, and by resisting his efforts to keep her alive, she indicates that she wishes to die. Her husband does not accept that fact and forces her to take nourishment. When she resists, he finally snaps and kills her by suffocating her. Movie audiences gasp in horror at the scene. Most of the viewers would probably agree that he should have helped her to complete the process of dying, but the suddenness and violence of his action properly draws a negative response.

What is perhaps the most morally problematic situation is that a person can be diagnosed with an incurable disease that is debilitating, but the disease itself is not fatal. Someone with Lou Gehrig's disease (ALS) has the prospect of losing all bodily functions while remaining mentally alert. It is understandable that a person who is afflicted with a terribly debilitating but not fatal disease may conclude that his or her life has now reached completion. Our medical terminology does not call the disease terminal, but the body is closing down, and the lifelong process of dying has reached a crisis point.

Not every person with a terrible handicap or sickness sees it that way. There are examples of people who, despite their illness or disability, live with the ordinary range of human joys and sorrows, or even make spectacular contributions to the common good. But if someone has lived with the problem for a long time, has been given the best of care, and has given serious thought to all the circumstances of his or her condition, can anyone say with certainty that his or her wish to reach the end of life is wrong?

A person who has ALS has a condition in which the body has already shut down most of its functions. The person may continue to have the strength and the help to participate in the human community. But at some point the person may not wish to continue the struggle. Anyone who aids the person in his or her desire to die is hastening the process of dying, which began at birth and has now reached its concluding phase. Most of us can barely imagine how it feels to be in that condition. The act of helping such a person to die seems to make moral sense.

A significant percentage of people who are on kidney dialysis simply stop the treatment. Are they killing themselves? In our usual language, the answer is yes. Their choice does involve an end to their life, but instead of wishing to die, they wish for a life without kidney failure. They participate in the cause of what kills them, but so do many people in less obvious ways. They are not committing suicide; they are allowing the disease to run its course.

People do not die of dementia; most dementia patients die of infection. Dementia patients are often subjected to multiple surgeries for infections. If an infection is not treated, the patient will die, but the dying can usually be free of serious pain. A physician with the agreement of the person's next of kin may decide not to perform surgery. The physician and the loved one know that the patient will die, but the intention is not to kill; it is to allow dying in the most humane way available.

This position of allowing and possibly hastening death differs from most writing today in favor of euthanasia. Writing on euthanasia today tends to be consequentialist—that is, what counts is the result. When the *New England Journal of Medicine* said that stopping treatment of a disease is different from intending to kill, James Rachels said that "of course it is exactly that, and if it were not, there would be no point to it."[11] Catholic moral tradition has always taken account of more than the consequence of an action.

An action can have results that are not intended by the actor. Catholic tradition included an important principle that came to be known as "double effect." The principle was taught in theology with exotic examples, such as whether it is allowable to throw someone off a lifeboat so that the other passengers can survive. That kind of discussion obscured the fact that the principle of intended and unintended results operates in practically every decision. Modern ethicists are skeptical of distinctions that came from theology, but this one is indispensable for reflecting on the morality of an action.[12]

The intended and unintended results are not parallel, but neither is one simply the means to the other. The person is intent on accomplishing a result; he or she has to take account of what is possible, likely, or certain to accompany the intended action. The military has given a bad name to what it calls collateral damage. While there may be a great effort to be precise in dropping bombs from the sky, violence done to people nearby is entirely predictable. It is difficult to claim one is innocent of collateral results if one begins by acting violently. The case is different when nonviolent protests for justice spark violent reactions.

If the intended result is to allow a patient to die peacefully, the means should be nonviolent, and the actor has to be as clear as possible about the motive of an action or an absence of action. A caregiver who does not want the burden of care any longer does not make a good judge about allowing the end to occur. Can we ever be entirely certain of our motives when facing difficult decisions? Perhaps not. But that the motive is allowing the person to come to a peaceful end is reflected in the means used for hastening death. When the means is sudden and violent, a humane completion to life is absent. But caring for a person until the last moment of life can include actions or omissions of action that have the unintended effect of death.

Modern medical devices such as a respirator or a nutrition line have been wonderful inventions that can temporarily be a substitute when a person is incapable of the actions of breathing or eating. These devices can artificially extend life until ordinary life can be restored. But if it is clear that there is no hope of the person rejoining the human community, indefinitely perpetuating mechanical activity does not humanly make sense. At some point, preserving life can obscure what is most important—namely, the life of a person.

Removing a respirator from a dying person has become legally accepted in many places. The action allows dying to take its course. It should not be described as suffocating a patient. The lungs and heart are no longer functioning; if there is no hope that they can be repaired, then death is imminent.

There has been more resistance to removing a feeding tube. Inflammatory language, such as "starving a person to death," is not helpful for people who are faced with dilemmas and tragedies.[13] Some people think that removing a feeding tube is an act of violence, but it is usually a recognition that the inability to eat is a sign that the body is preparing for death. When the body cannot digest food, it can be a violent act to force-feed a patient.

Actions or lack of actions that result in an end to life are morally acceptable when the whole context makes sense, including that the person has come to this decision after reflection on the circumstances of his or her condition. Laws allowing suicide in the Netherlands and in a few states of the United States have included such conditions. There are dangers that physicians will subtly encourage suicide or, especially in the United States, that money will become the primary motivation for hastening death. The movement for legalized suicide is being oversold with the phrase *dying with dignity*, meaning suicide. In hospices, dying with dignity means providing the best care possible to a dying patient.

One cannot trust the courts to decide what is moral. The Supreme Court has enough trouble trying to establish legal principles. The Roman Catholic Church has a long tradition that would be helpful to its participation in a national conversation on the care of the dying. The church's official teaching on end-of-life issues is much more nuanced and humane than critics of the church assume. A usual claim is that "the Roman Catholic Church is the sternest, most vigilant, and no doubt most effective opponent of euthanasia, as it is of abortion."[14] It is true that the church has always condemned euthanasia, but the meaning of euthanasia has changed in recent decades.

Throughout most of its history, the term *euthanasia* has meant mercy killing. The term has now been extended to cover any actions or nonactions that result in death.[15] What the church has always allowed is now being included in *euthanasia*. As a result of this change in the meaning of the term, a condemnation of euthanasia by church officials is ineffective and misleading. I think it is unfortunate that the term *euthanasia* has been extended in meaning to include not using all means in all circumstances to keep a person alive. But whether or not one likes the change in terminology, church officials have to be aware of the change when talking about euthanasia.

Church officials need to listen to the people who regularly confront these complex situations in nursing homes, hospitals, and hospices today. Complicated cases of morality are not solved by just applying abstract principles. Anyone who wishes to make a helpful contribution to a national and international discussion of issues around dying has to be willing to enter a genuine conversation on new problems that the world is facing.

Chapter 7

A Healthy Attitude toward Grief and Mourning

Everyone knows that death awaits, but we assume it will come later when we are better prepared for its arrival. Death is not a minor event in anyone's life. Thinkers from Plato to Freud have argued that all we do in life is governed by our views of mortality, which we almost but not quite succeed in banishing from consciousness. We are blessed with the power to foresee that we are going to die; we are incapacitated by our refusal to accept this fact of life.

For nearly everyone who dies, there are people who are traumatized by the death. They are grief-stricken that there is now a hole in the world that will never be filled. When the grief is for one's child, parent, spouse, or closest friend, one may feel that it is not worth continuing to live without that person's presence. As far back in history as we can trace, the human community has surrounded the death of a loved one with a ritual for stabilizing the community, lest its members swirl out of control. No one avoids grief; toward the end of life, it will become a constantly recurring experience. Human beings, besides being the rational animals, are the grieving animals.

The Christian movement was a bold attempt to deal with death by accepting it and going beyond it. At its center was the death-resurrection of Jesus of Nazareth. The church took over the idea of resurrection from

Jewish religion and linked this idea with celebration of the rebirth of nature that is found in other religions. Resurrection was a statement about the universe, not just a puzzling fact about Jesus. Dying is still painful for each person who dies; grief is still a burden for those who survive. The funeral rites surrounding the Christian's death were a paradoxical mixing of sorrow and hope. On the subject of death, church rituals have a long and rich history. Catholic tradition is a storehouse of possibilities that might speak to today's world.

As is true with most of the Catholic tradition, the good has been mixed in with the bad. When education in the church did not keep pace with the need for it, Christian doctrine was simplified in a way that focused on the dramatic and crude: "Jesus died for your sins in the most painful way imaginable. Each person is a sinner whose life will be exposed to harsh judgment by a just God." The rituals surrounding funeral and mourning continued to have consoling elements of support. But the fearful and frightening part of the liturgy came to predominate. By the late Middle Ages, death was portrayed as a court trial when there would be a final temptation. It was believed that as the person reviews his whole life on his death bed, he will be tempted either to despair or to vainglory.[1]

That attitude of fear was captured in the booming medieval hymn "Dies Irae," which was sung at Catholic funerals up to the 1960s. "Day of wrath and doom impending/David's word with Sibyl's blending/Heaven and earth in ashes ending. Oh what fear man's bosom rendeth/When from heaven the Judge descendeth/On whose sentence all dependeth. Lo! The book exactly worded/Wherein all hath been recorded/Thence shall judgment be awarded. Worthless are my prayers and sighing/Yet, good Lord in grace complying/Rescue me from fires undying."

The shift in tone of the funeral liturgy was one of the most dramatic results of the Second Vatican Council. Hope and joy replaced the attitude of fear and trembling. On the whole, it was a welcome change; it would be difficult to imagine that anyone would prefer a return to the precouncil atmosphere of funerals. One might still ask whether jumping from sorrow to joy had the danger of not acknowledging that the response to the death of a loved one is a deep sorrow that cannot be quickly replaced with joy. A period of bereavement that lasts for months is still a necessity to absorb the blow of death.

Geoffrey Gorer in a 1970s study of mourning found that the modern world did not handle mourning well.[2] He found two groups that were exceptions: Orthodox Jews and Roman Catholics. That may still be true today, given that practices around death are the most resistant to change. But there should be concern lest in this area the Roman Catholic Church adapt all too easily to the modern world and try to cover up the wound that the death of a loved person inflicts on the mourner. Much of the modern world prefers to manage death in a few days and then pretend that nothing significant has happened.

If, as it is often said, death is hidden in our culture, then one should not be surprised that mourning is, too. The dying cannot help what is happening to them; they stir up sympathy for their plight. But the mourner is more likely to generate impatience and resentment. "Get on with your life" is the frequent advice given to the mourner. When mourning is hidden or suppressed, it does not go away; it operates quietly but endlessly. As patients can be put on life-support systems that maintain only a semblance of life, so millions of people go on mourning with no end in sight.

A few distinctions in the use of terms would help in setting out the problem and getting some bearings in the use of resources. *Grief*, *mourning*, and *bereavement* are the terms most often used in referring to a response to death in the lives of survivors. Grief is a feeling of sorrow that follows upon a loss; most commonly it is used as a noun. Grief connotes a burden that a person carries when someone who had shared the burdens of life is now gone. Grief is the territory for psychologists and grief counselors who try to unlock the feelings of grieving individuals.

Mourning is helpfully distinguished from grief as its outward expression. Most commonly, mourning is used as a verb; to mourn is the activity of expressing grief. An individual mourns as a community member; that is, the main agent of mourning is a community or a group, while the individual both gives and receives as part of the community's process of mourning. The mourner can be a whole nation at a time when the nation has lost a leader and occasionally when a nation has lost its soul. Psychologists know much about mourning, but they are not the final experts. Every community has wise adults who have learned both to comfort and to mourn.

Bereavement is a state or condition in which mourners exist. The related adjective bereft is not used much in English, but it still carries the powerful image of feeling deprived and desolate. The noun *bereavement* is also not very common because a set period for mourning is no longer in fashion. People are supposedly freer to express their grief as they wish and for as long as they need to do so. But a bereavement having form and length survives among some religious groups and might actually be more supportive of personal freedom. Bereavement is capable of including both meanings of end: a fixed purpose and a termination point. The good thing about bereavement is that it ends.

Freud has a helpful essay on the difference between mourning and melancholy.[3] Both are feelings of loss, but melancholy is without end. The sad person who is afflicted with melancholy, says Freud, loses his or her own life and becomes impoverished emotionally. In contrast, the mourner "bit by bit, under great expense of time and ... energy returns to reality." The existence of the lost "object" remains in mind. In the grip of mourning, the world becomes poor and empty; in melancholy, it is the ego itself that is emptied. The absence of joy in one's life may paradoxically be due to an inability to mourn.

Public Mourning

Mourning is a personal and communal act that can only be understood as a relational response. If there is no community with rituals for mourning, then feelings of grief cannot be accepted and dealt with in a healthy way. What increasingly is the situation today is a dichotomy. On the one hand, there is intense private mourning that saps bodily and spiritual strength, and on the other hand, there is an ostentatious public mourning that promises what it cannot deliver. Public displays of mourning, such as the recent practice of victims confronting criminals at a court sentencing, supposedly bring closure, but more often than not they interfere with people coming to terms with their grief. Similarly, each time the nation relives a national calamity, most citizens simply repeat the grief.

Geoffrey Gorer's study compared mourning in the twentieth century to sex in the nineteenth century. The attitude was that everyone is known to do it in private, but one should not speak about it in public. Things have changed in the decades since Gorer's study but perhaps not as much as the surface would suggest. The place of sex was changed by adding public displays. There is endless talk about sex in the culture. But the main activities of sex remain intensely private and often contorted. Mourning, too, has acquired splashy public displays, but feelings of grief might remain bottled up in a private sphere.

The bridge between private and public spheres is rituals of community life that sustain interpersonal relations. Community rituals are external performances that allow for varying degrees of private feelings. Rituals of their nature are conservative; they connect us to the past. They are always vulnerable to being attacked as outdated and irrelevant. But at the most intense moments of their lives, humans need to be buoyed by routine gestures that hold the world together until new and reasonable actions can begin again.

Rituals have to grow organically; they cannot simply be invented. The best rituals are hundreds or thousands of years old. Rituals can change without losing their effectiveness, provided the change slowly emerges out of past experience. What can be especially corruptive of rituals surrounding death is the exploitation of tender feelings for the sake of profit. The commodification of grief, including books, workshops, and chat rooms, has boomed in recent decades.

The beginning of the grief industry was in the 1840s when the profession of undertaker or funeral director was born. The casket (a word taken from the jewel industry) replaced the plain, wooden coffin. Embalming became a standard practice to keep the corpse looking natural when obviously it is not. The funeral parlor gradually replaced the home as the setting for the mourners to gather. One cannot expect a funeral industry to reflect better attitudes toward death than does the culture as a whole. Death education is not primarily a matter for mortuary schools, or even for schools. It starts with the way parents provide an example of mourning to their children, and the education continues by way of the many groups and organizations in which people participate.

Television, now joined with the Internet, is one of the great variables in the modern expression of grief. Television is now old enough to have its own rituals. It can be an unsurpassable bond at moments of great sorrow. It can also be an instrument for the manipulation of mostly manufactured emotions. When John Kennedy was killed in 1963, rituals on television and the ritual of television itself were relatively new. The assassination of a president, who had projected youth and vigorous action, came as a genuine shock to the nation and the world. Television provided a calming effect. The funeral was elegantly designed with admirable restraint in its form. For four days the nation stopped its business and felt the reality of death.

It probably was not possible that television could ever repeat this simple and restrained approach to the need for national mourning. Just five years later, the deaths of Robert Kennedy and Martin Luther King Jr. evoked some of the same feelings as did the assassination of John Kennedy. But the country's mood was much different, and television could not heal the divisions that these deaths embodied. The artificiality of television's grief was evident. Since then, the death of a famous person—rock stars, movie actresses, athletes—sets the grief machine in motion.

The regular occurrence of mass shootings in the United States now guarantees public shrines and a string of political speeches on how terrible this event was and how it must never happen again. When the shooting takes place in a school, there is a special poignancy to the mourning and a more intense demand for action. A flurry of proposals follows: restrictions on gun ownership, better identification of people who are mentally disturbed, and improved treatment of the sick. Legislators would prefer not to get themselves involved in sticky situations; the gun lobby is known for its effective opposition to any control of firearms, even guns designed for a battlefield. One has to suspect that the public mournings are largely the result of media attention. The mourning disappears when the television crews leave.

In the United States, the event that bears closest comparison to John Kennedy's death is the bombings on September 11, 2001. The date itself became an immediate marker of anger, grief, self-pity, and insecurity. The spontaneous shrines that appeared the next few days in Manhattan represented genuine grief and the need to mourn in an appropriately public way. Television's part was a mixture of the best and the worst. For the first few days, a cadre of television reporters who were close to the scene delivered graphic and calming reports. But television's voracious appetite for news has no built-in restraints.

Some of the memorials at political, athletic, and educational gatherings during subsequent weeks expressed grief in a visible and solemn form. But after listening to a hundred renditions of "God Bless America," many nations that had shared in the US grief reached the limit of their sympathy. It was time for the United States to put its grief into world perspective. That did not mean to forget the event but to situate it in a way that is helpful for itself and for other nations. It is unclear whether the United States has yet come to this perspective.

Washington, DC, which Philippe Ariès described as a city of monuments to the dead, has one memorial that is different. The Vietnam memorial, a plain dark wall with 58,235 names on it, has done as much as any one thing to heal the division caused by that disastrous war in Southeast Asia. The designer, Maya Lin, who was a twenty-one-year-old student at Yale, accomplished a near miracle in getting the monument built. National monuments seldom carry such power because mourning (in contrast to grief) requires interaction. People rather than stones are the ordinary basis for interacting.

The genius of Lin's design is that, unlike so many recent memorials that merely relive the past horror, the Vietnam memorial has a narrative, a powerful story that begins with the grim facts but then moves the visitor beyond the grave. "I had an impulse to cut open the earth," wrote Lin. "The grass would grow back, but the cut would remain." One walks down until one is overwhelmed by the dead, but then one walks up and out. Perhaps the only comparable memorial in Washington is the Holocaust museum, filled as it is with the ordinary stuff of life and the extraordinary means of death. The museum is most powerful for

Jewish people, but as the crowds of visitors indicate, its stark simplicity crosses both ethnic and generational lines.

Personal/Communal Mourning

For most people most of the time, mourning is possible because there are a few people who are physically present to share the grief. The correlative of the verb *to mourn* is *to comfort*, a word that means to bring strength. The comforter brings strength mainly by being there. To comfort and to mourn are reciprocal actions; they can move back and forth in exchanges between mourner and comforter. Often the mourner ends up comforting the one who has come to offer support. No matter; the comforter and the mourner share the burden of grief and also share the healing that comes from genuine human encounters in dark times.

A ritual for coping with death has been central to most religions. Death runs counter to human plans, human hopes, and human love. Rational explanations in the wake of death are not very convincing. Comfort is provided by the presence of a few people who share a common history. They do not have to say anything; it may be better not to try explaining. Harold Kushner in *When Bad Things Happen to Good People* says that Job's friends did two things right: they showed up, and they stayed. Where they went wrong was in trying to answer Job's question, why did this happen?[4]

Religious rituals contain formulas that everyone in the community knows well. Such fixed formulas can be criticized as clichés or empty formalism. But in the midst of profound grief, few people are able to come up with fresh and brilliant insights that fit the situation. Most of us are stuck with saying "I'm sorry" or some other inane-sounding phrase. It is the strength of ritual sayings that they carry people through their sorrow. The standard Roman Catholic practice at wakes was to say the rosary, "a decade of the beads." The repetition of a prayer formula without much thought to the words can be a blessing. Jewish religion probably has the most precisely specified gestures and words from the moment of death throughout the week that follows.[5]

The Process of Bereavement

The funeral service usually gives support to the grievers for the period immediately following death. The same cannot be said of the mourning period that comes after the funeral. Widows complain that their friends and colleagues shun them for months and then pretend that nothing has happened. The writing of a letter of condolence is something of a lost art, but cards and letters are still an important form of comforting during the weeks and months after a death. Whether the card comes three days or six months later, it is always welcome. Today's e-mail lacks some of the desired formality, but it does have the advantage of providing easy access to worldwide communication. A parish church is an obvious place for programs to support widows and widowers.

Contemporary culture finds it difficult to accept that there is no substitute for time when it comes to mourning. The saying *time heals all wounds* is demonstrably false, but, nonetheless, time is an indispensable factor if wounds are to heal. The closer the person was, the more intense is the body's reaction. This closeness includes someone who was not necessarily loved but who nonetheless had an intimate bond with the survivor. A son or daughter who has been estranged from a parent or who constantly fought with a parent will often be surprised at how intensely he or she feels the loss.

Confucius said, "If a man ever reveals his true self, it is when he is mourning his parents." Middle-aged people today are likely to have one or both parents alive. It might seem that having one's parents alive until one's forties or fifties should make it easier to let go when they die, but it does not work that way. Middle-aged people whose parents die are inevitably surprised when the word that comes forcefully to mind is *orphan*. It is embarrassing to admit feeling like an orphan at the age of fifty. Always there had been a generation in front. The death of the parents means moving to the front pew at funerals.

The novelist Saul Bellow wrote to his biographer, "When my father died I was for a long time sunk." One tries to come up for air and coast along with the current. Many people insist after a few days that they have their feet back on the ground. The truth may be that they have postponed the reaction, which is sure to be more severe a month, six months, or a year later.

Most of the policies that allow leave from work provide three days to mourn one's parents. That is nowhere near enough for most people. In some work settings, coworkers can be very helpful in providing a stable environment, but returning to work immediately after the death of a parent, spouse, or close relative can be an evasion of the time to mourn. The arrival of insurance agents, real estate brokers, and tax accountants the day after the funeral is not the kind of interaction one needs.

The death of one's child is almost a different species of grief. The sense of loss at a parent's death is balanced by the recognition that life has its natural cycles; after fullness of life, there is inevitable decline and death. The death of a child is a screaming denial of what we assume are the ways of God or nature. Unless the parents can find a way to mourn together, the child's death will put a terrible strain upon their marriage. The parents need to talk and to talk to each other, but the situation makes talking difficult if not impossible. The sudden death of a child raises the mortality rate of the bereaved parents five times above the average.

There is strong resistance to the idea that the nature and length of a process of mourning can be universally charted. Certainly, anthropology has made us aware of the cultural variations surrounding death, disposal of the body, and mourning. More important, however, is anthropology's finding that every culture does have rituals for the funeral and a period of mourning. Today's culture is the odd one in dissolving almost all the trappings of a bereavement process. Perhaps that represents progress, but the medical and psychiatric toll suggests otherwise.

Stages of Mourning

It is surprising that stages of mourning have not been studied more extensively. People often refer to Kübler-Ross's book, *Death and Dying*, as describing the stages of grief.[6] But her study was entirely focused on stages of dying. The assumption that the two processes can be equated makes some sense, but there are some obvious differences. Mourning starts where dying leaves off (or possibly a little earlier). The end of the two processes differs. *Acceptance* might apply to the process of mourning as well as to that of dying, but the connotations of the word in the two situations are not the same.

In many cultures, there are two funerals or a funeral in two parts. The first funeral directly signifies the dying of the individual and the disintegration of the community. After some weeks or months, a second funeral is held; the remains are moved to a final resting place. Order has thereby been reestablished both for the community and for the dead person who has been reintegrated into life.

In the second funeral, men and women traditionally have different roles, and the ceremony includes sexual imagery. There is nothing shocking in the close association of sex and death. The struggle of life to overcome death is represented by the mixing of young men and young women. From ancient Greece down to the modern Irish wake and African burial rites, funerals have always been a choice time for finding a sexual partner.

Modern cultures do not have two funerals. But in some religions, the body is quickly disposed of, and a memorial service is held later. Friends and relatives for whom travel to the funeral was impossible can plan ahead for the memorial service. The mood of the second gathering is still somber, but the life of the dead person is now celebrated along with his or her death being mourned. Favorite stories about the dead person are recalled by each of the living participants. A eulogy means speaking appreciatively of the dead person.

For many people, of course, this second part of the funeral follows immediately after the first. The sadness at the cemetery gives way to a robust meal and sometimes overly robust drinking. The juxtaposition can seem incongruous, but, like sex, eating and drinking are the human challenge to death's finality. The drawback in the modern practice is the impatient attempt to settle everything in a few hours rather than letting time have its place.

The essence of Kübler-Ross's stages of dying is a three-part sequence: 1) a no to death that is a yes to life, 2) a yes to death that is a no to life, and then 3) a yes to life that includes death as part of life. The third moment is not really a stage so much as the synthesis of the two stages that have preceded. The two stages can be repeated any number of times. Kübler-Ross documented four stages of dying, but she implies that there could be six, eight, or another even number. The final synthesis, which is acceptance, can be reached only after the dialectic of yes and no has moved the elements toward embrace.

The stages of mourning have this same structure. If anything, the stages are more obvious in the case of mourning than in that of dying. One criticism of Kübler-Ross's stages of dying was that not everyone has a lengthy period in which to think about their fatal disease. Kübler-Ross acknowledged that point in granting that people reach acceptance only if they have sufficient time. In the experience of mourning, a lack of time is not the problem. Indeed, the problem here is finding a place to end the process of mourning. Some people are still mourning the death of a child fifty years later.

For many people today, the period of mourning begins before death. When a patient is on a life-support system for years, the family is likely to mourn the loss long before the system is discontinued. The experience of the survivors is that the organism is still living, but the person has departed. A similar and sometimes more agonizing experience occurs in the case of dementia, such as Alzheimer's disease. The person is still there but living in a different world. African tribal religions have a time between life and death when the person is "living-dead"; modern medicine seems to have created such a state in the nursing home or the intensive care unit of the hospital.

Stages of dying are most evident in long, drawn-out instances of dying. In sudden deaths, such as by automobile crashes or shootings, it is difficult to imagine anything called stages of dying. In contrast, stages of mourning are most evident in sudden and unexpected deaths. The survivor is plunged into one emotion and sometimes quickly reacts in an opposite direction. In such cases, when someone is informed that his or her spouse or child or close friend has died, the person reacts in the same way that a person does when informed that he or she has a terminal illness: "This cannot be true; there must be some mistake; I don't believe it."

As with the denial of dying, denial in grieving is a good thing that can go bad if persisted in for too long. When the dead body has not been seen, the denial might go on for years despite there being overwhelming evidence of the death. Each time the door opens, the unrealistic expectation of the dead person's appearance is renewed. Children who have been lied to about a parent's death, as often happens in cases of suicide, are especially prone to living in denial for years. "Mommy is away on a long trip, but she will come home someday."

The attempt to deny mourning indefinitely is likely to have repercussions. Grief is a burden that the body carries; the grief needs to be shared so as to be lightened. Erich Lindemann was among the first to document that some diseases commonly occur either when mourning is delayed or when denial is followed by an exaggerated reaction of grief. What Lindemann describes as morbid grief can have life-threatening effects.[7]

The danger in studies of mourning is that mourning itself may be seen as a sickness whereas mourning is actually the cure, to the extent that cure is possible. The experience of being somewhat depressed for a period of time is not a sickness. Whereas denial is a no to death, withdrawal is a yes to death, or at least a partial acceptance of death. Denial insists on affirming life. In contrast, withdrawal is a refusal of life, an unwillingness or an incapacity to take part in the affairs of ordinary life. Withdrawal is for healing, for letting the land lie fallow.

In the past, there were rituals for the time of bereavement. Details for its observance varied, but they typically referred to how people dress, how they are addressed, what they eat, where they travel, who visits. Weeping is a usual way to express sorrow, but religions provide a framework lest the wailing be excessive.[8] It may seem silly or even cruel that the widow had to wear black and did not go out in public for months. However, such practices did provide space in which the mourner learned quite literally to breathe again.

If one has stepped out of ordinary life, there is a risk of not returning. To mourn permanently is to be one of the dead among the living. Catholic tradition, like many other religions, avoids this result by supplying a series of markers, at the third day, the seventh day, a month, and a year. A period of bereavement is not a wandering in the desert; it is territory charted by hundreds of thousands of ancestors. At each marker along the way, a cloud of witnesses, a gathering of the community past and present, encourages a cherishing of memory in the context of a renewal of life.[9]

The final step in mourning is not a stage but a reintegration of the mourner into ordinary life. The mourner comes to a place where life wins out over depression and despair. One does not return to the same old things; instead one finds a new life with a new dimension. One will never again see life with the same eyes. The mourner now becomes capable of giving comfort to other mourners.

One paradoxical way of reintegration happens with the death of the mourner. There are numerous cases where the death of one spouse is quickly followed by the death of the other. Sometimes the second death seems to come from depression, and the widow or widower dies of a broken heart. But sometimes widows or widowers, having gone through a period of mourning, have shown that they are capable of resuming ordinary life. But then they die shortly afterward. Reintegration in such cases is with the departed spouse. The bond with the dead is stronger than any bond with the living.

How long should the period of bereavement be? Six months to a year would seem an appropriate time of bereavement for most people in most situations, presuming that the mourning was not delayed. The objection raised these days might be that a year is not enough time. While that is a genuine possibility, the objection may be due to blurring the difference between grief and mourning. The end of a period of mourning—bereavement—is not the end of sorrow and grief. For parents of a dead child or for a surviving spouse in a long-term marriage, the sorrow is unlikely to ever go away. Life will never return to what it was before the death.

Thus, *acceptance*, if the term belongs here, does not mean reaching an end point where sorrow at a death is no more; it means reaching the end of bereavement but not of sorrow. Acceptance means that the death of a loved one has become a permanent part of one's life. Not a yes to life and a no to death but a yes to life that includes the death of someone who will be forever loved.

Chapter 8

Gays, Lesbians, and Homosexual Orientation

Until recent centuries, there was some excuse for inaccurate moral teachings because accurate knowledge was not always available. Human sexuality is an area where the human race in the past has mainly depended on myth, ignorance, intolerance, and word of mouth. And by no means is the current sexual scene one of universal enlightenment and healthy practices. Despite ignorance in the past, human beings did learn from experience and concluded that some sexual practices were good, some were suspect, and a few were bad. There may be some wisdom stored in the human memory bank, along with myths and factual errors.

Human sexuality has always been integral to power relations. What was deemed sexually unacceptable depended in part on which groups could get their voices heard. For centuries, men controlled the public voice while women's voices were kept private.

Recently, men have had to come to grips with the fact that human sexuality could not be well understood if women did not have a public voice.

Another large segment of the human race that until very recently did not have a public voice is people who are oriented homosexually—that is, persons who are gay or lesbian. The emergence of gays and lesbians has opened further questions about sex, reflected now in reference to the LGBT community: lesbian, gay, bisexual, and transsexual people. No one knows where this rapidly changing picture is taking the human race, which could use a few guiding principles as it tries to assimilate a large body of new knowledge and new challenges to set ways. The Roman Catholic Church, by drawing on its long tradition, might have been a conservative guide instead of being widely perceived as one of the chief enemies of a gay/lesbian or LGBT movement.

As in most moral questions, the language used in asking the question sets the limits of any possible answer. What is notable about homosexuality is that until the end of the nineteenth century there was no language at all to address the question. It can hardly be doubted that homosexuality has always been a fact of human life. But in past centuries any reference to that reality was veiled and indirect. Roundabout phrases were used, but such descriptions did not necessarily mean what the term *homosexual* has come to mean in the twentieth and twenty-first centuries.

Homosexual was coined in the 1870s. The word is a peculiar combination of Greek and Latin. The term was invented as the name of a disease or a crime. To this day, homosexual used as a noun is usually disparaging in meaning. Homosexuals, it is feared, are a different kind of human being, who if they are not willing to be cured must be kept away from ordinary human beings. The young are supposedly susceptible to their influence so that there is fear that homosexuals may be teaching our children and leading them to debauchery.

Fortunately, this attitude is now that of a shrinking minority in the United States and many other countries. The change has happened with almost unbelievable speed. Ireland's 2015 legalization of same-sex marriage by a nearly two-to-one vote is one index of how dramatic has been the shift in attitude. In the United States, the Pew Research Poll in 2014 found a 60 percent approval of same-sex marriage among Catholics; that is higher than the 54 percent of the general population. The church may soon find the gap between official teaching and its members' attitudes on homosexuality to be as large as what exists for the official position on contraception.

Homosexual as an adjective has always had more flexibility than the noun. The adjective did not stamp a group of people as a subspecies of the human. The adjective homosexual can be a reference to one aspect of a person's life. A person who is oriented to same-sex attraction and love is not different in most respects from a heterosexual individual. What the differences and similarities are can only be known through ordinary conversation and scientific study.

The adjective homosexual in the course of a century shifted into a good or at least a neutral meaning; however, old meanings do not easily disappear. The phrase *homosexually oriented* was coined for an acceptance of homosexuality as a natural characteristic. Or at least the idea of orientation was the basis of tolerance by people who did not accept the full legitimacy of homosexuality. It is helpful to distinguish between a person's basic constitution and his or her behavior. However, the distinction can lead to an unrealistic separation between orientation and behavior. Today, gay, gay/lesbian, or LGBT tend to be the preferred terms of self-identification. However, *homosexual* is a term that is not likely to disappear any time soon.

The term *gay* is sometimes used to characterize a community or a culture. Groups that are oppressed or discriminated against often choose or are pressed to form a community as a means of resistance and survival. The linking of many such communities creates a culture of language and practices whose meanings are largely hidden from the oppressor. As intolerance toward the group eases, the need for a distinct culture lessens. But similar to the women's movement, which could not succeed without changing men, a gay movement is not likely to succeed if it does not change the perception of sexuality in the *straight* culture. The testimonies of gay and lesbian Catholics are important for changing Roman Catholic teaching, not only on homosexuality but on sex in general and sexual pleasure more particularly.[1]

Bases of Official Teaching

The two bases for the Roman Catholic Church's official teaching on homosexuality are its invocation of natural law and its citation of texts from the Bible.

119

Natural Law. The Roman Catholic Church's concern for what is natural and what is unnatural is the strength of the church's moral teaching. The church can rightly claim a tradition of trying to protect what is natural from violation and destruction. The firm basis of the church's moral teaching is its principle that what is *contra naturam*—a contradiction of nature—is immoral. This principle, however, does not logically mean that the moral and the natural are the same. The natural world of God's creation has been put in the hands of human beings for better and for worse. What can be affirmed from Catholic tradition is not that humans should submit to nature but that humans should act in accord with their nature, a nature that is constantly being reshaped artistically, politically, religiously, and sexually.

One of the most frequently used words describing homosexuality is *unnatural.* In the not-so-distant past, homosexual behavior was assumed to be a perversion of how people should act. Today, the weight of science and research is that a significant percentage of the human race is oriented toward same-sex love. Even more important than the science is the testimony of gay and lesbian people whose voices could not be heard in the past. Same-sex attraction and homosexual behavior are examples of a wonderful diversity that the human race has recently been coming to appreciate. The Roman Catholic Church, one might think, could celebrate these expressions of human-nature.

The church's official teachers often speak about a set of laws "imprinted" in the individual that allow for a simple naming of what is right and wrong.[2] But in much of life, it is not at all apparent if something is in accord with human-nature or destructive of this nature. In many cases, the best test is the test of time. Some things condemned as unnatural eventually get acceptance; other things that may seem harmless can turn out to be destructive. The individual, therefore, is not always the best judge of what is bad for him or her. But a tradition is not a help if it is not constantly being rethought in the light of new experience and knowledge. Homosexuality is a dramatic example of assumptions about human-nature that needed to be reconsidered on the basis of new information.

Alfred Kinsey's study of the sexual behavior of men in 1948 caused an uproar. He did not do a study of morality; his intention was simply to count instances of behavior. That fact was enough to get his study condemned in many quarters, but it was also the strength of what he accomplished. He was not an advocate of homosexual activity or any other kind of sexual behavior. He was in search of facts. What he discovered was a range of behavior that surprised many people, although there must have been millions of people who breathed a sigh of relief on discovering that they were not strange after all.

Kinsey found that up to 40 percent of men had engaged in same-sex intimacies. He estimated that 5 to 10 percent of men were homosexually oriented. Although critics protested that those numbers must be false, the data have generally stood up in subsequent studies; precise statistics are still impossible to get.[3] The most important thing was not the exact numbers but that Kinsey was able to distinguish same-sex activity of heterosexual men from the activity of men who are genuinely homosexual by nature. Henceforth, it was important to distinguish but not separate orientation and behavior. The term *homosexual behavior* should not logically be used for people who are heterosexual; the same-sex activity in those cases is the result of either experimentation or assault.

Bible. The second basis for the Roman Catholic Church's condemnation of homosexual behavior is the Bible. Here the Roman Catholic Church joins forces with some of evangelical Protestantism. Similar to the protest against abortion, the Roman Catholic Church and the most conservative wing of Protestantism make strange bedfellows. On most moral issues, the Roman Catholic Church's appeal to the Bible is secondary. The general tenor and outlook of the Bible is referred to, but proof texts have become less important, given the advance of biblical scholarship in the Roman Catholic Church.

The church has tried to reset the center of morality around the life and teaching of Jesus. The chief tenets of that teaching are to love God and to love one's neighbor. If homosexuality were a big moral problem, would one not expect guidance from the gospels? Church officials make no appeal to the gospels for their condemnation of homosexual behavior. The reason is simple: there is nothing in the gospels to appeal to. Jesus was a single man whose public life was mostly spent among a group of men. Did Jesus ever whisper to John, "the beloved disciple," that he should be careful about expressing his affection for one of the other disciples? If so, there is no record of any warning by Jesus about same-sex love.

Before any text in the Bible is cited as condemning homosexuality, the first and most important thing to be noted is that the Bible has *nothing* to say about homosexuality. The Bible had no term for homosexuality and no idea of homosexuality. The biblical authors could not condemn what they did not know and what they could not name. Contemporary authors sometimes acknowledge this fact of language and then proceed to cite texts in the Bible that supposedly condemn homosexuality.

The appeal to the Bible for condemning homosexuality consists of a strange selection of isolated texts.[4] The book of Leviticus plays a central role. Why Christians would follow the teaching of Leviticus on this question while disregarding almost everything else in Leviticus is a puzzle. As part of a long list of practices that excluded a man from the community, Lev. 18:22 says: "You shall not lie with a man as with a woman; it is an abomination." The condemnation is repeated in Lev. 20:13: "If a man lies with a male as with a woman both of them have committed an abomination." However, when these two texts are invoked, the second half of each verse is omitted—namely, "They shall be put to death, their blood is upon them." If the first half of the verse is given total validity, why is the second half of the verse dismissed as not worth mentioning? Actually, what seems to be the most relevant biblical text in Leviticus for discussing homosexuality is verse 19:20: "You shall love your neighbor as yourself."

The author of the book of Leviticus did not have the word *unnatural*; there was no such concept or term in ancient Hebrew. The word *abomination* that he used was to indicate a violation of the ritual code. Abomination took on a quite different meaning in later history.

In the New Testament, St. Paul, who was writing in Greek, did have available the term *nature*; he could therefore refer to some things as unnatural. However, his use of the term was unsystematic. In Romans 1:26–27, Paul applied the word *unnatural* to men having sex with men (interestingly he also included women with women, which would have been unthinkable in Leviticus). But he also thought that long hair on men was unnatural (1 Corinthians 11:14). He even describes God as acting contrary to nature in grafting Christians into the cultivated olive tree of Judaism (Romans 11:24). If St. Paul were to come back today, what would he think of men having sex with men, if the two men were, by nature, same-sex oriented? No one can say. However, he would surely condemn most of the sex between men in our prisons because it is not properly called homosexual behavior but (heterosexual) rape.

The texts in Leviticus and Romans are the usual evidence brought forth that the Bible condemns homosexuality. Church documents toss in a few other references to shore up the case, but that only reveals how weak the case is. The story of Sodom is still cited even though modern scholarship (as well as ancient sources) gives no support to the belief that the story is a condemnation of homosexuality. The name Sodom supplied the English term *sodomy* that usually means anal sex, but the term can be extended in meaning to other sexual practices. Of course, anal sex, oral sex, and sex with animals are not restricted to gay people, but sodomy laws that were enacted in many states were aimed at gay men.

The origin of sodomy is the story in Genesis 19 about a city named Sodom in which Lot provides hospitality to some men (or angels?) who are visitors to Sodom. Some of the townsmen demand that the visitors be brought out to have sex with them. At the least the townspeople show a lack of hospitality, and beyond that their intention is rape. Lot, horrifyingly, offers as a substitute two of his daughters "who have not known men … Let me bring them out to you, and do to them as you please." Eventually, Lot, his daughters, and the visitors escape the destruction of Sodom. The Bible in numerous places refers to the fate of Sodom, but never is same-sex behavior referred to as being the wickedness of the city. The city is regularly condemned in the Bible because the poor are oppressed and the needy are crushed (Amos 4:11).

Other texts of the Bible that are occasionally included as a condemnation of homosexuality are in lists of *uncleanness* or *wickedness* (for example, 1 Timothy 1:10 and 1 Corinthians 6:9). One of the references in these lists is claimed to be homosexuality. But since there was no such term, the references are always ambiguous, veiled, and obscure.

There are hundreds of passages in the Bible that condemn the oppression of the poor. The Bible also makes abundantly clear that killing your brother is unacceptable behavior. And there are clear commands in the gospel to put aside vengeance and seek peace. If same-sex love were a terrible violation of God's law, should we not expect something clearer in the Bible than what is regularly offered up in church condemnations?

Roman Catholic Church Documents

I will examine in this section some of the documents on homosexuality that have come from the Vatican's Congregation for the Doctrine of the Faith and from the United States Conference of Catholic Bishops. It is easy to summarize church officials on homosexual behavior: they are against it. However, both the Vatican officials and the US bishops have found it necessary to respond to the revolution happening all around them. The documents are painful to read because they keep trying to find a way to condemn all homosexual behavior while at the same time protesting that they are not condemning homosexual people. The Vatican and the US bishops had some differences in their approach to this tension. The US bishops tried to find a way to sound less negative about "homosexual persons," but their position came out as no more logical.

As the gay rights movement was picking up steam in 1975, the Vatican thought it was necessary to put forward a declaration that reaffirmed the church's position on homosexuality.[5] The document raises some hope in its opening sentence: "According to contemporary scientific research ..." But by the end of that paragraph, the foremost concern is not scientific research but "licentious hedonism." It is difficult to find any appreciation of "contemporary scientific research" in the document. It does express some sympathy with adolescents struggling with masturbation but still insists that "scripture condemns this sin" and that each act can be a mortal sin (section 9).[6]

The declaration confidently asserts that the church "ceaselessly preserves and transmits without error the truths of the moral order, and she authentically interprets not only the revealed positive law 'but also ... those principles of the moral order which have their origin in human nature itself'" (section 4). The authors of the document do not seem to think that it is necessary to learn about "human nature itself" from contemporary research and human testimony.

The declaration does make a bow to contemporary discussions by saying that "with some reason" it is possible to distinguish between two kinds of "homosexuals." The first kind is "homosexuals whose tendency comes from a false education, from a lack of normal sexual development ... and is transitory, or at least not incurable ..." In contrast, there are "homosexuals who are definitively such because of some innate kind of instinct or a pathological constitution judged to be incurable" and, while they may not always be personally responsible for their behavior, "homosexual acts are intrinsically disordered" (section 8).

The Vatican document distinguishes here between two kinds of homosexuals, but the distinction is false. Their first kind of homosexual should have been described as heterosexuals engaging in same-sex behavior. Their second kind of homosexual are actual homosexual people, "homosexuals who are definitively such." In acknowledging "some kind of innate instinct," the authors of the document seemed close to agreeing with the widespread view that people do not choose to be homosexual; they are homosexual by nature. However, that hint of openness is immediately dashed by equating this innate instinct with "a pathological constitution judged to be incurable." The category of homosexual person is accepted, but the condition of being a homosexual is said to be a sickness.

Rather surprisingly, the Vatican felt it necessary in 1986 to address homosexuality again in *On the Pastoral Care of Homosexual Persons.*[7] The reason they give is that in the reaction to their 1975 declaration, an "overly benign interpretation was given to the homosexual condition itself." Apparently, many people, including some US bishops, were willing to go with the Vatican's language of "some kind of innate instinct" and to disregard "a pathological constitution judged to be incurable." Because the declaration distinguished between "homosexual condition" and individual homosexual actions, some people thought it possible to condemn the actions but view the homosexual condition as "neutral or even good."

This new Vatican document makes no admission that by calling people "homosexuals who are definitively such" it created its own dilemma. It would seem that if there are "real homosexual persons," they have to act as homosexual persons. This new document refers to a "homosexual condition or tendency" as a way out of the dilemma, but that phrase only raises further questions. What reality is acknowledged for a "condition" that is lifelong and that is also called an "objective disorder"?

The most astounding passages in this 1986 document are sections 11 and 16 in which the term *sexual orientation* is brought up but only to be condemned. In section 11 the church is said to be defending the liberty and dignity of homosexual persons against "the unfounded and demeaning assumption that the sexual behavior of homosexual persons is always and totally compulsive and therefore inculpable." Here orientation is said to be the cause of compulsive activity instead of its referring to activity that is in accord with being a homosexual person. Section 16 states that "the human person, made in the image and likeness of God, can hardly be adequately described by a reductionist reference to his or her sexual orientation." Why is the term *sexual orientation* reductionist when it is simply an acknowledgment that people are primarily oriented homosexually or heterosexually?

The US bishops were undoubtedly affected by the pressures of the gay rights movement, which was particularly strong in the United States. The US bishops would not, of course, disagree with the Vatican. However, individual bishops used the term *sexual orientation* in the early 1980s, which probably upset Vatican officials. It is surprising, therefore, that in the bishops' 1990 statement on sexuality, even after the Vatican "clarification," there are eight paragraphs headed "Persons with a Homosexual Orientation." Were the bishops trying to distance themselves from the Vatican, or were they simply using the language at hand? The answer is not clear from the discussion at their 1990 meeting that led to this document. Most of their debate was about how much weight they should give to the Vatican's use of "objective disorder." The bishops rightly suspected that the terms *sexual orientation* and *objective disorder* did not go together.

In subsequent documents, the US bishops continued to express compassion for gay and lesbian people. In *Human Sexuality: A Catholic Perspective for Education and Lifelong Learning* in 1991, they invite homosexual people to have an active role in the church. In their pastoral letter of 1997, *Always Our Children*, the bishops express understanding of the difficulties that homosexual people face, and they encourage patience. They use the term *sexual orientation* but still condemn homosexual behavior. Looking back on these documents, retired Bishop Thomas Gumbleton frankly admits, "We need to face the reality that there is a basic incoherence in the church's teaching on homosexuality."[8]

By the time of their 2006 document, the US bishops seem to have learned to conform to Vatican language. The title, *Ministry to Persons with a Homosexual Inclination: Guidelines for Pastoral Care*, indicates their term of choice: *inclination*. One might think inclination is just a synonym for orientation. The bishops may have been suggesting that there was not much difference between those two terms, and some readers thought that the bishops had made progress. But while they use inclination in the singular, it would have been more honest for them to have used it in the plural. That is, in the bishops' thinking, instead of people having an inclination that constitutes them as homosexual, they repeatedly have inclinations to (sinful) homosexual activities.

The homosexual inclination is said to be not a sin but a temptation to sin. The bishops say that the "tendency or inclination" is a sin only "if one were voluntarily to entertain homosexual temptations or to choose to act on them" (page 5). The bishops' advice for resisting this temptation is, "It would not be wise for persons with a homosexual inclination to seek friendship exclusively among persons with the same inclination. They should seek to form friendships among both homosexuals and heterosexuals" (pages 10–11). The bishops wish to say positive things about homosexual persons who have a temptation to homosexual behavior, but the dilemma in the bishops discussion is, can persons who are homosexual act morally as the persons they are?

The US Catholic bishops, to their credit, did not wish to condemn a whole segment of the human race. Particularly during the 1980s, there were bishops who were sympathetic to the gay and lesbian cause, in private conversations if not in print. But the path to rethinking the church's position on homosexuality was blocked by the Vatican. Today any restating of the church's doctrinal position is more difficult than it would have been in the 1970s and 1980s.

Statements from the US Bishops Conference, similar to statements from the Vatican, focus on pastoral care. It is safe to talk about respecting the dignity of persons with a homosexual tendency and of ministering to them. The bishops even say that "it is important that Church ministers listen to the experiences, needs, and hopes of the persons with a homosexual inclination to whom and with whom they minister." But the bishops are not ready to listen to the widespread testimony of people who say that their *inclination* is part of their identity and that their way of sexually expressing their person is by same-sex love. Why? The bishops' answer is, "The natural law shows what we should do (as does divinely revealed law, such as the Ten Commandments)."[9]

Sex and Same-Sex Marriage

The church's condemnation of homosexuality is part of a larger problem. Church officials praise marital sex that is "open to life" but find little else positive to say about sex. Homosexuality reveals the cramped view of sexuality that church officials have. Homosexual persons or persons with a homosexual "tendency" are supposed to fit into the proscription of all sex outside marriage. In its praise of the monastic tradition, the Roman Catholic Church puts great value on celibacy or consecrated virginity, but it insists that only people with a special calling from God can live in this state. What advice can church officials give to homosexual persons who do not have marriage as an option?

These days, of course, same-sex marriage has rather suddenly become an option for gay and lesbian people. The United States has followed Ireland in the legalization of same-sex marriage. In Ireland, 62 percent of the voters endorsed same-sex marriage. In the United States, it was left to the Supreme Court to decide the issue. The way that the case for same-sex marriage was argued involved disingenuousness on both sides. The first problem was that opponents of same-sex marriage argued that marriage has had the same meaning for millennia. Advocates replied that marriage is always changing. Neither side has been entirely forthcoming. The US Catholic bishops said after the decision that "marriage remains unchanged and unchangeable." That statement is simply a denial of reality. Marriage has obviously undergone changes over the centuries; there is no eternal essence of marriage. But one has to respect the history of an institution to decide which changes do or do not make sense.

The second problem is the phrase *marriage equality*. It is an effective slogan because if equality is the issue, opponents are in a corner. Do they really want to be on the side of inequality? But like most slogans, marriage equality clouds the issue rather than clarifies it. People who argued against same-sex marriage logically raised the question of what are the limits of that equality. In an essay entitled "Is Polygamy Next?" William Baude argues for polygamy as the next extension of marriage equality.[10] He concludes the essay, "Once we abandon the rigid constraints of history, we cannot be sure that we know where the future will take us." Indeed, once we abandon those rigid constraints of history, we can call anything by any name, but there is nothing left to argue about.

A plural marriage could conceivably fit within some logic of marriage, but the case would have to be made within the perception of an historical evolution. The marriage of one man and several women is nothing new, and it could even be construed as regression. These days there would presumably be an inclusion of one woman and several men, as well as all numerical combinations of men and women. But what is the limit? Can five people have a marriage? Is there any advantage in calling a union of five people a marriage rather than, say, a kind of community?

Same-sex marriage has some logic to it by reason of the way that the idea and the institution of marriage have evolved. In the distant past, marriage was about a man's property, which included a woman or women who could bear the children that he would father. In contemporary speech, men still father children; mothering is something that happens after birth. The conclusion of Justice Kennedy's majority opinion that marriage makes "two people greater than they once were" is almost comical in the light of history. Even in the nineteenth century the common-law rule of coverture collapsed the woman's legal identity into that of her husband's. A wife was legally invisible.

It has been a long journey for women to get to the place where marriage could realistically be called a mutual relation. Not much progress toward such a partnership had been made until the human race began producing more babies than two parents could manage or the earth can sustain. The Roman Catholic Church had always maintained a matrimonial ideal as a mutual covenant between a man and a woman. Unfortunately, when the Council of Trent in 1563 legislated a rigid set of requirements for a valid marriage (in a church, before a priest, and with two witnesses), the effect was to undermine the idea of marriage as mutual consent and make Catholic marriage more closely resemble the legal contract of secular society.[11] It is surprising and perhaps ironic that the women's movement of the nineteenth century and the feminist movement of the early twentieth century brought marriage closer to the Catholic ideal of a mutual covenant.

The big sexual revolution in the twentieth century occurred in the 1920s. The sexual behavior of women changed dramatically in that decade. There was discussion at that time of two kinds of marriage, traditional and companionate. Margaret Mead, who was one advocate, called the two kinds individual marriage and parental marriage.[12] Even the Roman Catholic Church in the 1930s accepted companionship as a secondary purpose of marriage; the primary purpose, according to the church, was still the birth and education of children.

The church altered its position in the 1960s by saying that there is no hierarchy of ends. Vatican II said that "marriage to be sure is not instituted solely for procreation ... as an unbreakable compact between persons ... marriage persists as a whole manner and communion of life, and maintains its value and indissolubility even when offspring are lacking."[13] In that framework, the Roman Catholic Church could be a supporter of same-sex marriage, which is suited to the companionate function of marriage and presents no problem of interference in the process of pregnancy and conception.

The church might acknowledge same-sex marriage as a conservative movement to shore up a troubled institution. I am somewhat puzzled why gay people have been so anxious to join an institution that fails more often than it succeeds. The upper classes in this country still consider marriage a mark of respectability, but a sizable part of the straight population has disconnected marriage and babies. And a great many of them also have doubts that sexual companionship is helped by the stereotypes that still burden the idea of marriage.

Ten years ago, I, like most of the country, was not a supporter of same-sex marriage. I was not against it; I simply did not know how big the issue was for gay couples. I thought that perhaps heterosexual couples would increasingly join gay couples in establishing sexual unions with desirable economic protections and social approval. But why would sexual partners wish to get involved in all the husband and wife stuff where equality is still a problem? Parenthood does involve more complicated questions than a stable sexual partnership so that some of marriage tradition makes sense for the upbringing of children.

The problem with all the attention given to who can marry is that the related question of who takes care of the children can get underemphasized. The term *marriage* could have been rerouted to its historic role of a contract to start a family. Gay couples raising a family could have strengthened or reconnected the bond between marriage and family. The government could then have concentrated on the quality of childcare in this country where one out of five children is born into poverty. Other stable sexual unions could be blessed by the church while the government stayed out of the sex lives of straight and gay couples who wish to contribute to society in ways other than by parenting.

The moment has passed when that linguistic direction could have been taken. The legal recognition of same-sex marriage is progress insofar as it provides gay people with the respect they deserve. But a confusion about the nature of marriage remains. Same-sex marriage is more likely to strengthen than to weaken the institution of marriage, but the institution needs more help than the addition of a new population. The country needs an honest discussion of how to improve family life and get government policies that help rather than undermine families.

The Roman Catholic Church has begun a massive change in its attitude toward gay couples adopting children. In 2003, the Vatican denounced gay marriage and family, claiming that "allowing children to be adopted by parents living in such unions would actually mean doing violence to these children." No evidence was offered for that claim. There is only a reference to the United Nations' *Convention on the Rights of the Child*, which contains nothing on this issue. In a welcome change of tone, the synod in 2014 said that "the Church pays special attention to children who live with same-sex couples and stresses that the needs and rights of the little ones must always be given priority."

The Roman Catholic Church could make a great contribution to society by continuing to affirm that the two ends of marriage are not hierarchically ordered. They now constitute two kinds of marriage that could be sacramentally distinguished. They might be called family marriage and partnership marriage. Straight and gay couples who intend to raise children need the support of family-friendly policies by the government and the support by the church. Other married couples need legal recognition of their economic partnership, and they also need social support for their union. If the Roman Catholic Church were to come on board, a new way of looking at marriage might emerge that respects tradition but acknowledges the irreversible trends of the last seventy-five years. Women's equality and help for family life could be given the attention they deserve.

The Roman Catholic Church's good intention has been to protect the integrity of family life, but the bond between marriage and children was severed a long time ago. Many gay and lesbian couples who wish to adopt children are on the same side as is the church. In his address to the US Congress, Pope Francis made only an oblique reference to the church's problem with same-sex marriage. Instead he focused on family. And the next day's editorial in the *New York Times* noted in reference to the pope's statement, "I can only reiterate the importance and, above all, the richness and beauty of family life," is "a point that same-sex couples would certainly embrace."

A thorough defense of the official Catholic teaching was published immediately after the Supreme Court ruling. Ryan Anderson's *Truth Overruled: The Future of Marriage and Religious Freedom* was bitterly attacked for being antigay although the author was simply defending the claim that marriage is a union of a man and a woman oriented toward the birth of children.[14] His position would not be far from what is outlined here except that he treats the marriage of infertile couples as an exception to the rule instead of it now being more rule than exception. If he could view the changes of sex and marriage not as unfortunate aberrations coming from the 1960s but as developments during at least a century, he could acknowledge a second form of marriage centered on a stable sexual union between two individuals. Because the Roman Catholic Church does accept marriage for reasons that do not involve pregnancy and birth, one could logically extend the word *marriage* to homosexual unions. Of course, the main question is not whether gay marriage is acceptable but whether gay sex is accepted.

On homosexuality and other sexual questions, contemporary Roman Catholic Church officials have not listened enough to their own people. A particularly sad example is the case of Jeanine Gramick and Robert Nugent who tried to build a bridge between the Roman Catholic Church and gay/lesbian groups in the United States.[15] Their New Ways Ministry had success in doing just that. It would be difficult to find two people who were more devoted to the church and who were careful not to attack church doctrine. However, as happens frequently, the Vatican goes after people who are having success in reaching out to groups that are alienated from the church. Obviously, people who are doing such work have to emphasize some aspects of the church and go easy on other things.

Gramick and Nugent were vulnerable as members of religious orders. They have the distinction of receiving their own Vatican document of condemnation, which concluded that "their position regarding the intrinsic evil of homosexual acts and the objective disorder of the homosexual inclination are doctrinally unacceptable."[16] That is, they were required to profess unqualified belief in "intrinsic evil," "objective disorder," and "homosexual inclination," philosophical concepts that are at best of doubtful validity. Gramick and Nugent took their unfair condemnation and survived with their dignity intact. The Roman Catholic Church's alienation from gays and lesbians continued.

The Synod of 2014–15

Early in his papacy, Pope Francis famously made two references to homosexuality in his seemingly offhand style. Both remarks were in the form of a rhetorical question: "Who am I to judge?" and "When God looks at a gay person, does he endorse this person with love, or reject and condemn this person?"[17] His nonjudgmental attitude was hailed as a breakthrough and raised expectations of change. His use of the English word *gay* may have been more significant than even he realized.

The Synod on the Family in 2014 followed the pope's lead in an open discussion of how the church should be a place of welcome for homosexual people. A strong reaction against the first week's report led the synod to pull back in its final report, which disappointed many people. But there is little doubt that in the history of the Roman Catholic Church, the Synod on the Family in 2014 will be seen as the moment when the church officially changed its attitude on homosexuality and began the long-overdue process of accepting gay and lesbian Catholics.

Two uses of language reveal the change that occurred as well as the distance that church officials still have to travel. The discussion at the synod and its documents still refer to "the homosexual," a usage that reflects a contrast between them and us. It was too much to expect that the synod would talk about gay and straight Catholics, but the bishops could stop talking about "the homosexuals" as an alien species. (On statistical grounds alone, one has to presume that some of the bishops are gay.) Pope Francis led with his use of the term *gay*, but neither the news media nor the synod seemed to notice this big change.

The important change of language at the synod, which some bishops probably were not even aware of, is in this line: "Are our communities capable of this [being a welcoming home to homosexual people], accepting and valuing their sexual orientation …" No Vatican document had ever suggested that the church accept, let alone value, the sexual orientation of gay and lesbian people. The Congregation for the Doctrine of the Faith had avoided the term *sexual orientation* or attacked the idea.

Lacking a knowledge of Vatican documents, journalists missed how revolutionary was this change. Even *Commonweal* said that the synod report contained just one paragraph "repeating Vatican statements on homosexual orientation."[18] Horrified opponents of any rethinking of homosexuality did not miss the significance of the use of homosexual "orientation." They succeeded in having the final synod document in 2015 regress to talking about homosexual "tendency" or "tendencies."[19] The acceptance of the category of sexual orientation is the necessary condition to the acceptance of homosexuality and same-sex marriage.

The rapidity of change in public attitude toward gay/lesbian marriage has been astounding. No one should expect the Roman Catholic Church to change at a similar speed. But if companionate marriage is now accepted for straight people, a change in attitude toward same-sex marriage is at least possible even if not likely.[20]

Chapter 9

∞

Catholic Tradition and Passive Resistance

C atholic tradition has always embodied a precarious tension between condemnations of violence based on the teachings of Jesus of Nazareth and a philosophical/political tradition that has grappled with the reality of force, violence, and war. In the earliest part of church history, noncooperation with the war-making powers was emphasized. After the fourth century, the church became part of the political, economic, and military power of imperial rule. Voices of opposition to the use of violence were never stilled, but they were in the minority.

This chapter recounts the rebirth and expansion of traditional protests against violence. I will comment briefly on Jesus's teachings and on the approach to nonviolence today. My main focus is on the past century, more specifically on those who have witnessed nonviolence as a way of life. While Roman Catholic protest is rooted in New Testament teaching, it usually has a philosophical side. For better and for worse, the last two thousand years of history is part of the tradition.

The Bible and Nonviolence

The Christian version of the Bible includes what Christians call the Old Testament as well as the books of the New Testament. The life, death, and resurrection of Jesus are set within the context of this complex literature. Each Christian group gives particular emphasis to some parts of the Bible, thereby arriving at various interpretations on how a Christian should live. While all Christians would claim to be followers of Jesus, the interpretive prism of St. Paul's Letters or the importance of the fourth gospel may be strongly determinative of how a Christian group or an individual is defined as a follower.

During the 2000 presidential campaign, George W. Bush was asked who his favorite philosopher is. He answered, "Jesus Christ." The response triggered ridicule or horror in many places. But if one asks what is wrong with the answer, I think it is the second of the two words. If Bush had simply answered "Jesus," he would have found himself in the company of Gandhi and Martin Luther King Jr.

The reason for suspicion about Bush's answer is his addition of *Christ*, which is a Christian liturgical term and an article of belief. Although it is common to refer to "Jesus Christ," anyone sensitive to the meaning of "Jesus (the) Christ" would not refer to a philosopher named Jesus Christ. If philosophers are the question, then the teachings of Jesus of Nazareth have to be placed in comparison to other thinkers rather than cited as words coming directly from God. That is a risk that Christians take if they wish to enter the political arena in order to persuade people who are not Christians on the value of these teachings.[1]

When Christians do live by the challenging teachings of Jesus, they find a positive response from many Jews, Muslims, Buddhists, and people with no religion. Jewish scholars are particularly helpful in explaining the core teachings of Jesus. There is little doubt that Jesus belonged to the peace party in the reformations of his day.[2] He opposed both Zealots who advocated war on the Roman forces, as well as the Roman authorities who tried to appropriate a halo of divine approbation.

The Sermon on the Mount is taken to be the center of Jesus's teaching on peace and nonviolence. It is regularly praised as a personal ideal. But a practice common to both Christians and non-Christians is to dismiss the Sermon on the Mount as irrelevant to the practice of realistic government policies. That attitude has a long history, but it was given forceful expression by Max Weber in a famous essay that contrasted two ethics, an ethic of intention and an ethic of responsibility.[3] The Sermon on the Mount, according to Weber, epitomizes an ethic of good intention in which the person is unconcerned with results. The politician, however, has to be "responsible"; he has to achieve results with means that include the use of violence.

The critics who dismiss the teaching of Jesus often show little knowledge of the teaching beyond a few phrases taken out of context. "Turn the other cheek" is an oft-quoted phrase that supposedly sums up Jesus's teaching. Many Christian authors accept the claim that the Sermon on the Mount is not relevant to politics. Reinhold Niebuhr's early work, *Moral Man and Immoral Society*, had high praise for the Sermon on the Mount as the ethical inspiration for the "moral man."[4] Unfortunately, these moral individuals have to live in an immoral society where the only thing realistic is to use violence in a responsible way. Niebuhr's split of ethics had a profound influence on Christian ethics in the twentieth century and continues to be influential. Barack Obama's speech when he received the Nobel Peace Prize explicitly followed the separation of ethics into a personal code of nonviolence and the ethics that a president has to follow in using violence to defend the American people.[5]

Jesus's teaching needs to be set within a temporal and geographical context, wherein he was commenting on the texts of his people. He was not rejecting that tradition but emphasizing particular aspects of it. The assumption that Jesus was advocating a supine attitude in the face of oppressors is not borne out by the sermon as a whole, nor by the tradition of which it is a part. The purpose of the teaching, as careful students have recognized, is to de-hostilize enemies in order to win them over. "Do good to those who hate you" is a political strategy requiring skill, courage, and persistence. Jesus recognized that there is no way out of an escalation of mutual retaliation unless someone refuses to act violently and instead responds asymmetrically. Reconciliation will benefit the hater as well as the hated. Nonviolent activity does not exclude forceful activity and inevitable conflicts. Nonviolence makes the world safe for conflict.

The Jewish philosopher Hannah Arendt has a remarkable passage in her classic work, *The Human Condition*, in which she affirms that "the discoverer of the role of forgiveness in the realm of human affairs was Jesus of Nazareth."[6] It was important, she writes, that Jesus taught that forgiveness has to start from human beings, and then God will do likewise. Forgiveness is the only action that can save men and women— and nations—from a cycle of violence that is met with more violence. Forgiveness, like nonviolence, is more complicated than it might seem. It requires working through a whole range of attitudes so that when one says, "I forgive you," it is action that releases a person from the past and makes possible a new direction in life. Forgiveness does not come easily to anyone, but it is supposed to be a hallmark of a follower of Jesus.

"Love your neighbor," so often repeated without much thought, would be better translated as "love to your neighbor." Jesus was commenting on Leviticus 19:18: "Love your neighbor as yourself; I am the Lord." Christian love is neither selfish nor altruistic; it is a love of both neighbor and self, grounded in the recognition of God's love for every creature. Special attention is given to victims of human unkindness, disadvantaged people, and those who come last in political calculations.

The fundamental attitude of Christian love is not pity, a characteristic that was one of Nietzsche's complaints about Christianity. Instead, the Christian attitude is sympathy for and with the suffering of people, which is a rousing call to action. Martin Luther King Jr. described his nonviolent army by contrasting it to the armies that maim and kill. To be a member in those armies, King said, "one must be physically sound, possessed of straight limbs and accurate vision. But in Birmingham, the lame and the halt and the crippled could, and did, join up."[7] Gandhi, another activist inspired by Jesus's teaching, found that "individuals who neither submit passively nor retaliate to violence find in themselves a new sense of strength, dignity and courage."[8]

Postbiblical Tradition

The early Christian Church believed that Christians should not take up arms. The Greek fathers of the Church were generally united in their attitude against participation in war. Clement of Alexandria, Justin Martyr, and Cyprian were among the outspoken opponents of Christians participating in war. The greatest of these writers, Origen, set out a theory in which he argued that Christians should not serve in the military but that they are still responsible for serving the commonwealth.[9]

Over the centuries, the Catholic Church's teaching on war was encapsulated in the phrase *just war* theory. At the least, that phrase is a misleading translation of *jus ad bellum, jus in bello.* There are conditions that need to be fulfilled before going to war, and there are rules for limiting the violence in the execution of a war. Church writers offered these rules for going to war and for fighting a war on the assumption that war is inevitable. The rules did not guarantee justice. The rules might be summarized as how to do the least injustice in wars that are thought to be necessary.

The Christian writer's name most closely associated with the term *just war* is Augustine of Hippo, an African bishop of the late fourth century who set the direction for much of Western Christianity. Augustine was no enthusiast for war.[10] He thought that the Christian, in imitation of Jesus, should not use violence to defend himself. However, he believed that the Christian has a responsibility to aid a victim under attack.[11] It is difficult to argue against Augustine's principle of defending the vulnerable. But it is even more difficult to move from the image of a man protecting his wife or child to the reality of a nation-state at war in the twentieth or twenty-first centuries.[12] Thomas Aquinas, who always tried to avoid directly contradicting Augustine, worked at subtly making changes in Augustinian teaching. Aquinas, however, raised little challenge to what became just war theory.[13]

It is hardly surprising that nations regularly believe that the conditions for a just war are fulfilled when they are ready to go to war. That is, they think that 1) the cause is just, 2) their intention is good, 3) a competent authority declares the war, 4) success in war is likely, 5) war is the last resort, and 6) the war is proportional in its means. And then, of course, in the midst of war, nations claim to be following the rules for a responsible use of violence. They are careful to distinguish between combatants and noncombatants, trying not to kill innocent people. During the last century of war, that has meant following international agreements on the limits of war. It is always the other side that commits war crimes.

Opposition to war survived in the Christian Middle Ages, mainly in the mystical tradition. The mystics sought a unity beyond conflict. Mysticism is often dismissed as apolitical and otherworldly. While mysticism does not fit in with ordinary politics, its political reverberations are considerable. As the Marxist Ernst Bloch phrased it, "He who believes that he is in union with the Lord of Lords does not, when it comes down to it, make a very good serf."[14] Cut loose from the moorings of ordinary life, mysticism can easily turn violent, as often happened in the late Middle Ages.[15] But on that same basis of challenging ordinary politics, mysticism could also point to unity as the end of politics, and peace as the means to that unity.

The greatest mystic of the Middle Ages was the fourteenth-century preacher, Meister Eckhart. His pleas for peaceful reconciliation went unheeded in his own day. However, Eckhart's writings continue to inspire people. At times, Eckhart has been pictured as a misplaced Buddhist, but he was firmly rooted in the New Testament and Christian tradition. He was keenly aware that the passionate preaching of justice for the poor might unleash more conflict, but he was convinced that there was no true peace without justice.[16] His sermons denouncing the rich for their oppression of the poor would still stir up strong passions today.

The most outstanding medieval essay on peace, *Peace Protests*, belongs to Desiderius Erasmus. Erasmus was a great humanist of the early sixteenth century, one of the world's first cosmopolitans. Erasmus was dissatisfied with a choice between just war theory and opposition to war. He thought that war is insane, but he also thought that simply saying one is in favor of peace is inadequate as a response to the violence all around us. Erasmus presciently saw the need for structures of mediation that could work through international conflict. Almost four centuries later, the world is slowly coming to accept what Erasmus saw as indispensable for peacemaking.[17]

The Twentieth Century

The story of the Roman Catholic Church in the twentieth century is one of a gradual shift toward skepticism about any claims for a just war. Some impetus for a Catholic Peace Party was provided by papal statements and individual bishops. More often, official statements lagged behind Catholic groups who were willing to take a radical stand against war.

When Pope John XXIII was elected pope at age seventy-nine, it was widely assumed he would be a caretaker pope. He startled the world by moving swiftly to engage the Roman Catholic Church with the political and economic realities of the twentieth century. His elegant plea for peace is an encyclical *Pacem in Terris* (*Peace on Earth*). In this document, the pope expressed an opposition to nationalism and condemned the arms race. His emphasis on nonviolence was an attempt to transcend the opposition between just war theory and pacifism. He called for structural reform of the international political and legal systems. Notably missing from the document is an endorsement of the right of self-defense for peoples and states, a doctrine commonly put forward as justification for war. Pope John concluded that in an age such as ours that prides itself on its nuclear power, it is contrary to reason to hold that war is a suitable way to restore rights that have been violated.[18]

A year after the publication of *Pacem in Terris*, twenty-five hundred bishops of the Roman Catholic Church met in Rome for the Second Vatican Council. A discussion of the ethics of war took place during the council's third session in 1964. A condemnation of nuclear weapons initiated a vigorous debate that continued into the fourth session in 1965. Conservative Catholic groups from the United States argued that the condemnation of nuclear weapons would put US Catholics in the difficult position of opposing either their church or their government.

Nuclear weapons and other extraordinary means of destruction had been unimaginable in earlier discussions of the morality of war. The council said that "these considerations compel us to undertake an evaluation of war with an entirely new attitude." This new attitude included a recognition of nonviolence in resisting war: "We cannot fail to praise those who renounce the use of violence in the vindication of their rights and who resort to methods of defense which are otherwise available to weaker parties, too, provided this can be done without injury to the rights and duties of others or of the community itself." This praise of resistance to violence was hardly a rousing call for a policy of nonviolence. Nonetheless, it represented progress in that direction.

The Vatican Council, in accepting the right of a nation to defend itself, would not condemn all war or the possession of nuclear weapons. But it did condemn total war, the use of nuclear and other weapons that cause indiscriminate killing. In previous councils, the church was often ready to pronounce condemnation of any perceived heresy. At the Second Vatican Council, the word *condemnation* was used only once: "Any act of war aimed indiscriminately at the destruction of entire cities ... merits unequivocal and unhesitating condemnation."[19]

After the Second Vatican Council, the US bishops began moving toward a more critical stance on military policies. In 1982, the United States Catholic Conference issued the document *Statement on Central America*, a call for liberation and peace. The bishops opposed the US government's anticommunist crusade, declaring that "the dominant challenge is the internal condition of poverty and the denial of human rights."[20]

In 1983, the bishops' pastoral letter *The Challenge of Peace* seemed to many people a drastic change of course for the Roman Catholic Church. The US government had counted on the staunch anticommunism of the bishops as a support for US foreign policy. The White House tried to influence the bishops in their writing of the letter. The government was concerned because the bishops were not young radicals who might reverse themselves when fashion dictated. The bishops had slowly and agonizingly argued themselves into the firm conviction that just war theory is inadequate in the age of nuclear weapons.

The bishops acknowledged that "the nonviolent witness of such figures as Dorothy Day and Martin Luther King Jr. has had a profound impact upon the life of the church in the United States."[21] Thomas Gumbleton was one of the most important voices in the bishops' stand on peace. Bishop Gumbleton gave credit to peace activists such as Daniel Berrigan for the evolution of his own thinking: "I have to face the question they faced: Is the war moral or immoral? I think people who are ready to put their whole lives on the line forced me to do some thinking."[22]

The bishops received praise for their document, although they were not given the credit that they deserved for contributing to the emerging thaw in the Gorbachev-Reagan dialogue of the 1980s. The bishops' letter has continued to influence the thinking of US Catholics about the issues of violence and war. The Catholic Church has tried to develop what Cardinal Joseph Bernardin called "a consistent ethic of life."[23] The church's opposition to war has been tied to opposing the state execution of prisoners and to protests against abortion. For most of the country, including many Roman Catholics, the bishops are so obsessed with the abortion question that they do not pay enough attention to violence outside the womb. However, if liberal critics of war invite the support of the Roman Catholic Church, they have to pay attention to the bishops' concern with all forms of violence, including abortion.

Individual Leaders

In his address to the US Congress, Pope Francis somewhat surprisingly singled out Dorothy Day and Thomas Merton as models for contemporary US Catholics. Those two people may be remembered today as advocates of peace and reconciliation, as indeed they were. But they were also hated and reviled in their lifetimes for their uncompromising resistance to US wars. In what follows, I discuss the courageous actions of Day and Merton, and I add a third great Catholic resister to violence and war, Daniel Berrigan.

Dorothy Day. Together with Peter Maurin, Dorothy Day founded the Catholic Worker movement in 1933. Day was born of Scots-Irish Calvinist parents. She worked with the Anti-Conscription League in World War I and the women's suffrage movement, for which she was arrested and jailed in 1917. After conversion to Catholicism in 1927, Day wrote for several Catholic magazines.[24]

The Catholic Worker movement began as a struggle for social justice and for the rights of the poor. Day took on voluntary poverty to side with workers and to launch a social and moral regeneration. From 1933 to 1941, thirty-two Catholic Worker houses were founded. The houses were soup kitchens, meeting rooms, clothing centers, and schools rolled into a single revolutionary headquarters. To spread the word, Day began a newspaper, the *Catholic Worker,* which sold for a penny a copy and has continued with the same price. Its circulation during the 1930s grew to 185,000.[25]

People sometimes confused Day with isolationists, most notoriously with Father Coughlin, whose preaching degenerated into anti-Semitism. Day, however, was an internationalist or trans-nationalist. She based her convictions on the Christian gospel and maintained her opposition to war even during wartime.[26] In August 1940, Day wrote an open letter in the *Catholic Worker* opposing all preparation for war.[27] She called for opposition to the manufacture of munitions and to the purchasing of defense bonds. Day had always seen the connection between the oppression of the poor and the destruction from war. However, many people who were ready to join with her in the fight against poverty were not prepared to stand against the United States government's call to arms.

The immediate results of Day's uncompromising nonviolence were disastrous. Twenty of the thirty-two Worker houses were closed. The *Catholic Worker* lost over 100,000 subscribers.[28] The movement might have seemed finished. Instead, Day's integrity and consistency under the most trying conditions provided a foundation for a Catholic Worker movement that still attracts bright and dedicated people. The Catholic Worker is also an inspiration for other communities that are trying to sustain a nonviolent way of life.

Very few Catholics opposed the United States's part in World War II. The war seemed to fulfill the traditional criteria for a just war. Toward the end of the war, however, as the United States engaged in obliteration bombing, some Catholics, including a few bishops, condemned these actions. The policy of firebombing Japanese cities reached its culmination with the bombing of Hiroshima and Nagasaki. For most people at the time, the use of atomic bombs did not seem to cross any new boundary.

The Vietnam War was the occasion for a significant shift in the attitude of Catholics toward war. At the start of the Vietnam War, Catholics were more hawkish than other US citizens; at the end of the war, they were more dovish, and remained so.[29] In contrast, US bishops lagged behind the people and were resistant to condemning the war as immoral.

Dorothy Day was in most respects a conservative Roman Catholic believer. She had no interest in attacking bishops or launching liberal reforms of the church. When she was asked why she recited the rosary, she said that when you are being carted off to jail, it helps to have something to hold onto.

Thomas Merton. One of the leading voices of protest against the war in Vietnam was that of Thomas Merton, a Cistercian monk. Like Dorothy Day, Thomas Merton came to the Catholic peace movement in the United States from an unusual background. He was born in France of a Quaker mother. After studying at Cambridge University, he came to the United States and completed a master's degree in English at Columbia University. He became a Catholic in 1938 and entered a Trappist monastery in 1942. Cloistered in a Kentucky monastery, Merton was an unlikely candidate to lead a peace movement. But he drew upon a long Catholic tradition that he appropriated with critical intelligence. He provided a calm but penetrating view of the turbulent 1960s. Merton's writings have continued to inspire generations of Catholics.

Thomas Merton described the paradox of his being a peace activist in his monastic cell: "To adopt a life that is essentially non-assertive, non-violent, a life of humility and peace is in itself a statement of one's position ... It is my intention to make my entire life a rejection of, a protest against, the crimes and injustices of war and political tyranny which threaten to destroy the whole race of man and the world with him."[30]

In 1964, Merton wrote an open letter to the bishops of the Second Vatican Council. His two chief concerns were the right of a Catholic to be a conscientious objector and the moral problem of using nuclear weapons. He found support for his positions in the statements of Pope

Pius XII and Pope John XXIII. Merton was instrumental in bringing the council to condemn what it called "total war."[31]

Merton did not live long enough to develop a complete theory of peace-making. He was highly critical of the Augustinian theory of a just war with its stress on the subjective purity of intention. He also found it impossible to call himself a pacifist because of the term's connotations, including its sole dependence on the conscience of the individual and a lack of concern for the oppressed.[32] Toward the end of his life, Merton had begun a dialogue with Zen Buddhism and found support for nonviolence in traditional Eastern thinkers.

While he passionately pleaded for justice and peace, Merton refused to dabble in the hatred that often affected the 1960s movements. Inspired by Dorothy Day's gentle but unyielding stance and aware of Martin Luther King Jr.'s evolving tactics in the 1960s, Merton never lost sight of the aim of peace, which requires a method of peace. Without criticizing by name some Catholic activists and their tactics during the protests of the late 1960s, Merton worried that direct political action against violence inevitably becomes entangled in violence. In one of his last statements, he said, "The language of spurious nonviolence is merely another, more equivocal form of the language of power ... Nonviolence is not for power but for truth. It is not pragmatic but prophetic. It is not aimed at immediate political results but at the manifestation of fundamental and critically important truth."[33]

Gordon Zahn, commenting approvingly on this statement of Merton, notes "Merton's insistence that the action not be measured by results." I do not think that is quite right. A crucial word in Merton's statement is *immediate.* Like anyone passionately dedicated to a cause, Merton wanted results, but he was not prepared to sacrifice a disciplined and patient approach for the sake of getting instantaneous and impressive results. He was properly suspicious of how modern news media, which can be used by protesters to get attention for their cause, can also become an obstacle to a quiet, determined, and long-range search for peace.

Merton, in the company of Dorothy Day, was willing to stay with a course that many people dismiss as too passive.[34] Like Day, Merton was not inclined to divide the world into friend and enemy. He wrote: "A test of our sincerity in the practice of nonviolence is this: are we willing to learn something from our adversary? If a new truth is made known to us by him, will we admit it? Are we willing to admit that he is not totally inhumane, wrong, unreasonable, cruel?"[35] The Roman Catholic Church lost one of its strongest advocates of nonviolence when Merton was accidentally killed in 1967.

Daniel Berrigan. The Jesuit priest Daniel Berrigan is associated with the activist side of antiwar protest. With his brother, Philip, he will be remembered for bold actions that directly confronted the United States government, actions that sent both men to prison for long stretches. It should also be noted that Dan Berrigan was a poet and a theologian before becoming a peace activist. And he never became a simple political activist. He maintained a serenity and a sense of humor in the midst of conflicts with the government and with his own church. He was sustained by his religious devotion to the scriptures and the religious practices of his community. It is an unusual activist who says, "Don't just do something; stand there."

What the news media called "the Catholic Left" had a brief history, emerging into public view with a break-in of a government facility at Catonsville, Maryland in May 1968, and effectively ending with a trial in Camden, New Jersey, in May 1973. It is easy to see the whole period as a clumsy and unsuccessful attempt to stop a disastrous war. But while most of the radical left in politics disappeared with the end of the Vietnam War, the Catholic peace movement continued in communities of resistance, peace organizations, and an episcopal leadership that shifted its teaching on war and peace.

The most dramatic form of protest during the Vietnam War was to break in to government offices and pour blood on draft records. This highly symbolic act, which echoes the church's sacramental practice, was dramatically effective and caught the attention of the news media. But breaking into a building and destroying property raised serious problems, legally, ethically, and strategically. Many passionate opponents of the war thought that such concerns were irrelevant, but for people sensitive to how any violence can undermine a commitment to peace, the issue had to be carefully addressed.

Many religious pacifists were skeptical about a manner of protest that was in danger of generating violence, even when the violence was not intended. Both Dorothy Day and Thomas Merton expressed qualified support for the action of Dan Berrigan and his associates. Thomas Merton wrote of Catonsville: "This was an attempt at prophetic nonviolent provocation. It bordered on violence and was violent to the extent that it meant pushing some good ladies around and destroying some government property. On a long-term basis, I think the peace movement needs to really study, practice, and use nonviolence in its classic form with all that implies of religious and ethical grounds."[36]

The FBI was several times successful in planting informers in the protest group. In the government's most ambitious trial against the protesters, the case relied almost entirely on an informer, Robert Handy. Strangely, however, Handy ended up testifying for the defense. He said that FBI policy in making arrests was first "to make sure the defendants commit as many crimes as possible and destroy the draft files." Handy also testified about the people he informed on that "they are the finest group of Christian people I have ever been associated with. They are not even capable of hurting anyone." But he concluded his description by saying that "as far as mechanical skills and abilities, they were totally inept … It definitely wouldn't have happened without me."[37] When the protesters were set up and captured in the Camden government office, J. Edgar Hoover and Attorney General John Mitchell exulted, "We have broken the back of the Catholic Left."[38]

What the news media called the Catholic Left may have come to an end in the early 1970s, but numerous small groups continued to protest against the further militarization of the United States and a policy of nuclear retaliation. In less dramatic fashion, organizations, such as Pax Christi USA, continued to awaken opposition to war and violence. Pax Christi was founded in France at the end of World War II; a US branch was begun in 1973. Respectful of church tradition and sensitive to the range of feelings among Catholic believers, Pax Christi seeks to educate Catholics about the realities of violence and to work for alliances with other peace-making groups. By 1981, the group had five thousand members, forty-six of whom were bishops. It openly criticized

US military policy and called for the end of draft legislation. Pax Christi USA has continued to be a voice for Catholics and an influence on the bishops even after the militarization that began in September 2001.

The overall record of the Roman Catholic Church in opposing war and advocating nonviolent tactics does not fare well when measured against the Sermon on the Mount. Starting with St. Augustine, the attempt to control the number of wars and the injustices inherent to war was well-intentioned and may have had some good effects in earlier times. The Geneva Conventions are a modern variation on this tradition. But we are past the time when war itself should be declared illegal and immoral.

In the United States, Roman Catholic anxiety about not being thought sufficiently patriotic often took precedence over the demands of the gospel. The Roman Catholic bishops and clergy were all too ready to endorse the policies of the US government, including its twentieth-century military build-up. A population composed mainly of immigrants wanted to avoid the taint of being insufficiently American. Only a few brave souls protested the World Wars and the policies of the Cold War. The expectation of a peace dividend, which was common in the 1980s, now seems quaint and naïve. In 2001, the nation shifted into a war mentality that seems to be without end.

It can at least be said that within the Roman Catholic Church the party of nonviolence is no longer relegated to the margin. Recent popes, especially Pope Francis, have been strong advocates of world peace. The Roman Catholic Church is one of the few institutions that extends throughout the world and does not operate from a perspective of national self-interest. Its own history includes examples of horrible and indefensible violence, but it is possible that the original impetus of the Christian movement can be reasserted as the core of Catholic teaching. That is the value of tradition. The teachings of other great thinkers in history can easily get forgotten when their immediate disciples die. The influence of Jesus's teaching is clearly still present in young Catholic lives.

Given the church's checkered history of violence and entanglement with empires, Roman Catholics have to be restrained in their claim to be the party of peace. Big institutions are always compromised in their professions of being on the side of goodness. Reinhold Niebuhr was not wrong in reminding Christians that we cannot escape inclinations to act from motives of fear, greed, and selfishness. Institutions are even more inclined toward moral obtuseness than individuals are. Nevertheless, institutions are the way that individuals can multiply the effects of their actions for good or ill.

Popes and bishops in the Roman Catholic Church control the levers of institutional change, but they are often in the position of catching up with nonofficial members of the church. Personal witness that draws upon the best of Catholic tradition is indispensable to the church and the nation. The testimony of Dorothy Day, Thomas Merton, and Daniel Berrigan continues to sound in the land and call the nation to recognize that violence has to be resisted if the nation is to have a future at all.

Chapter 10

Revelation: Divine, Not Christian

When Pope John XXIII called an ecumenical council in 1959, many people were puzzled as to what would be the agenda. Officials in the Vatican presumed that documents from such a council would do little more than reassert the unchanging message that the church has for the modern world. The documents prepared in advance of the council's first session and the procedures in place for approving these documents reflected the belief that lengthy deliberations would be unnecessary. However, at the first meeting of the council, a few bishops balked at the rules of procedure. Subsequently, the members of the council sent back to committee those documents that were judged to be unacceptable.[1]

The officials who had prepared the documents for Vatican II presumed that especially in the foundational area there was nothing new to be said. The Council of Trent had definitively ruled on the nature and sources of revelation. The First Vatican Council had defined the nature of faith in precisely stated propositions. The Second Vatican Council had no intention of rejecting the teaching of these previous councils. Nevertheless, the social and political context of that teaching had drastically changed over the course of the centuries. Old truths may need reformulating even to preserve the truth of what has been previously stated.

What began with that first session of the Second Vatican Council was a long period of church upheaval that has continued to the present. Some people had expected that after a brief flurry of changes, the Roman Catholic Church would settle back into a placid condition with some minor adjustments. But the changes initiated by the council have been intensely debated in recent years, and the debate is ultimately about the significance of the council and its relation to the centuries-old tradition of the Roman Catholic Church. There is a denial in some Vatican offices that Vatican II was an "event," by which they mean a "ruptured continuity" with the tradition.[2] This whole debate of whether there has been a discontinuity in the Catholic tradition misconceives the nature of tradition that is always in a process of change.

The focus of this chapter is the foundation of church life as a community responsive to God who is present in creation and who speaks to believers in the Christ-centered tradition. Two categories that have shaped the church's life and its authority pattern are faith and revelation. This chapter explores faith and revelation not as two separable things but as the poles of a divine-human relation. I argue that *revelation* as a term to describe the divine side of this relation needs complementing by the metaphor of God speaking. And for positing a dialogical relation between divine and human, the form of the church has to be a community of speaking and listening.

Finding the Question

I began graduate school as the Vatican Council was in preparation. I discovered that there had been far more intellectual ferment in the Roman Catholic Church since the 1930s than I was aware of. During my first semester, I took a course entitled Introduction to Theology. For my first term paper, I chose the relation between scripture and tradition. I discovered that there was a new Catholic-Protestant discussion of this question, which surprised me. Starting in elementary school, I had been taught that Protestants believed revelation is in the Bible, while Catholics believed that the Bible was supplemented by other truths in tradition. I was always puzzled that Protestants could not see that we had more truths than they did.

153

My term paper turned out to be a more ambitious project than I had anticipated. There were lively discussions of the question among Catholics, among Protestants, and between Catholics and Protestants. The amount of material was manageable, but most of the discussion had taken place in European journals. What confused me was that some Catholic scholars seemed to be saying that all revelation is in scripture, and some Protestant scholars were insisting on the need for tradition. Was it possible that the two camps were switching sides? I tried sorting out the differing views without pretending to have an answer. I could not have imagined then that more than fifty years later I would still be working at the best way to formulate the question so as to get a better answer.

My term paper turned into a master's thesis by the end of that school year, and then it was accepted for publication during the summer. My modest volume appeared in a series called *Questiones Disputatae*.[3] While I nervously awaited publication of my book, the Second Vatican Council began and immediately took up a document entitled *The Sources of Revelation*. The document restated the formulas of the Council of Trent. A few bishops, especially from missionary countries, knew that the proposed document was inadequate. A key figure in the rejection of the document was a young advisor to Cardinal Frings of Cologne. The theologian was Josef Ratzinger, who had done a provocative study in the 1950s of Bonaventure and revelation.[4] If there had not been a majority vote to reject the document, along with Pope Paul VI's intervention, the major changes in thinking that occurred at the council could not have happened (and my book would have been irrelevant before it was published).

The best thing that my master's thesis did for me was that it gave me a topic for a doctoral dissertation. From trying to make sense of the argument over sources of revelation, I concluded that there might be a deeper problem with the idea of revelation itself. The amount of writing on that topic was surprisingly thin. A major study by René Latourelle, *Théologie de la Révélation*, was published in 1963.[5] Nothing as comprehensive existed in English. Treatments of revelation found in textbooks tended to repeat standard formulas without any indication that there might be room for questioning.

What I imagined myself doing was drawing out the implied meaning of revelation in recent literature on grace, sacraments, moral theology, the Holy Spirit, tradition, and biblical studies. I was studying in a program of religious education that provided a liturgical context for biblical studies. It seemed to me that this biblical-liturgical material required a rethinking of a philosophical or theological doctrine of revelation.

I finished my dissertation in the spring of 1965 and began preparing it for publication. In the summer of that year, I obtained a copy of the revised document on revelation that was to be discussed in the last session of the council in the fall. I trusted that there would be no major changes in the final version, and I prepared my manuscript with spaces that were left to insert quotations from the council. The document entitled *Dei Verbum* was approved in December 1965, and my book, including appropriate quotations from the council's text, appeared just over a month later. I did not claim that I was deriving my book from the council, but I was claiming compatibility with its document on revelation.

My dissertation was published as two books, *Theology of Revelation* and *Catechesis of Revelation*.[6] An important source for my reflection in both books was the high school religion courses I had been teaching previous to beginning graduate studies. The second book, on catechesis, appeared to be an almost paragraph-by-paragraph application of the first book. In fact, however, the process often ran in the opposite direction; that is, my experience and convictions from educational practice informed the theology. I would not have tried to invent a theology to fit with the teaching of religion. Nonetheless, it was educational practice that pointed a direction and confirmed the pattern of what I was piecing together from theology.

The most important principle that I thought was necessary for education is that *God's word* is spoken in the present. My question was whether that conviction was compatible with Catholic tradition. To some people, a *present revelation* was obviously heretical. Undeniably, I was running up against some doctrinal formulas, such as the (nineteenth-century) statement that "revelation closed with the death of the last apostle." For my part, I thought I was taking seriously the liturgical proclamation of the scripture, that God's word is spoken to you today. The British edition of *Catechesis of Revelation* was published with the title *God Still Speaks*. Although I was not consulted about the change of title, I had to admit that it was a better title than I had chosen.

Like many books that present a systematic argument, my attempt to think through the nature of revelation in *Theology of Revelation* was often reduced to a slogan. I still meet people who identify me with the phrase *continuing revelation*. Perhaps that phrase suggested to some people what I was trying to do, but that was not my formula of choice. The idea of a continuing revelation was a widespread theory of liberal Protestant theology in the late nineteenth century. In that literature, scientific knowledge was believed to be brightening the path of human life and leading to unending progress. The Bible and early Christian tradition were thought to be an early stage of this revelation (or enlightenment) while today's lights are much stronger. The Bible was thus relegated to a first stage of this continuing revelation.[7]

I think some people saw my work as anti-biblical or an attempt to undermine the place of the Bible. Instead, I was trying to provide an adequate context for the Bible. To this day, it is generally assumed that revelation is the domain of biblical scholars, but that assumption is not a service to the Bible or to biblical study. References to the Bible as "the revealed word of God" go counter to modern biblical study that describes the Bible as written by human beings under divine inspiration. "Dei Verbum," or the "Dogmatic Constitution on Divine Revelation," was mainly the work of biblical scholars. They made the document come alive with the spirit of the gospel, saving the document from the Roman Curia's sixteenth-century theology. They did not try to go further than the Bible. The question of revelation cannot be answered from within biblical studies or Christian theology.

Revelation and Faith

Faith, similar to revelation, tends to become an object. In my childhood, *the faith* was very well defined; it was the set of beliefs and practices presented to the individual Roman Catholic. When I became an adult, I was aware of the limitations of that meaning of faith, but it took me a long time to find the right way, or at least a better way, to relate faith and revelation.

Faith is the word that is popularly used to sum up the difference between religious people and the nonbeliever. Opponents of Christianity direct their attack at faith, which they assume is a collection of irrational ideas and practices. Where *revelation* was once used, *faith* now seems to be used by believers as a term more defensible than *revelation*. That can have the unfortunate result of faith being directed at faith. A book on mourning that I once used in a college course on death encouraged the mourner "to have faith in whatever beliefs you have."

The term *Christian faith* in the Middle Ages usually referred to the faith that is Christian in nature—that is, centered on Christ. Christian faith is a meaningful term, but it should not be overused to refer to all aspects of the Christian's religion. For example, in Joseph Ratzinger's writings, he uses "Christian faith" hundreds of times. More often than not, *Christian faith* in his writing refers to Catholic doctrine or the Roman Catholic Church.[8]

Today's conversation among Christians, Jews, and Muslims is misleadingly called "interfaith" dialogue. Christians, Jews, and Muslims differ in their beliefs but not in their faith. Neither the Bible nor the Qur'an recognizes a multiplicity of faiths. Dialogue requires the assumption that one's interlocutor is speaking in *good faith*. A conversation involving Christians, Jews, and Muslims would best be called an *interreligious dialogue*. Such a dialogue can be based on a unity of our believing in God together with differences in our beliefs and religious practices.

There are two distinct verbs of believing, *believe in* and *believe that*. Even in secular usage, people distinguish between believing in someone and believing that a statement is true. The English language provides a direct translation from the Latin phrases that Augustine and early church writers developed. For the authors of the creed, *"credo in unum Deum"* did not mean "I believe that there is one God" but rather "I place my trust in the only God there is." This distinction between *believe in* and *believe that* was regularly obscured in Catholic-Protestant polemics. Luther's "every man must do his own believing" was met by the Roman Catholic Church's insistence on the individual accepting "the faith," by which was meant accepting every doctrine of the Roman Catholic Church.

The beliefs that an individual Roman Catholic has may stand in some tension with the belief system of the Roman Catholic Church. The question for the individual and for church officials is whether a person's beliefs are sufficiently congruent with the greater church tradition so as to mark him or her as a church member. The Roman Catholic Church is admirably concerned with consistency and with the continuity of its beliefs. But hunters after heresy should realize the limitations of their job. A loyal member of the church who has led an upstanding life should not be treated as an enemy because of a single belief that he or she holds that differs from official teaching. The Congregation for the Doctrine of the Faith makes judgments pertaining to *doctrines about faith.* It is not in a position to make judgments about anyone's Catholic or Christian faith but only whether a statement is at variance with a defined doctrine of the Roman Catholic Church.

The church from earliest times has carefully attended to how beliefs should be formulated in statements. That proper concern for beliefs should not hide the fact that faith as *believing in* is also expressed in nonverbal ways. The church's concern has to be *ortho-praxis* as well as orthodoxy—that is, how faith is embodied in a person's actions. In the description of the last judgment in the New Testament (Matthew 25:31–46), the basis of judgment is not whether someone has said "Lord, Lord" but whether the person fed the hungry, clothed the naked, sheltered the homeless, visited the imprisoned, and hungered after justice.

If faith-revelation is used as a description of the divine-human relation, then faith can be described in detail as a human activity. In contrast, there is not much that one can directly say of the religious use of revelation after saying that it is activity on the divine side of the relation. The two guidelines for a religious use of *revelation* are as follows: the word can be used only as a verb, not as a noun, and the word can be used only in the singular, not the plural. The term *revelation* does have to be explored but always with the recognition that the church does not have a revelation from God. It may claim to have what is a result of the divine activity of revelation; modern biblical study presupposes that principle. However, this meaning of revelation is constantly obscured in theological and catechetical documents that speak of an "objective content to revelation" or a "revealed message."

John Noonan is a brilliant historian who has uncovered facts about the Roman Catholic Church's history that officials would sometimes have preferred were left in the dark. His book, *A Church that Can Change and Cannot Change*, has some devastating facts, for example, that the Roman Catholic Church did not oppose slavery until after much of secular society had seen the light. While medieval commentators thought that usury is "against nature," they had difficulty seeing that slavery surely is. At the end of this long tale of a very slow awakening, Noonan writes, "Development does occur in the understanding of the demands of Christian revelation. No new revelation is made. The revelation itself does not change. Yet change occurs. How does it occur? As Vatican II answers this question, by deepening the understanding of revelation."[9]

Noonan obviously does not wish to oppose the foundation of the Roman Catholic Church, but he surely must suspect that that paragraph makes no sense. To be compatible with the history that he has just recounted, something better is needed. He might be relieved if he knew that there are no "demands of Christian revelation" because the category of Christian revelation is a sixteenth-century invention. The claim of a Christian revelation subverts an understanding of a divine revelation that is present throughout creation. The Roman Catholic Church, along with other religious bodies, has to respond to that divine activity with all of its human activities.

Noonan is not unusual in assuming the existence of a Christian revelation. It is a standard premise of theologians. If a question is raised about such a category, their reply is that they deal with the content of Christian revelation; exploring the idea of revelation is the work of biblical scholars or philosophers. A professor of dogmatic theology, moral theology, Christology, or ecclesiology cannot be expected to explore in any depth the premises of theology. But the casually used term *Christian revelation* is a modern distortion of the idea of revelation. Thomas Aquinas makes no references to "Christian revelation" despite many writers attributing views on Christian revelation to Thomas; the term did not exist before the sixteenth century. *Christian revelation* arose from the struggle between Catholics and Protestant for possession of the true religion. The question was who had control of God's truth, the revelation that is truly Christian. Today the question is whether the category of revelation makes sense. There are innumerable things that can be called revelations, but what would a revelation of God mean?

Revelation is not a prominent term in the Bible. Like many terms in Christian tradition, revelation was a Greek import, a translation of apocalypse. In this case, the earliest Greek meaning—to enlighten— had been overlaid with a mixture of Middle Eastern religions that claimed to know secrets about the end of the world. These religions provided a context for the Jesus movement and the early church. The last book of the New Testament, called Revelation or Apocalypse, describes the end of the world; the revelation is a vision of a new heaven and a new earth. Vatican II's *Constitution on Divine Revelation* shockingly has no mention of the last book of the Bible, Revelation/Apocalypse.

The claim to know the secrets about the end of the world has always been a volatile element in the Christian religion, never more so than at present. The book of Revelation has provided comfort to Christians during periods of persecution.[10] But from the earliest era of the church, Revelation was recognized as a dangerous book when it is isolated from the rest of Christian belief. People who are certain that they know the final secrets of God's plan for the universe may think it unnecessary to study the rest of the story. Not surprisingly, the meaning that most people have of *apocalypse* is violent destruction. The impatient attempts to bring the world to apocalypse/revelation have regularly involved violence.

As soon as it became clear that Jesus's second coming was not imminent, the Christian Church understood that its mission is to live in the in-between time. Its liturgical practice is oriented to remembering the past and hoping for the future while living in the tension of the present. *Creation* is a present activity of God, but the term orients our minds to the past. *Revelation* is a present activity of God, and it is a term that encourages us to see in the present the quickening possibilities of the future.

The *Constitution on Divine Revelation* begins with a first chapter entitled "Revelation Itself." The five paragraphs string together biblical quotations. For many people—not only church opponents—the document seems to say that the revelation of God is in the Bible because the Bible says of itself that it is the revelation of God. Some degree of circularity in religious belief is probably unavoidable, but the issue needs to be examined and given the best formulation possible. In the Roman Catholic Church after the Reformation, apologetics tried to break out of a circular argument by proving from reason alone the foundation of theology. Some proponents of natural law still presuppose this framework for their opinions on moral issues. Vatican II wisely avoided this language of supporting a "supernatural revelation" with a "natural revelation," but it precariously left a "biblical revelation" without much visible support. Revelation-faith as expressive of a divine-human relation has to be an intelligible idea, supported by biblical material but not exclusively derived from the Bible.

Karl Rahner was the theologian who perhaps exercised the single greatest influence on the thinking of Vatican II. Rahner was genuinely conservative in often going back or down to a seemingly dead formula and tracing where the formula came from and what it could still teach us today. Rahner thought that the work of Vatican II on revelation was only a first step in thinking through the idea of revelation for a world Christianity.[11]

To most people, "the Christian revelation" quite logically means something fixed in the distant past that the Christian Church claims to possess. Church officials understand their job to be one of preserving and passing on the Christian revelation. Any change in that body of material is construed as a distortion. It is useless to criticize bishops for doing what they believe is their solemn obligation; they need help to reimagine their job. The second chapter of the *Constitution on Divine Revelation* is entitled "The Transmission of Divine Revelation." The church cannot transmit revelation; it can transmit doctrines and practices of the tradition. While a church would have no right to alter a revelation of God, it has to constantly rethink what are doctrinal attempts to understand a divine revelation. The past is a necessary guide for understanding the divine-human relation in the present.

A conversation between Christians and other religious people is indispensable today, but it will not get started with the term *Christian revelation*. A conversation can only be based on the premise that there is one God, one creation, one divine revelation to which Christians, Jews, Muslims, and others respond with their own best lights and faithful lives. Each of the religions may claim—probably must claim—that their interpretation of divine revelation is superior to all others. That belief does not stop a conversation. The diversity of interpretations can be a rich source for reflection, learning, and debate.

What a Roman Catholic brings to the table is a complex set of doctrinal beliefs that distinguishes Catholic Christians from Muslims, Jews, Protestant Christians, and other religious people. The Catholic tradition does not lop off beliefs from the past on the basis that they seem out of fashion in the present. The two thousand defined doctrines of the Roman Catholic Church are a kind of kaleidoscope through which to view reality. Some of the doctrines make no sense to me, but I am not inclined to oppose them. Perhaps the doctrine will make more sense to a future generation and in a different context. Or perhaps we still have to puzzle out what a previous generation was trying to get at. In any case, Catholic tradition can be an endlessly fascinating storehouse for intelligence, imagination, and playful possibilities.

At the beginning of modern science, most scientists and theologians wished to avoid a direct conflict with each other. A compromise was worked out whereby enlightenment or natural revelation was the work of the sciences, and a supernatural or special revelation was given over to the Christian Churches. The split between the public world of the sciences and the private world of religion generally succeeded in keeping the peace. But the price for the churches was to be cut off from both the natural world and politics. Recently, in both Catholic and Protestant Churches, there has been a refusal to stay in the private space that the modern world has assigned to religion.[12]

Pope Francis's encyclical *Laudato si* could be read as a meditation on divine revelation. Inspired by Francis of Assisi, the pope calls attention to every creature as a manifestation of the divine. But one jarring sentence calls into question the seriousness of what is said about God speaking through all of creation. Using a quotation from Pope John Paul II, Pope Francis says that "alongside revelation properly so called, contained in Sacred Scripture, there is a divine manifestation in the blaze of the sun and the fall of the night."[13] That would be a badly formulated statement anywhere and anytime, but in the context of a twenty-first-century reflection on the humans and their environment, the statement undercuts much of the encyclical's message.

The split between "revelation properly so called" and divine manifestations in "natural" events reflects the seventeenth-century's bargain in which empirical science was in charge of the natural world, and Christianity had a supernatural revelation, *contained* in sacred scripture. Trying to add a natural revelation to revelation "properly so called" has never worked and cannot work. The only way to overcome the dichotomy is to affirm divine activity everywhere and at every time. The place of a holy scripture, a religious community, and the person of Jesus as Christ have to be worked out from within the one creation, one revelation of God. That is the basis for dialogue among religions and dialogue of the church with secular society.

In summary, if the Roman Catholic Church continues to use the term *revelation*, as I assume it will, its meaning should be restricted to a metaphor for divine activity. This visual metaphor of unveiling what had been secret has to be supplemented by a dialogical metaphor that is more consistently used in the Bible. The divine revelation is the illumination of creation that still lives partially in darkness while awaiting the birth of a new creation. In the Christian view, a brilliant light came into the world at a particular time and place. It should be noted, however, that Genesis opens not with the words "let there be light" but "God said." Similarly, the fourth gospel does not begin with "the light shines in the darkness" but rather "In the beginning was the Word." Revelation or enlightenment is not alien to the Bible, but it is subordinate to the metaphor of speaking-answering.

Divine Speaking, Human Answering

The central metaphor of both biblical and Qur'anic traditions is that God speaks. The part that humans play is to listen and then respond. Prayer is thus imagined as a conversation with God. To be sure, it is a strange kind of conversation because God does not speak any of the standard dialects that a human recognizes. Nevertheless, in an extended sense of language that can include gestures, symbols, and actions, the tribe of Abraham believes that God speaks in natural phenomena and human events. The Bible and the Qur'an are attempts to use human words to convey both the divine speaking and the human responses. Religious scriptures are a lens by which to read reality; they point beyond the written text to all of creation as "Word of God."

In his book *Man's Search for Meaning*, Victor Frankl recounts a conversation he had with a woman who survived the Holocaust.[14] He asked her what kept her going in the prison cell where she was confined for several years. The woman said that there was a slit in the wall through which she could see a tree, and the tree spoke to her. "What did the tree say?" asked Frankl. The woman replied that the tree said, "Life, life." Did the tree really speak? One could say that for someone who is immersed in biblical imagery and belief, a tree and everything else in the universe can speak.

It is ironic that the Christian movement was in large part responsible for the invention of the book (which is what *bible* means). Muslims refer somewhat misleadingly to Jews and Christians as "people of the book." Modern Jews seem to have no problem with calling their scriptures the Bible, though their religion has employed not a book but the reading of scrolls. The Christian religion at its beginning was spread not with a book but by the spoken word. When the New Testament came to exist, it was written in the popular spoken Greek of the time, not literary Greek. Only gradually did the collection of gospels and letters assume the form that we identify as a book. This book had an *old testament* for its beginning and *revelation* for its conclusion. In between the beginning and the end was the story of Jesus's life, death, and resurrection. Once a story is put between the covers of a book, it loses some of its vitality. The obvious advantage of creating a book is that the story can be shared more widely, including with future generations.

The particular danger for the church was the impression a book gave that God revealed secrets until about the year 30 CE, and then God went silent. Christianity is viewed by some people as only of interest to archeologists, historians, and literary theorists. A God who delivered a message to one group of people during one short period of time does not seem believable as the God of the universe. A further problem is that an ancient revelation can seem to deliver the answers to life when most schoolchildren and many adults are still trying to discover what the questions of life are. *Revelation* is not flexible enough to deal with this issue; it is not a dialogical term. Revelation means that the secret is now known, the mystery is resolved, no further questioning is necessary.

An early Christian formula asserted that the rule of faith is set by the rule of prayer.[15] The liturgy, even when it has been mishandled, has kept alive the language that "God speaks now," and the congregation responds with "amen." The words spoken in the liturgy are not the revelation of truths; instead, they are words of invitation, challenge, and comfort, which are complete only if there is a human response of faith. The church's mission is not to save the world but to be a place where the Word of God takes human form *through* Christ and *in* the Spirit. This relation can include the visual metaphor of revelation— the church as a light to the nations. But the church should not try to compete with science in enlightenment or revelation. The sciences are successful, sometimes spectacularly so, in opening our eyes to the physical dimensions of the universe and in producing solutions to many human problems. Modern science understands the world empirically and mathematically; once science goes beyond appearances, its answers to problems are in numbers.

There are other kinds of human problems in addition to the empirical and mathematical. The Christian tradition calls these problems mysteries, and they are faced by every generation and each individual.[16] We are no closer to solutions of these mysteries than were people of millennia past. Why is there a world? Is there a meaning to human life? Does anything survive death? Why is there suffering? Directly or indirectly, every individual wrestles with these questions. Just when we may think that our private world does not include these pesky religious questions, a tragic happening or a moment of unalloyed joy shakes up our ordinary routines. In moments of crisis, we listen for words of comfort and direction from a trusted friend or a wise tradition. At such moments in life, the point is not how to get an answer to life but how to rethink our response to what life now offers.

In recent years, the term *dialogue* has been used to describe Christian-Jewish and Christian-Jewish-Muslim relations. Dialogue between religions presupposes dialogue within a religion. Dialogue among Christians is closely related to an understanding of divine-human dialogue, which is at the heart of Christianity. This dialogue with the divine has to be taken up anew every day. The church has to engage in one of life's most difficult tasks: listening. In the Roman Catholic Church, there are officially appointed teachers, but, as Vatican II said, they can teach only if they first listen for the word that God speaks. They too are the "church taught," part of the "faithful" in the divine-human dialogue.[17]

The interior working of the Roman Catholic Church has not often been imagined as a continuing conversation in which the whole church seeks to hear a divine word. Early Christian thinkers already recognized that in the paradox of the divine-human Christ the elimination of the human was the greater danger. It was easier to believe that Jesus was God under a human appearance than to believe that Jesus was in dialogue with his Father and that the Christ was both Word of God and word of man. The Christian Church throughout the centuries has struggled to maintain the almost unbearable paradox of Son of God, Son of Man. No human language is available to adequately express this relation; the most that the church can do is preserve the mystery by fending off simplistic solutions. In one of Soren Kierkegaard's brilliant formulas of belief in Christ, he wrote: "Never has any religion brought God and man so close together but neither has any religion so protected itself against that most shocking of all blasphemies, that when God decided to take the step, the step should be taken in vain."[18]

When the paradox of the Christ is obscured, the Christian Church takes on divine trappings and forgets that its role is to be a respondent. Church officials then act as if they possess divinely revealed truths while neglecting the fact that no one has access to divine truth except through and in human language. The church, as the Second Vatican Council said, "is a kind of sacrament or sign of intimate union with God and the unity of all mankind."[19] The church as "original sacrament" points to the whole universe as sacramental. The seven activities that the Council of Trent called the sacraments are the standouts in a sacramental universe of divine revelation.

The language that has been used by church councils at their best has been "not this, not that, keep going." The First Vatican Council's pronouncements on faith can be read as condemning the rationalism of the nineteenth century while also rejecting the romantic reaction that undervalued reason. Faith is not simply rational, nor is it irrational. As for defining faith, the First Vatican Council was saying, "Keep trying to understand faith but don't expect to find a final answer." Similarly, at the end of the Second Vatican Council, Pope Paul VI said that there were many issues that the council could not resolve.[20] He could have added "and that the church will never resolve."

Community

The necessary context for faith in a revealing/speaking God is a living community where the presence of Christ and the Holy Spirit is credible. If revelation is assumed to mean that truths were once revealed and are now possessed by the Christian Church, then dialogue is at most an optional feature of church life. However, if divine revelation is the present activity of God requiring a response of faith, then dialogue has to be at the center of church life. Listening, care, compassion, and love are hallmarks of a human community.

The basis of a community is that everyone knows and cares for all the others who constitute the group. An organization of millions of people cannot be such a community. However, an organization can shelter under its roof the development of many communal groups; the large size of an organization is then an advantage to the existence of communities. Only if a large organization is composed of communal units will modern means of communication support a unified purpose for an organization.

The United States was originally built on individualism. Immigrant groups, especially Catholics and Jews, brought a sensibility to the country that differed from individualism. In time, these tightly knit communities tended to get absorbed into the individualistic ethos of the country. Jews, because of their small numbers and because the United States is suffused with Christian symbols, have been more insistent than other immigrant groups on maintaining a distinct community. Roman Catholics at first faced a struggle similar to Jews, though not as severe in relating to US society. For better and for worse, Roman Catholics have progressed far along the way at being assimilated into US social patterns. Nevertheless, Roman Catholics, at least to the present time, retain a sense of community as more than a collection of individuals.

Communities can be of many kinds, but the term *community* connotes a human bond that goes beyond membership in an organization, or working on a task force, or being a colleague at work. The Roman Catholic Church of the 1950s was an impressive organization that provided community experiences in family life, within parishes, and in religious orders. That experience was sometimes helped and sometimes hindered by the church's larger organizational apparatus. Before Vatican II, there was a distinct sense of church communities, but that sense no longer exists. The Roman Catholic Church cannot and should not try to reestablish its 1950s organization.

In today's world, most of us live in many communities, or at least in many fractured forms of community. Whether our new technology of instant and incessant communication will help the bonds of community remains to be seen. People still need other faces and voices that are etched in their memories. As Aristotle said, "nobody would choose to live without friends even if he had all the other good things."[21] The liturgical community of the church is not a substitute for other community experiences nor should it be in competition with them. The liturgical community is not necessarily worse off today for being only one of the communities that Roman Catholics identify with. Roman Catholics still go to Sunday Mass in great numbers, even if attendance is far below what it once was. There is still an opportunity to provide a link to the richness of Catholic tradition and some connection to the wider world of Christian Churches.

The deeper experiences of community emerge from both planned and unplanned events that invite participation of family, friends, and interested strangers. A reunion of a school class, a meeting of a professional association, or a picnic by family members can sometimes spark a sense of community. Such communities cannot be directly transposed to parishes, but lessons can be found there for the internal working of a parish and for events that might give some operational meaning to the word *community*. The sacraments when based on ordinary experience can be places where God speaks and Christians respond in faith. The sacramental system of the Roman Catholic Church offers a developmental scheme that extends from birth to death. These events still offer possibilities of community experience.

The Roman Catholic Church is a main source for small groups who are committed to fighting injustices and taking care of the downtrodden. Working in disaster relief is a sacramental practice in which the presence of God is made credible. The clerical sex scandal has done incalculable harm to victims of sexual abuse and to the authority of the Roman Catholic Church. The great work of Catholic groups at home and in missionary lands has been obscured by this scandal. The Roman Catholic Church will survive this crisis despite the inept response of many church officials. The Catholic tradition has riches that are often buried beneath the shards of organizational corruption and incompetence. God still speaks in the lives of people and their dedicated work. There are still people who believe in and are open to the Spirit of God and who respond with the activity of faithful lives.

Chapter 11

Responsibility, Obligations, Rights

T he idea of responsibility follows directly from revelation
as a divine activity calling for human response. The term
responsible originated from a mixture of Jewish, Christian, and
Roman elements about two thousand years ago, especially through the
emergence of the human individual—the child of a heavenly father—in
pharisaic Judaism. Another necessary element for responsibility was
the sense of judgment, the belief that the individual must answer for
his or her life's actions. The apocalyptic religions that were prominent
at the time of early Christianity played a part in this evolution. The
legal thinking that blossomed in both Latin Christianity and Rabbinic
Judaism was also influential in producing a description of the human
being as responsible.

Responsibility has always been more important than one virtue
among many. There are no classical accounts of a virtue of responsibility
and no medieval treatises on the subject. The word itself lay mostly
hidden until the eighteenth century, but it underlies the Jewish and
Christian sense of what a human being is: the being who listens and
responds to the one who is creator of the universe and its ultimate judge.

The omnipresence of the term *responsibility* in ethics and popular
speech today is both an encouraging sign and a somewhat suspect
development. The term is constantly used as if everyone knows what

responsibility is, and that the only problem is that we do not have enough of it. Responsibility is one of the terms that the contemporary world holds on to from the past, although the premises of the idea may have been lost. Humans in the past were thought to live under a judgment about their lives as a whole. Today, *responsibilities* are simply asserted as a price paid for *rights*.

Environmental literature comes the closest to recognizing the problem. Why should humans act ethically? The answer given is that they should do so because they have a responsibility to the earth that gave them life and continues to nourish them. This acknowledgment means that human beings are not autonomous—a law unto themselves— which has been a principle at the heart of modern ethics. Human lives depend on an unimaginably complex web of life. A religious or mystical attitude surrounds much of environmental literature. Unfortunately, responsibility to the earth or to nature does not move most people to change their behavior.

Responsibility is a characteristic of all human beings and some nonhuman beings. The root meaning of responsible is "able to answer to what has been spoken." What is spoken can be human speech or a metaphorical extension of it. And the answering can be performed by every human being, including infants, people who are judged mentally retarded, hardened criminals, and people dying of old age. The response need not be in the form of words. A physical or mental act could be the acknowledgment of what has been heard. Some nonhuman animals clearly fall within this meaning of responsible. They listen and then answer. Anyone who spends time with a dog, a cat, a horse, or a chimp knows that at least some animals are able to respond to a word that has been spoken to them.

Moral Responsibility

There are two crucial distinctions that are needed for understanding how a *human* being is responsible. The first distinction is between the kind of responsibility that many animals are born with and a *moral* responsibility that applies only to human beings. Various degrees of responsibility can be attributed to animals. A horse or a dog can be disciplined (taught) by a trainer to respond in one way rather than another.[1] If a pit bull attacks a child, it is likely to be restrained or killed. Words such as vicious, savage, or criminal are sometimes used to describe the animal. We stop short of imputing guilt to the dog, but we do hold it responsible for what it has done, even though the dog's owner may be largely responsible for the dog's bad behavior.

The call for people to be responsible is often empty rhetoric insofar as human beings are born responsible. Every action that is attributable to a human being is a responsible action; that is, the human being causes the action to occur in response to the external world. *Moral* responsibility, however, involves a person being aware of having a choice between outcomes that are either good or bad. Conscience is simply awareness that our responsibility involves a freedom to do either what is right or what is wrong. Moral responsibility takes time to develop. Somewhere during childhood, morally responsible actions become possible, but a line between actions that are moral and nonmoral is not always clear.

We often do not know if a person is morally responsible for a bad action, even when we judge that the behavior (the external aspect of human action) is unacceptable. Courts have to judge whether a defendant is legally responsible—that is, guilty or innocent before the law. Fortunately for all of us, the judgment of *moral* guilt can only be tentatively and fallibly rendered by any human court of opinion. If there is an evaluation of one's life as a whole, it cannot be done by any human judge.

Responsible to, Responsible For

The second distinction in human responsibility is between *responsible to* and *responsible for*. The process of acting responsibly is a dialectical interplay between listening and answering. The first moment of responsibility is being responsible to someone or something. The second moment is responsibility for the action that follows upon listening. This dialectical exchange then issues in a third moment—namely, *responding to* what one has been *responsible for*. The interplay continues throughout a person's lifetime. At any moment, I can only be responsible *for* what I am responsible *to*. But what I am responsible *to* is dependent on what I have previously been responsible *for*.[2]

This interdependence of *responsible to* and *responsible for* may seem to doom the human being to a closed cycle of determined behavior. Can there be any moral progress if I am responsible for an actions only insofar as I am aware of that responsibility, an awareness that is itself dependent on how moral I am? Human beings are, indeed, strongly conditioned by genetic makeup, early experiences, and their physical and social environments. It is easy to show that human beings do not have free will in the sense that people imagine they are free. No one can simply will to be a different person. Some of evolutionary biology today seems ready to close the circle and exclude freedom of choice.

The human being would indeed be left to fate if the sense of *responsible to* is underdeveloped or goes unnoticed. Freedom depends upon attentiveness to what is happening and on a capacity to reflect upon previous actions in a way that gradually widens the cycle of responsible to and responsible for.[3] A failing in responsibility very often lies in what is not done because we are unaware that it should be done. The failure to attend—to be *responsible to*—is often at the base of moral fault. Ignorance can be culpable (morally if not legally) when we could have known and should have known, but we were selectively unaware.

Responsible to: Until the late nineteenth century, the word *responsible* was nearly always followed by *to*. The action of a person depended on to whom or to what it was a response. One of the first uses in the *Oxford English Dictionary* refers to a legislature being responsible to the people. Of course, it was assumed that responsibility for particular actions would follow, but the basic meaning of the word was listening to someone or something.

To whom and to what should one listen for moral guidance? The short but comprehensive answer is one should be open to everyone and everything. Obviously, that is not an efficient strategy. We need help to sort out the many voices in our head and to interpret what we are summoned to. We need the help of a trusted guide. Nevertheless, at particular moments the important word might be spoken by friend or stranger, young or old, living or dead, brilliant or slow-witted, human or nonhuman. Responsible human listening cannot in principle be closed to any source as a possible moral guide.

In practice, all of us adopt guides and guidelines that we believe are trustworthy. A parent or a friend may be the chief guide when we are young. A scholar or a school of thought may later gain our trust. A religious tradition is a guide for how to interpret the whole of reality. Jewish and Christian traditions say that God is more likely to speak here rather than there, but listen carefully because it could be just the opposite. Those who demand a premature certainty are likely to become attached to one set of ideas that increasingly filter out much of the beauty and meaning in life. The best alternative to a system of fixed certainties is a gradual growth in certainty as one's life is lived in response to the best lights that one has at any moment.

Morality begins with the readiness to receive. Giving and receiving are opposite ends of a single relation; there is no giver without a receiver. In human exchanges, receiving is a form of giving oneself; the giver therefore receives in giving.[4] Human gifts keep moving until they return to the giver. If the circle is too small, the sense of gift may become replaced by the calculation of a narrow self-interest. If, in contrast, one passes on the gift to another person without calculating the return, the circle keeps expanding.

We generally think of our neighbor as someone who lives close by. But the test of who is my neighbor was conveyed in the Hebrew Bible by the question, what will you do for the stranger who is in need? This understanding of the love of neighbor was illustrated in many of Jesus's parables, such as the story of the Good Samaritan. If a fellow human being is in a bad way and I am the person who can help, then that person is my neighbor.[5]

The meaning of *responsible to* should be as broad and as deep as possible. In practice, breadth and depth stand in tension so that we have to look for the best combination of them. One friend's advice may be too little, but the advice of ten colleagues may be too much, especially if none of the advice comes from the depths of friendship. Ten historical documents are not more revealing than one document that speaks to the heart of the matter. There are no clear rules for how each of us combines a broad-based response and a response from the depths of the self. We are not certain of the best way to respond in a given situation, but we can be sure that a narrow and shallow response is the wrong way.

Responsible for. If we are responsible *to* in the best way that we know how, we will get a more precise understanding of what we are responsible *for.* A vague, narrow, or shallow understanding of what we are responsible *to* will lead to a distortion in what we are responsible *for.* One such distortion takes the form of an aggressive seizing upon some activity as a quick resolution of life's problems. People make decisions to change careers, choose a marriage partner, lose fifty pounds, or quit school, without attending to important voices that are outside themselves and without lining up support within their own bodies for whatever is decided.

The extreme case of this distortion is the terrorist who takes responsibility for a bombing. All the terrorists in the world seem to speak the language of responsibility. I suspect that having been hectored to take responsibility for his life, the terrorist says, "You want me to take responsibility. Here it is." This distortion of responsibility by a terrorist is easy to recognize, but there are many subtle distortions in relation to what we are responsible for. We are often mistaken in understanding our responsibility 1) for other people, 2) for our own life, and 3) for things.

1) I am not responsible for other people, except insofar as they cannot perform some needed act. We are regularly urged to take responsibility for others. So widespread is the belief that we should be responsible for other people that the opposite is judged to be morally reprehensible. The favorite phrase here is the Bible's "my brother's keeper." The murderer Cain asks, "Am I my brother's keeper?" When the phrase is invoked today, the assumption is that the obvious answer is yes. But in the Bible, God does not deign to answer the question. If God had answered Cain, the reply might have been, "No, I did not ask you to be your brother's keeper. Brothers are neither for keeping nor for killing. I asked you to be your brother's brother."

In a world of isolated individuals, the question would be, should I be responsible for myself alone or should I also be responsible for other people? But in a relational world, the question is, should I be responsible *for* other people or responsible *to* other people? The latter activity is the way that my responsibility respects the freedom of other people and discovers what they need. Then the action that follows will be in the best interest of what relates us: if a brother, love; if an enemy, reconciliation; if a stranger, care for her or his needs. Professional people, such as politicians, physicians, and priests, need to be regularly reminded that responsibility should not creep over into paternalistic usurpation of the other's freedom.[6]

The exception for taking responsibility for others is that each human being does have times when he or she cannot do some things for himself or herself. That is the case for all of us when we are very young; a one-year-old cannot prepare its dinner or change its diaper. The same case may be true for us when we are very old and near death. That situation of an old person not being able to act for himself or herself has become increasingly common in our society. But one need not wait to get old for this condition to appear. Throughout the life of each person, events may temporarily prevent one from acting on his or her own behalf. If a person's incapacity to act is temporary, someone else has to supply actions for as long as and to the extent that the person is incapacitated. Toward the end of life, this incapacitated condition may be permanent, and someone may have to decide to continue or discontinue keeping a patient alive. Continuing to use a respirator or a feeding tube is a human decision just as much as is terminating its use.[7]

When someone else has to be responsible for our actions, we hope that it will be a close family member or a friend who has our best interests in mind. Lacking that, we can hope for an ethics committee in a hospital to defend our interests. Any of us may become responsible for acting on behalf of a stranger. If I come upon a crime or an accident and a person needs medical help, I can be morally responsible for getting that assistance. The United States does not have a Good Samaritan law that would hold the bystander legally responsible. Nevertheless, if I am the person on the scene, some action is morally called for, if only to call 911.

2) I am not responsible for my life; I am responsible for those actions over which I have sufficient control. Each of us is the product

of heredity, environment, and early nurturing that leave some of our behavior beyond direct or immediate control. Some people have truly severe addictions that make their lives a mess. Each of us has impulses, drives, and attachments that are incomprehensible to ourselves. But except for extreme cases, people retain the ability to reflect on their actions and to take a step away from their worst behavior.

Freedom consists mainly in the ability to say no. The self that we are has several possibilities that are present. Choice consists in saying no to all but one of them and accepting *that* possibility as future reality. At times—for example, in a prison cell, within an unhappy family, or on a needed job—there may not be much else that one can do except to say no, but that action can be the difference between retaining the dignity of a human being and sinking into an inhuman state. By a person repeatedly denying that any of the choices available is morally acceptable, he or she may gradually widen the area of behavior over which he or she has moral responsibility.[8]

In referring to actions over which I have *sufficient* control, the qualifier is necessarily ambiguous. Sometimes I am certain of being morally responsible for an action; the action is thoroughly mine. Sometimes I am uncertain if I am morally responsible because of external or internal pressures. If I sometimes cannot judge my own moral responsibility for an action, all the more is it true that I cannot judge other people's moral responsibility.

While I should accept responsibility for some actions, I think one should avoid the claim that "I take full responsibility." The person who makes that claim is usually caught within a complex set of circumstances. The person may have done some horrible deed and cannot understand his or her own motives. Or the person is a member of an organization that is involved in some serious wrongdoing. In such cases, the individual cannot take full responsibility because it is not there for the taking. If the person is famous, the news media demand that he or she come forth and take full responsibility for whatever bad thing has happened. There is a public ritual in which the person says, "I am sorry. I take full responsibility for what I did." And the news media then lose interest.

Instead of this ritual of saying, "I take full responsibility for what happened," the person who understands responsibility would say, "I accept responsibility for my part in this wrongdoing. I do not fully understand how this happened. I am taking steps a, b, or c to get further understanding and prevent a recurrence. I am going into rehab, or I am joining a support group, or I am resigning from my position in the government."

Telling someone to "take responsibility for your life" is not helpful and can be depressing and counterproductive. The person who receives such advice cannot get control of his or her life by a decision. What a person can do is accept some responsibility for the action that he or she is about to perform. In taking that one responsible step, the person might begin to reorient his or her life.

3) I am responsible for the things of creation that cannot be responsible for themselves. Ironically, we often assume that we are responsible for people but not for things, but it is things for which we are clearly responsible. The things sometimes include nonhuman animals although the ability of animals to decide many things for themselves should be respected. Vegetative life and nonliving things, as far as we can determine, cannot decide anything. Human beings need to accept responsibility for protecting the physical environment and caring for individual elements within the environment. Sometimes that means aggressive action on behalf of a river, a forest, or an oceanfront. Sometimes human responsibility is exercised by noninterference, leaving intact the cycle of living things.

Pope Francis's encyclical *Laudato si* has a strange sentence in commenting on Genesis II: "This implies a relationship of mutual responsibility between human beings and nature."[9] The statement might just be dismissed as clumsy, but it suggests a failure to understand both the terms *responsibility* and *nature*. The pope surely does not wish to endorse the modern personification of nature as a name for God or a replacement for God. Instead, the statement reflects a tendency to overuse both *responsibility* and *nature* in vague and abstract ways. Someone can have a degree of mutuality with a dog or a dolphin. To the extent that the dog is an agent that responds to one's actions with agreement or disagreement, a human and a dog are responsible to each other. Some people might argue for extending that way of speaking to a plant's relation to a man or woman. But there is no way a human being can be mutually responsible with an abstraction called nature.

Responsibility as Personal/Corporate

If responsibility is to everyone and everything, there is no reason why moral responsibility should exclude impersonal relations. For that to happen, however, one must start with a distinction that relates the personal and impersonal. Responsibility is always both personal and corporate; that is, every act of responsibility is a personal action from within a corporate or bodily structure. At the center of responsibility is the understanding and freedom of a personal being; surrounding that center is corporate existence that begins with the physical organism and extends into innumerable bodily organizations.

The structure of personal responsibility is always complex. Libertarian critics of government have no difficulty in cataloguing inefficient and incompetent actions by government agencies. When asked for the alternative, the critics answer that everything would be fine if everyone would be individually responsible for themselves. That answer may seem obvious, but it is psychologically, socially, economically deluded. Every human decision takes place within a web of relations that we can hardly begin to imagine, let alone control.

The term *personal* carries connotations that the term *individual* lacks. An *individual* is a unit in actuarial tables, economic forecasts, and scientific studies. A *person* is an actor, one who plays a role in the drama of life. The word *person* means to speak through a mask; the person is always partly hidden but is present by way of speaking. Person suggests a dialogue that is internal to the self. When playing many scenes, the actor in life's drama may be unclear as to how that scene fits into the overall plot. The actor has to trust that, by playing each scene to the best of his or her ability, a unity of personal existence will eventually emerge.

The person as actor always has conflicts in reaching a coalescence of character.[10] No one is transparent to himself or herself; one's own motives are never entirely clear. The lack of unity in a person is not best described as a conflict between body and spirit or as an opposition between reason and passion. In a negotiation of speaking and listening, the choice is between a superficial reason and a deeper reason that includes passion. We often wonder, why did I do that? Should I have acted differently? Hannah Arendt wrote that only bad people have clear consciences. The rest of us live with moral ambiguity, aware of our failures and the need for forgiveness.[11]

A corporation is any organization, institution, or body in space and time. A human body is a corporation, as also are the Boston Celtics, the United States Senate, the city of Rome, the American Medical Association, or Exxon Oil. It may seem quixotic to attempt retrieving the term *corporation* from its nearly exclusive control today by the business world. In support of such a project, I offer three considerations: First, there is no etymological reason why the business world has any more right to the term *corporation* than any other body. Second, corporations outside of the business world have been recognized as legal or artificial persons for almost a thousand years.[12] Third, many religious, political, and educational organizations today retain a share of the term *corporation* as nonprofit organizations.

The continuity of the personal and the corporate does not preclude distinguishing between natural persons and a variety of artificial persons. The 2010 Supreme Court case *Citizens United v. Federal Elections Commission* allowed business corporations to spend unlimited amounts of money in political campaigns. The deficiency in the decision was not the consideration of corporations as (artificial) persons. The decision was obtuse in not acknowledging that the size and economic power of some artificial persons can overwhelm the electoral process. The Supreme Court's 2014 decision in *Burwell v. Hobby Lobby* recognized a for-profit corporation's religious belief in opposing the contraception mandate of the health care law. The problem again was not the recognition of a corporation as an (artificial) person; the problem was confusing the religious beliefs of its owners with a business corporation that does not have religious beliefs.

Business corporations should be acknowledged as (artificial) persons that are responsible agents with both rights and duties. An artificial person needs to have a structure for the responsible exercise of its power on the world around it as well as for its own members. Max Weber was correct in saying that modern capitalism makes it difficult to say who is responsible for what. The problem should not be exacerbated by a radical individualism that regards institutions as completely impersonal—that is, other than us. Responsibility on the part of a natural person requires listening to and responding to the artificial persons that are extensions of a natural self.

On extreme occasions, a person's responsibility can involve a refusal to cooperate with one of the formative institutions of one's life. For example, one might resist fighting in an immoral war or selling a company's deadly product. An exercise of one's moral responsibility may require one to leave the country, go to jail, quit one's job, or blow the whistle on one's employer. No such steps should be taken precipitously without exploring other possibilities for action and without measuring one's ability to bear the burden of heavy responsibility. Most of the time, less dramatic responsible action is called for. In most jobs, one can exercise responsibility by responding to one's boss, letting him or her know if something is wrong. If there are no other available means, then one's responsibility may include trying to develop them. Going to the local television reporter or to *60 Minutes* is a last resort and not usually a career-enhancing move.

No one has the luxury of thinking that he or she is uncontaminated by the ethical problems of today's artificial persons. Our responsibility varies in an organization according to the position we occupy, such as employee, member, director, or owner.[13] If I buy a product from a company, I share responsibility—if only in a minuscule way—for the corporation's policies. If I am a member or employee of the company, I associate myself and my reputation with the ethics of that corporation. If I am a member of the governing board or executive council of the company, I share a direct responsibility for the corporate decisions. In that role, I am morally responsible and may be held legally responsible for crimes committed by the corporation.

It should be noted, however, that an employee or even an owner of a corporation does not invest the whole of his or her personhood in an organization. People invest themselves to varying degrees, according to the nature of the organization and their personal inclinations. One would expect deeper investment in the roles of father, citizen, or church member than in following a business career or belonging to a country club. Responsibility can be particularly dependent on whether we have the option of exit from a corporation. If there is no possibility of leaving an organization, one's responsibility for the organization's decision is greatly diminished. The distinctions here are more complicated than is generally assumed, and we lack an adequate language to formulate questions.[14]

In the Roman Catholic Church, a bishop has a greater responsibility for ecclesiastical decisions than other church members. The bishop of Rome has added responsibility, but it is still set within the history and present organization of the church. Pope Francis in commenting on the clerical abuse scandal said, "I feel compelled to take personal responsibility for all the evil that some priests—many in number although not in comparison to the totality—to assume personal responsibility and to ask forgiveness for the damage caused by the sexual abuse of the children."[15] The clumsy syntax of the sentence is indicative of confusion about responsibility. No one can take "personal responsibility for all the evil that some priests" have perpetrated. It might have been helpful for the pope to say, "As the chief spokesperson for the Roman Catholic Church, I apologize in the name of the church to those people who suffered these indignities." It is important for presidents and CEOs to make such apologies followed by a plan for the corporation to never repeat the failure.

Responsibility and Time

Responsibility that is always both personal and corporate helps to fill in how the relation between past and present is constituted. A responsibility to everyone and everything includes a responsibility *to* the past. At least in principle, this responsibility to the past is clear. It means that responsibility includes my listening to the voices of the past for guidance in the present. But can a person today be held responsible *for* actions committed in the past?

The moral responsibility for my own past goes back as far as my childhood. Can it go back further? Is a Christian born in the twenty-first century responsible for the persecution of Jews in fifteenth-century Toledo? Is a German born in 1947 responsible for Nazi atrocities? Is a white citizen in today's United States responsible for the horrors of slavery? To all of these questions an answer other than no seems grossly unfair. Yet such questions do not go away. In discussions of these issues, someone typically says, "Of course, I don't believe in collective guilt," and then goes on to attribute a kind of collective guilt that spreads back into the past.

Germany, the Roman Catholic Church, and the United States of America are not fictions, nor are they collections of individuals. They are corporate realities or artificial persons that are responsible for actions. A present member of one of these organizations is morally responsible for accepting or rejecting the actions of the body. As a member of the organization at a later time in history, he or she is still responsible for opposing—in the form of present actions—something that was clearly immoral in the past. Adult voices in the United States were needed in 1945 to protest the progressively immoral bombings of Tokyo, Hiroshima, and Nagasaki; at the time, few voices of protest were heard. There is still a need for opposition, although it obviously takes a different form more than half a century later.

A United States citizen is not responsible *for* those actions in the past, but he or she should be responsible *to* those past actions. Responsibility to the past leads to being responsible for present actions. Nothing is gained by having people feel vaguely guilty for crimes that they did not commit. The rest of the world does not expect the United States and its citizens to wallow in guilt for past transgressions. But other countries would like to be assured that the United States is responsible to its past, to the bad memories as well as the good, so as to learn some lessons. Responsible action in the present has to be grounded in such knowledge of the past. The same principle applies to members of the church.

Acceptance of the past in the present is connected to how we view the future. In a strange way, the past (the meaning of our past) depends upon the future (our projection of a future in the present). The common image of time as a series of points creates a false symmetry of past and future. The past obviously exists in a way that the future does not. Our responsibility to the future is fundamentally different from our listening to the voices of the past. One cannot be responsible to voices that have not yet spoken. We also cannot be responsible for our actions in the future because those actions have not yet been performed. Nevertheless, we still sense a responsibility that we have in regard to the future.

Responsibility understood to be both personal and corporate reveals two definite connections to the future: corporations and children. By means of membership in an artificial person, the actions of a natural person can influence the future. One of the main differences between natural and artificial persons is that the former die, but the latter can be chartered in perpetuity. My present responsibility is mediated to the future by political, religious, environmental, and business corporations. I am responsible to the future, and I am indirectly responsible for the future insofar as I act within a corporation that will outlive me.

There is some irony in this fact. In the thinking of liberal theoreticians, progress has usually been measured by the individual's freedom from control by institutions. And yet our contribution to a better world depends upon the extension of our corporate selves into the corporate structures of large organizations.[16] A Roman Catholic can be responsible to the future well-being of the world by acting as a church member. A responsible church member has to know the tradition of the church and act from the best lights provided by that tradition.

The other link to the future is children. One can be responsible to the future and indirectly responsible for the future by caring for children. Adults have a responsibility for children to the degree that a child cannot be responsible for its own actions. Parents have a special responsibility for their own children's actions, but the parent has to slowly relinquish responsibility for a child's actions as the child gets older. The danger of well-meaning adults is that they substitute their decisions for a child's own responsibility. Adults have to provide a safe haven during the time that infants and young children try out their responsibility to their environment and their responsibility for what they can do by their own physical and mental powers.

A child's moral responsibility is not something that arrives all at once or even in one year. Modern studies have not significantly changed the traditional view that children can exercise a moral sense by about age six but that a developed moral responsibility for a breadth of one's actions is not present at least until the teenage years. If a young person commits a crime, the parents have to examine what went wrong. The parents possibly share some responsibility for the child's failure. However, efforts in the United States to make parents legally responsible for actions by their sixteen- or eighteen-year-old children are unfair.

Children, it is often said, are the promise of the future. The statement is true in the most literal sense. For most religious groups, children are God's special representatives. In Christian history from Augustine to the Puritans, children were often cast as vessels of sin who were in need of harsh discipline. In modern times, children are more often sentimentalized as the model of human innocence. Neither attitude does justice to children as the embodying of possibility, promise, and the hope for the future of the human race. In negotiations to end factional wars, no more important question can be asked than, "What about the children?"

Chapter 12

Human Rights and Catholic Tradition

I n most literature on human rights, religion is treated in one of two ways. It is either dismissed as irrelevant, or else it is seen as an obstacle to the realization of human rights. Both of those attitudes are understandable but are nonetheless regrettable. As Diane Orentlicher has argued, unless human rights are understood to be at least compatible with religious traditions, the human rights movement will not succeed.[1] I argue here for something more than that minimum—namely, that religions could be an important ally of human rights. The key to that occurring is a conversation among the major religions of the world and their convergence on themes that support the idea of human rights. That will happen only if there is a true ecumenical movement, one that is worldwide in scope and effects.[2]

The present essay is limited to the place of Catholic tradition in the understanding of human rights. This issue exemplifies my claim that Catholic tradition is much richer than is evident in official church teaching today. Catholic tradition had a central role in the evolution of natural rights, an idea that provides a backdrop to the twentieth-century's human rights. Some Catholic writers conclude that the basis of human rights can be supplied by Catholic theology. But it is a big jump from the medieval idea of natural rights to the emergence of human rights in the second half of the twentieth century.

The Roman Catholic Church during the last seventy-five years has often failed to carry through on the valuable principles that are part of its tradition. But in the case of human rights, the rich possibilities of Catholic tradition did manage to have an effect in some areas, such as opposition to war and to the state execution of prisoners. Also, the Roman Catholic Church has often been a voice for the poor. The tragedy is that some of its official teachings place the modern church either on the sidelines of the human rights movement or in direct opposition to it.

Human Rights

Human rights is one of the better ideas that the twentieth century produced. Some writers argue that human rights emerged many centuries before the twentieth. I think that it is a plausible argument that the idea of human rights was implied by philosophers or religious leaders at the beginning of the Common Era or even earlier. Indeed, one might say that human rights were implied by the first person who came up with the idea of humanity or the human race. However, the absence of the term *human rights* in earlier centuries is significant. There could not be a realization of rights applicable to every member of the human race until "human rights" was coined.

When exactly *human rights* was first used is difficult to say. A few people used the adjective *human* before the noun *right* without having a novel idea in mind. The use of the words *human rights* as a distinct term began to flourish only in the 1970s. There were scattered uses of the term in the 1930s and 1940s, but only a select group of people were familiar with the term. The earliest use of the term *human rights* that I have found is in the antislavery movement in the 1830s.[3] Frederick Douglass's use of the term in his 1845 autobiography suggests that Douglass was aiming precisely at the meaning of human rights that surfaced in the twentieth century, rights that are proper to every human being from the fact of being human.

It is also significant that the next use of the term *human rights* that I can find was at the women's convention at Seneca Falls in 1848. The

Declaration of Sentiments "resolved that the equality of human rights results necessarily from the fact of the identity of the race in capabilities and responsibilities." The women were demanding not women's rights (though they are also important) but the recognition of women as human beings.

Human rights was coined as the name for those rights that are universal in nature, claims that every person can make on the whole human community. Obviously, there are very few rights that can qualify as applicable to every individual in every culture and every nation. And because every language is particular, any *statement* of human rights lacks a full universality. One has to try to state these rights in a concrete but simple way that translates easily from one language to another.

For example, a right to life may seem clear, but a right not to be killed or tortured is clearer. "Free speech" can be powerful rhetoric, but the power to communicate with other people is a more accurate description of a human right. A right to basic subsistence is probably the best way to summarize the availability of food, shelter, air, and water that are necessary for every human life. No list of human rights can be definitively stated, but it is possible to indicate the most basic human needs.

The movement for human rights during the past few decades is nowhere near complete. The rhetoric has outstripped the realization. *Human rights* has become a favorite term among political leaders. But the fact that *human rights* is so widely invoked and almost universally praised can make one suspect that it is being used to cover up a multitude of problems. The term is used without much care for what exactly are human rights and what are the needed restrictions in its use lest the term lose all effectiveness.

The term *human right* obviously presumes a meaning for the term *right*. A right is a demand for a good that one person can make on another person or an institution. The concept of right is usually tied to legislation that provides moral protections for an individual or a group. A right is tied to some accompanying obligation. A person thus has civil rights on the basis that there is a political body that will protect an individual's exercise of a political function. An individual has a civil right to vote when it is guaranteed by a constitution or by specific legislation. Accompanying the right to vote, the voter has a duty to exercise the minimum conditions of citizenship.

Human rights, paradoxically, are unlike all other rights that people have. There is no legislative body that establishes these rights. Human rights are said to belong to a person simply by being a member of the human race. Does this make human rights a fiction or at most a useful piece of rhetoric to direct popular disapproval of something? Much of the literature on human rights comes close to saying that human rights have no basis in reality.

The result of thinking this way is that human rights literature is heavily sermonic. The role of sacred scripture is played by the United Nations' *Universal Declaration of Human Rights*. The literature on human rights concentrates on advocacy of those rights listed in the declaration and in some subsequent UN proclamations. Sermons are proper vehicles in church; they are based on the assumption that the congregation already has a common set of beliefs. The sermon is to motivate actions that flow from those beliefs. Secular sermons cannot presuppose a common core of belief.

The UN declaration in 1948 was a great accomplishment for the time, but it is a badly flawed document. The authors imagined their task as adding to political rights that were already established in Western democracies. The Soviet bloc opposed this approach, insisting that social and economic rights had priority. It was almost a miracle that any document was approved (the Soviet bloc abstained from the vote). But the flawed document that resulted includes far too many rights. Worse, it split the idea of human rights into political rights and economic rights, a dichotomy that undermines the meaning of *human* rights. A human right needs both political and economic dimensions as befits each human being.

In recent decades, international lawyers have been laying claim to owning human rights. But human rights cannot be established by international human rights law. It is indeed a welcome development that international lawyers have finally become interested in human rights. From its beginning in the eighteenth century, international law was what nation-states agreed upon. Individuals and their rights did not figure prominently. Piracy was against international law, but slavery was not.

Human rights, if they exist, are transnational; they cannot be based on what nation-states decide are the rights of a human being. The paradox of human rights includes the fact that human rights are supposed to be enforced by nation-states while nation-states are often the chief offending party. International law is needed to protect human rights, but international law cannot establish such rights.

Is there any way to provide a firm basis for human rights? The first step, as I noted above, was the concept of humanity or a human community. That idea was present in some parts of the world thousands of years ago. The book of Genesis has such an idea as do other religious traditions in the Middle East, in India, and in China. Philosophy in Greece as early as Plato's work in the fourth century BCE has an idea of humanity.

A second step was reflection on who is included within that concept of humanity. This reflection by a few thinkers in the human race was restricted in its comprehensiveness to what the thinker could know and imagine. Until a few hundred years ago, there were almost no world travelers and no worldwide flow of ideas. Immanuel Kant at the end of the eighteenth century referred to the "rights of humanity." The question remained: Who is included in humanity? Humanity does not have rights. Human beings have rights.

The human race, one can hope, has now taken the third step necessary for the emergence of human rights. The long evolution of the human race involved a growing awareness that the human race has had some terrible biases toward people who were different from whoever was making the laws. For example, it was widely believed that homosexuality was a "perversion" of human-nature. Historical and scientific studies, together with the testimony of gay and lesbian people, indicate that homosexuality is a part of human-nature. As a more obvious example, one might think that women and children were always recognized as beings who share fully in human-nature, but laws did not unequivocally endorse that view in the past and in some places still do not.

Beyond a small band of lawgivers who recognized that women and children and blacks and gays are human, these groups needed to be able to speak for themselves. They needed a public voice of their own. Thanks to modern means of communication and the shrinking of the size of the human world, every sizable minority in the human race now has some chance of getting its voice heard. The world is still only at the beginning stage of realizing in practice the rights proper to every human being. But there is no going back to an obliviousness of the human race's great variety.

Natural Rights

In the long run up to the idea of human rights, the concept of a natural right has an important though confusing role to play. Human rights have to be clearly distinguished from the earlier concept of natural rights. But an understanding of human rights is greatly helped by tracing the history of natural rights. Most people associate the idea of natural rights with the eighteenth-century revolutions in France and British America. Both Thomas Jefferson's *Declaration of Independence* and the French *Declaration of the Rights of Man and of the Citizen* made claim to natural rights or the rights of man.

What is painfully evident now is that these proclaimed rights were limited in application to adult white males. The fact that many of the founders of the United States were slaveholders undercuts any claim that the founders were fighting for the freedom of men and women everywhere. Slavery was not just a blemish on the founding of the country; it was this nation-state's original sin that has never been completely washed away. For the emergence of human rights, the antislavery movement, first in England and then in the United States, was much more significant than what Jefferson wrote.

If the eighteenth century had better understood what natural rights were, the journey to human rights might have been a briefer one. But at the time of the revolutions in France and British America, the meaning of *natural right* no longer had a connection with the tradition that nourished this idea. The revolutionaries used the term *natural rights* because it was traditional, but they were not aware of or were dismissive of the history of rights. The British Americans did look back to the seventeenth-century revolution in England. The more influential French Revolution announced that the world was now going to start over.

One of the ironies in the eighteenth-century use of *natural rights* is that these rights of man were asserted in opposition to nature. The primary meaning of nature had shifted radically in the seventeenth century, from referring to the essence of a thing to an object confronting man. Starting with Francis Bacon, it was said that man has both a right and a duty to conquer nature.[4] There is still a problem today in the relation between the rights that are proper to human beings and the need to protect the natural world.

Many environmentalists are skeptical of human rights because these authors continue to assume the framework of the eighteenth century in which the only choice is between man who is in conflict with nature and man who is in harmony with nature. Neither of those positions is an adequate description of human-nature that is in tension with the idea of nature. The humans should neither submit to nature nor do violence to nature. In that context, human rights are the rights of men, women, and children that arise from an affirmation of all natural beings.

Catholic Tradition

Catholic tradition is at the center of the history and the idea of natural rights. The only way to untangle the meaning of natural rights is to trace its history from the beginning. Natural rights evolved from natural law. The idea and the term *natural law* originated with Cicero and was a governing idea of the philosophy of Stoicism. In Stoic thought, man had to learn to obey nature; a man's freedom consisted of saying either yes or no to nature. If a man disobeyed nature, he would eventually suffer punishment. In the opposition between nature and man, nature in the form of death eventually triumphs.

Christianity absorbed much of the language of Stoicism, a fact that in retrospect can be seen as unfortunate because it caused much confusion. Important terms such as religion, devotion, piety, vow, sacrament, and nature found their way into Christian language. Sometimes it was obvious, as in the case of *sacrament*, that the term had a radically different meaning in Christianity. Sometimes it was not clear—for example, in using *nature* and *natural law*—that Christianity did not agree with Stoic philosophy. Christianity called not for obedience to nature but for living in accord with nature. Prayer, devotion, piety, and vows were directed not to nature but to the creator of nature.

In addition to a changed meaning of *natural* in the term *natural law*, Christianity attempted to change the meaning of law. This project was never entirely successful, but the attempt is still relevant to today's understanding of ethics and particularly to understanding human rights.

St. Paul began the effort by announcing that Christ had liberated the believer from the burden of law. Paul's unsystematic references to law were and still are open to various interpretations. He regularly identified law with the Jews, but the Jews were not the source of laws that stand in opposition to human freedom. In fact, the Jewish Torah was already an alternative to a conception of law as an external constraint. Torah is often translated as law, but *teaching* better conveys the meaning of that term. It is significant that the original meaning of Torah was the teaching of a child. One best teaches a child by providing a model of how to live. The Torah is a way of life. The purpose of Talmudic rules was "to build a fence around the Torah."[5]

The early Christian movement, while fighting against the tradition of the Jews, could not avoid depending on the Old Testament for reflecting on the life and teachings of Jesus of Nazareth. Those teachings reflected what was to be found in the pharisaic reform of law. Ellis Rivkin goes so far as to say that "the triumph of Christianity was thus, in essence, the triumph of Pharisaism."[6] Christian writers said that Christ frees us from law; that is, with the model of Jesus's life to follow, the Christian is not hemmed in by external rules. Perhaps the Christian movement should have used a different term than *law* for asserting how human life should be governed.

The history of monasticism is an important source for understanding what the Christian Church tried to do with the meaning of law. Revolutions are often not clear to the people who are leading them. The first writers in the monastic tradition grappled somewhat uncertainly with the philosophy of law and ethics that they were trying to articulate. From the earliest documents, however, they conceived of entrance into the monastic life not as accepting a legal document that would tell the novice how to live but rather as a profession to live in a community. The monk accepted a form of life that was modeled on the Christian gospel.

The word *rule* plays a large part in monastic history, but the "rule of life" is the basic rule; a written rule was consequent upon the rule of life. Bernard of Clairvaux writes that "no one at profession really promises 'the Rule' but specifically, that he will act according to the rule."[7] Instead of following rules of conduct, the monk followed a rule of life governed by the example of Jesus's life and teaching.

In Augustine's original monastic rule, there is no initiation ceremony for the pronouncement of vows. Vows did become central to monastic life, but the meaning of vow was different from what it was in Roman law. The Benedictine monk took a single vow to live in the community. What eventually became formalized as vows of poverty, chastity, and obedience were not promises to obey a code of conduct but a description of the community's life. The postulant, the one who was asking for admission, did not profess vows; he confessed his faith, and the community accepted him. He was "professed in vows," language that is still used in the Roman Catholic Church.

The implications of this radical shift in the meaning of law, rules, and regulations became clear in the Franciscan movement of the twelfth century. The tension was severe between the monastic morality of freedom from (external) law and writings of the new ecclesiologists. Francis of Assisi was in constant danger of being condemned because he found the divine in all creation and he renounced ownership of property. Some of his followers did go astray, lacking the personal discipline that is presupposed in Augustine's mantra of "love God and do as you please." Francis thought that Christian life, exemplified by his "little brothers," should be ruled by the example of Jesus. Poverty meant that the goods of the world should be used but not become property.

The writings of Thomas Aquinas are often assumed to be opposed to the simple piety of Francis. Thomas's detailed analysis of moral issues made him vulnerable to being used by later moralists who were intent on drawing up lists of don'ts. But Thomas was in agreement with Francis that "everything we have is on loan." The Christian should not be governed by an external code but by an informed intelligence.

The Christian view of natural law was not an external law but human-nature itself. Natural duties were what followed from human-nature, and natural right was a respect for that nature and its duties. One of the keys to Thomas's meaning of natural law is what he says of its promulgation, something that Thomas says is needed for any law: "God puts it into men's minds to be known naturally."[8] There is no external set of laws constituting a natural law. Rather, this natural law is promulgated internal to the human mind. This law is discovered by following the deepest inclinations of the human being. These principles have to be joined with "determinations" that are based on experience and accumulated knowledge. "God is only offended," wrote Thomas, "when we act against our own well-being."[9] There is nothing greater in creation, according to Thomas, than the person.[10] The person is not subservient to a code of natural laws.

The code of canon law that Gratian began to gather in the twelfth century in some ways epitomizes the cramped understanding of a morality governed by a detailed code of conduct.[11] However, there were some surprising discussions in the later Middle Ages about the relation between an objective law and subjective rights.[12] The natural law implied obligations to act in accord with human-nature; in turn, these natural obligations implied natural rights—that is, rights based on human-nature. This sequence that goes from law to obligations to rights sounds strange to modern ears. The assumption now is that we start by having rights, and because we have rights, we somewhat reluctantly acquire obligations. Unfortunately, that assumption leaves rights without any grounding.

The most important of these rights were called inalienable. No human being should be subjected to violations of these inalienable rights that belong to human-nature. There was extensive debate over whether property is a right of human-nature or is a result of sin. The contemporary world still has not clarified the ambiguities in the meaning of property and the need to limit an individual's ownership of property.

Seventeenth to Twenty-First Centuries

John Locke is famous for having said that the natural rights of man are life, liberty, and property. He was following one thread of the medieval debate about property, which held that property is natural and therefore inalienable. Locke has been criticized for saying that the chief end of government for men is "the preservation of their property." But in the preceding paragraph, he had described property as "their lives, liberties and estates."[13] Whether or not Locke was conscious of the origin of this meaning of property, he included "life and liberties" within the meaning of property. That meaning of property—what is proper to a person—is in accord with human-nature. But property as the amassing of riches without regard for how that may harm others is not what Locke advocated and is surely not a natural right.[14]

Thomas Jefferson, instead of defending property as a necessity of personhood, substituted for property the right to a pursuit of happiness. As a right, the pursuit of happiness is vague and puts no control on greed. Jefferson borrowed ideas from Locke and several Scottish philosophers, but he did not manifest a strong interest in the long tradition behind natural rights. Jefferson's explanation for the origin of inalienable rights is that they are self-evident truths, a denial of the need for tradition, intelligent discussion, and an ever-increasing inclusiveness. Jefferson's claim of self-evident truths was met by mockery in the eighteenth century. That reaction was deserved insofar as Jefferson the slaveholder could not even see how his words applied in his own yard.

The French declaration included property as a natural right.[15] In the nineteenth century, an untouchable right to property, including the ownership of slaves, dominated talk of natural rights. Natural rights became discredited in the minds of liberal reformers. The people who pushed the idea of natural rights were seen as the enemies of political reform. Karl Marx's critique was aimed at the French Revolution's attributing a right of property to abstract "man." That meaning of property removed the struggle for economic justice from the politics of actual men and women.[16] At the present, the defense of individual rights remains central to the platform of the political right wing. That phrase may sound similar to the movement for human rights, but *individual rights* is historically rooted in the language of nineteenth-century slaveholding.

Individual rights are especially concerned with the acquisition of property. There seems to be no limit to the acquisitiveness and greed of rich people. But the natural resources of the world are indeed limited. As environmental problems spiral beyond whatever controls are in place, the world may need to learn what Thomas Aquinas and Francis of Assisi taught—namely, that everything that humans have is on loan and that goods can only be possessed by being shared in a community.

Each person has inalienable rights to physical security and the means of subsistence. These rights should have the full support of each of the world's religions. Unfortunately, religions have a very mixed record when it comes to the recognition of rights for every human being. Religions are based on an affirmation of *my people* and what is due to every member of this particular community. However, the genuineness of a community is tested by its attitude toward the outsider and the stranger. Every genuine religious community has to be an affirmation of the whole human community.

Catholic tradition has a rich contribution to make to the basis of human rights. Human rights literature generally ignores any positive role of the church. It would be unreasonable to expect that writers on human rights investigate in detail the evolution of canon law or the history of early monasticism. But they should know that the discussion of respect for the person has a long history that includes religious and philosophical themes. Francis of Assisi is praised in environmental writing, but there is seldom any effort made to understand where he fits within Catholic tradition.

The natural law of Catholic tradition is not a code of conduct but a basic moral stance that violence against nature and natural beings is wrong. The term *natural law* may be unsalvageable, but the principle of *do violence to no one* is as important today as ever. Catholic officials invoke natural law in condemnations of contraception, abortion, gay marriage, and euthanasia. There is indeed a rich philosophical and theological history to be brought into the discussion of these issues. But the uncritical use of the term *natural law* gets in the way of respect for each person's human rights.

Official teachers in the Roman Catholic Church have no excuse for their ignorance. Their invoking of natural law as if there were a code of self-evident natural laws provides no support to church condemnations of specific practices. Church leaders have an obligation to learn about the complexity of Catholic tradition instead of treating Thomas Aquinas's writings as catechism answers (except when the answers do not agree with them). If church officials did some study of their own tradition, they would be better prepared to engage in political discussions of today, and they would have a credibility that they lack when they simply announce answers to questions before the issue has been thoroughly explored with the help of history, science, and contemporary testimonies.

Chapter 13

Catholicism and Environmentalism

T wo of the most important developments during the last half century have been the human rights movement and the environmental movement. The literature on human rights seldom makes reference to the environmental movement. Human rights are a demand upon the whole human community, but what are the implications for the rest of the world? Are human rights a claim to a human superiority that is destructive of the environment? On its side, environmental literature seldom refers to the movement for human rights, although there are frequent debates about who or what, if anyone, has rights. Do environmental concerns rule out special attention to human dignity and human needs? The failure to address the relation between human rights and environmental concerns distorts both of these important areas.

There is potential for a clash between these two movements because they are implicitly competing to be the religion of the twenty-first century. Both movements understandably bring out religious or quasi-religious passions on the part of their advocates who are concerned with issues of life and death. Both movements could use an awareness of the good and the bad sides of religious passion. A particular danger is that if a movement makes a religion its enemy, then it might create a new religion that simply reverses images of the religion being attacked.

Much of environmental literature is aggressively opposed to what is assumed to be the Christian view. The publication of Pope Francis's encyclical *Laudato si* was therefore a milestone in clearly placing the Roman Catholic Church on the side of concern with environmental problems and their solutions. It was somewhat disconcerting that people had lined up for and against the encyclical long before it appeared. The impression given was that the encyclical was simply to be a vote for or against what most scientists say about the origin of climate change. The pope would not have needed 37,000 words to register a vote. The pope's main concern was the connection between environmental destruction and the plight of poor and vulnerable populations. Whether many people were and are willing to hear that argument remains to be seen.

Environmental writing has embodied a religious orthodoxy that was remarkably shaped by a single brief essay in the late 1960s: "The Historical Roots of our Ecological Crisis" by Lynn White Jr.[1] Many of the key terms in environmental writing come directly from that essay. White was by no means an opponent of Christianity, but he provided material that has been wielded in anti-Christian arguments. The pope employs several of these terms without acknowledging their history, either because he was unaware of that history or because he thought he could simply twist the terms to his advantage.

I was hoping that with this pope's penchant for surprises he would challenge some of environmentalism's standard formulas, particularly involving the terms *nature* and *environment*. If church officials wish to insist that their moral teaching is based on human-nature, then the ecological question cannot be called the relation between man and nature, humanity and nature, or society and nature. It might seem clumsy to refer to "human-nature and other natures" or the "human world and the nonhuman natural world," but such formulas are a better description of what exists than the abstractions that dominate environmental orthodoxy.

The environmental movement has beliefs that are similar to ancient Stoicism. The similarity is not surprising in that Christianity began in competition with Stoicism. Central to Stoicism was the belief that humans have to acknowledge the superiority of nature. Nature is all-wise, whereas human beings are a troublesome species that is prone to claims of being superior to the other animals. Humans have to take themselves out of the center of the world and find their proper place as one species among nature's many offspring.

Both Christianity and Stoicism were seen as schools of how to live; there was not a clear distinction in that era between philosophy and religion. Both movements offered practical help for ordinary people and challenging speculation for the philosophical-minded. The Christian Church won the competition, probably because it offered a more hopeful view of human life and more effective daily rituals.[2] But as has often happened in history, the conquered party lived on in the language that the conqueror had absorbed. In Christianity, there were a dozen key terms, including *nature* and *religion*, that church writers adopted because they were the language at hand. These Latin words had been stamped by Roman use and the religious/philosophical speculation of Stoic thinkers.

Christianity therefore included a meaning of nature as the all-encompassing reality, but at the same time Christianity rejected the Stoic belief that nature is the mother of us all. For Christianity, a father God creates all natures, including a special *human-nature*. Humans were not reducible to one of nature's offspring. As the human race advanced in its development, a human claim to specialness was inevitable. No one else was doing the measurement or making the claims. *Nature* as a term for the All and as a source of life is a projection from human experience.

The Christian movement was central to human awareness of its own distinctiveness, but that did not imply a denigration of other beings of creation. Christian religion helped to inspire human respect for the world of physical beings and for the power of human intelligence. That attitude of respect for intelligence and for the intelligibility of the nonhuman natural world helped to provide the context for the emergence of modern science. Lynn White Jr. was one of the historians who traced the beginnings of science back to the eleventh century. The late Middle Ages produced the mathematical tools that were necessary for the development of the empirical sciences.

The seventeenth century developed a new language for the relation between humans and the others who make up the world of human experience. The call was for man to conquer nature. Man's new knowledge together with newly invented instruments of control were thought capable of freeing man from his ancient enemies of disease, war, hunger, and homelessness. Today's environmental movement is in many ways a revolt against the language of early modern science; today's scientists acknowledge the hubris of thinking that man can conquer nature. A new language of respect for nature could conceivably open up a dialogue with traditional religions. That has not happened.

Environmentalism has been very successful in achieving public awareness. It has been less successful in reaching practical solutions to the environmental problems that threaten life on earth. The new Stoicism has its attractive side, but it is not much practical help for addressing the problems that the human race has created for itself in the last two centuries. Environmental solutions require an affirmation of the human being and the distinctive power of the human race among all earthly creatures. That human role is not *man the conqueror* but humans as the responsible caretakers of the nonhuman natural world. Christian writers should be offering that alternative, but most of Christian writing on the environment accepts the new orthodoxy. There is a difference between accepting the overwhelming scientific data on an issue, such as climate warming, and accepting an assumed philosophical/religious orthodoxy.

The Environmental Movement

The environmental movement is most often dated from 1970. The previous decade had been one of fierce political conflicts. The movement for racial equality had led into the women's movement, the peace movement, the gay rights movement, and more. Suddenly there appeared a movement that seemed to transcend politics and could unite everyone. Surely no one was opposed to saving the earth. The assumption that there could be an apolitical environmental movement was a terrible illusion that created an orthodoxy.

A movement needs an enemy; otherwise there is no need for a movement. The environmental movement quickly identified the enemy as something called "Judeo-Christian tradition," a term that Lynn White Jr. provided for the environmental movement. Pope Francis unfortunately employed this term several times.

The problem with Judeo-Christian tradition is that it was invented in the 1890s as an ideology celebrating the supremacy of the individual and his control of the world. It was a strange phrase that did not immediately take hold. In the 1930s, *Judeo-Christian* was occasionally used by Christians who were trying to take a more positive outlook toward Jews. The term got a boost in usage as the plight of Jews in Nazi Germany became known. Some Christians were quick to claim that Hitler's terrible acts were directed toward the Judeo-Christian tradition, even though the obvious fact was that he was killing Jews.

The term *Judeo-Christian* became commonly used when environmentalists declared it to be the source of all our ecological problems. The political right wing took the bait and mounted a defense of "Judeo-Christian values" and "Judeo-Christian civilization." (*Judeo-Christian religion* is not a common phrase, because there is no institution of Judeo-Christianity nor any practicing Judeo-Christians). Judeo-Christian values are said to be under attack by Hitler's successors. *Judeo-Christian values* seem to have a great deal to do with authority, which is good, and sex, which is always suspect. But a concern with environmental degradation does not figure prominently in Judeo-Christian values, or it is dismissed as a plot against individual freedom.

Environmentalism thus has a logical enemy in the Judeo-Christian tradition. Unfortunately, this ideology reveals little about the Jewish tradition, the Christian tradition, or the diversity within each of those traditions. The one verse of the Bible that is relentlessly quoted in environmental literature is Genesis 1:28, on "man's dominion" over all the earth. The assumption seems to be that that one verse says all you need to know about the Bible, the Jewish tradition, and the Christian tradition. If one is going to attempt to summarize the Bible, it would be advisable to at least get to the second chapter of Genesis where the man and the woman are placed in a garden and told to dress it and keep it. "Guardians of the garden" is the most common image in the biblical exegesis of the rabbis and the legal ordinances of the Talmud.[3]

Environmental writers never refer to the large body of Christian literature that provides commentary on the book of Genesis. Most of the fathers of the church and medieval theologians wrote commentaries on Genesis. Christians may have fallen short in practice of what they profess to believe, but it is still worth consulting how leading Christian writers interpreted Genesis. For example, since Genesis pictured the human control of animals as that of naming them, the conclusion of most commentators was that killing animals is a sign of sin rather than a right given to the human race by God.[4] What environmental writers assume to be the biblical view of humanity is often a biblical description of what has gone wrong with humans.

The encyclical *Laudato si* has a long section that summarizes biblical scholarship touching these points. I am doubtful that many people will be able to assimilate the significance of this material without a more pointed reference to the accusation that the pope is implicitly responding to. I would have preferred a shorter and punchier summary that took direct issue with the lazy repetitions of what Judeo-Christian tradition says about nature, a word that did not exist in ancient Hebrew.

The overall record of both Jewish and Christian traditions in protecting the environment is not one to boast about. Particularly in Christian history, the emphasis on personal/communal salvation gave way to individual salvation, which led to the beginning of philosophical and political individualism. Emphasis upon individual man and the failure to attain what today is called gender equality distorted the power of man. Nonetheless, there is no reason why both Jewish and Christian traditions cannot be allies of a movement to care for what surrounds the humans and has been damaged by thoughtlessness and greed.

A strange aspect of much environmental writing is an apotheosis of Francis of Assisi as the one acceptable Christian in history. Even before someone studies the evidence for this claim, the claim on the face of it makes no sense. Francis was a great man who has had a profound influence on Christian history. It was because he was so deeply embedded in the Christian tradition that he could influence ordinary piety, the religious orders, and the Christian attitude toward divine revelation. The claim that he was "clearly heretical" is made to praise Francis while condemning the religious tradition that nourished him.[5]

Pope Francis, starting with the name he chose as pope, has consistently indicated his kinship with Francis of Assisi. As one would expect, the pope repeatedly refers to Francis of Assisi throughout the encyclical, starting with the title *Laudato si*, taken from Francis's well-known Canticle of Creatures. The pope is pleased to note that even many people who are not Christian praise the monk from Assisi. The pope could have pointed out that much of the praise for Francis shows little knowledge of his life, his thinking, and his place in the history of the environment.

Writers who use Francis of Assisi in their accusation against Judeo-Christian tradition rely on Lynn White's call for Francis to be the patron saint of ecology. White's summary of Francis is regularly quoted: "Francis proposed what he thought was an alternative Christian view of nature and man's relation to it … He tried to substitute the idea of an equality of all creatures for the idea of man's limitless rule of creation." White is wrong on both halves of that claim. Francis did not claim equality for all creatures, and one of the first principles of Christian tradition is that human control of the universe is not limitless.

Francis of Assisi's poetry calls our attention to particular animals and to particular elements in our environment. Although he has been appointed the patron saint of nature, he never used the term *nature*. "He did not call nature his mother; he called a particular donkey his brother or a particular sparrow his sister. He refused to see the wood for the trees."[6] That is the greatness of Francis and also his limitation. He was a poet, not a philosopher, nor a theologian, nor an economist. The pope helpfully invoked Francis in a condemnation of greed.[7] The pope is suspicious of the profit motive or self-interest, but he does not condemn them.

One of Francis's biographers says that Francis simply assumed the Christian conception of the world as "belief in divine creation, organized according to a plan that is hierarchical and unchanging, with all parts having their established positions and dependent on divine will and action." His attempt to live according to the example of Jesus continued and extended the monastic ideal of previous centuries. "In thinking of him as one who loved nature, we must not lose sight of the man who served Lady Poverty, tended the diseased, and risked or even sought martyrdom among the Saracens."[8]

One of Francis's biographers writes that "Francis's vision of the interdependence between humankind and animals was uniquely his own," and yet his basic values "were not innovations."[9] This description of Francis's uniqueness means that he was especially open to influence by the previous Christian tradition and the world around him. His life was a special demonstration of the uniqueness that can be found in every human being.

Humanly Unique

Pope Francis repeatedly refers to the human being as unique. He does not acknowledge that the claim to human uniqueness is at the center of the attack on the Judeo-Christian tradition. The pope makes no attempt to sort out the paradox embodied in the term *uniqueness*. Some writers on the environment assume that asserting rights for all human beings is opposed to the environment. An affirmation of human rights that are based on the uniqueness of every person is thought to be a problem for other species. For example, Peter Singer ridicules the phrase "uniquely human."[10] In doing so, he presumes a meaning of unique that is nearly the opposite of the meaning of uniqueness that can best describe the human relation to everything in its surroundings.

Uniqueness means to differ from all others. Actually, a unique thing is impossible. Each thing has some notes of similarity with other things; otherwise, it would not be a thing. Despite the admonitions of grammar teachers, people regularly use a modifier before unique. By *very unique* or *most unique*, they recognize that something is almost but not entirely different from everything else.

This process of differentiation can go in opposite directions. An object is (very nearly) unique by a narrowing down of space and time; what is here differs from everything that is there; what is now differs from everything that was then. This (nearly complete) difference occurs by a process of exclusion of notes of sameness. To the extent that humans are like objects, they share in this kind of uniqueness by a process of increasing exclusion. A human being can be described as one thing that is located in only one place and lives only at one time. It is (very nearly) unique in relation to other things.

However, the more important uniqueness of the human person is based on an increasing inclusiveness to others. All animals are open to the world around them; mammals are individuals that are particularly receptive and responsive to their environment. The human being carries the process further by being open to the whole world. As Theodosius Dobzhansky put it, "All species are unique, but humans are uniquest."[11] The human is unlike every other animal by being similar to all of them, a recapitulation and an embodiment of the full texture of life. As the ninth-century writer Erigena put it, "the humans are the workshop of creation."[12] Human life is wondrous in its complexity and incomprehensible to itself.

A unique living being is one that suffers or feels the world. The person as the uniquest being extends the meaning of world. Human uniqueness includes empathy for other sentient animals for whom suffering the world includes pain. Understandably, human empathy is the greatest toward the human's own kind. The humans as the uniquest animals are in the world with their whole selves. Reason is not a power above animal nature; at its best, reason is the transformative power of the whole self from within.

Some environmental writers argue that if only humans would recognize that they are an insignificant speck in the universe, they would stay in their place of equality with other species. The problem is that in relation to the power to destroy other species, the humans never were equal, and their power now has become enormously magnified. The attempt to downgrade the human goes in the wrong direction. Humility is not engendered by people being told that the world is very old and very big. Humility ("of the earth") is born of the recognition by each human being of its place in the human community.

Human respect for the uniqueness and greatness of each human being is needed to restrain humans from using violence against each other. Violence toward other humans inevitably spills over to violence against the humans' earth-mates. Conversely, if each human being were seen as uniquely important, an attitude of respect would extend to what the human being is related to—that is, to everything. In Christian terms, the humans are created a little less than the angels; they are the priests of all creation.

Humans and Their Environment

One of the terms that Pope Francis appropriates from environmental writing is *anthropocentrism*, a strange word that apparently was coined to parallel words such as racism, sexism, and ageism. Anthropocentrism is thought to be the last narrow-minded prejudice, a favoring of human beings over other species. In devoting a whole section of his encyclical to modern anthropocentrism, the pope does not seem to be aware that the term came into environmental writing as part of the attack on Christianity.[13] Lynn White Jr., once again, was the source in saying, "Christianity is the most anthropocentric religion the world has seen." Whatever White meant by that statement, Christianity was quickly charged with the crime of anthropocentrism.

On the question of where should humans imagine themselves to be in relation to the environment, the logical answer seems to be in the middle. The environment is what surrounds the humans; it is what humans necessarily interact with every hour of the day. A person can either take care of his or her environment or carelessly do violence to it. A community and the human race as a whole have the same choice. A person who is careless of his or her surroundings is foolishly oblivious of the interdependence of the humans and what surrounds them.[14]

Leading thinkers at the beginning of the modern era tried to remove themselves from the human place at the center of their environment and imagine themselves outside and above the world called nature. This was the human temptation to be eccentric (not at the center). What the seventeenth century assumed to be separate and above nature was not actual human beings but man, or more exactly the rational and controlling mind of man, which can conceive nature as an object to be conquered.

The promise of modern science and technology has been the liberation of man, which was from the beginning an unrealistic hope. "Man's power over Nature turns out to be a power exercised by some men over other men."[15] Each breakthrough in technology has been hailed for its power to set man free from conditions of poverty and hopelessness. But each of the new instruments of power enters a world where the existing power structure only becomes strengthened. The particular men whose lives have been made comfortable by technology ascend higher in the control of human and nonhuman lives.

In the nineteenth century and the first half of the twentieth century, the idea that nature is the source and explanation of everything coexisted uneasily with the idea that nature is whatever is to be conquered by man. Nature was a loving mother, bestowing natural rights on man, but nature was also an evil stepmother, which justified man's overpowering of nature with the marvels of technology.

In the second half of the twentieth century, man began to recognize that he was doing damage to his surroundings. Instead of conquering nature, humans needed a mutual relation with nonhuman beings in their environment. It was not a coincidence that the environmental and the women's movements emerged at the same time. Man could not solve the environmental problems that he had created; men and women had to cooperate in caring for the things in their environment. Unfortunately, some environmental writers never got the message and continue to talk about man and nature. Their alternative to claiming that man has been put above nature is to place nature above man. Those abstractions do not get at the problems of the environment or encourage men and women to care for their environment while caring for each other.

The story of man and nature can be exciting to study. But neither man nor nature exists in the world where individual men and women struggle with trying to make sense of their lives. One of the most prominent writers who has mastered his field of study and effectively written for a popular audience is Edward O. Wilson. He has been writing on the unifying of knowledge and the understanding of human life for half a century. Now eighty-five years old, he recently published a book with the modest title, *The Meaning of Human Existence*. His vast knowledge of biology seems to provide him with a meaning for his existence. He argues for cooperation between science and art, although science is the senior partner that provides the meaning of human existence. He is comfortable with atheism, finding it easy to demolish any arguments for the god of theism.

What is remarkable, however, is that Wilson seems not to have a glimmer of what a religious question is. He assumes that when people talk about the meaning of existence they are looking for scientific explanations of cause and effect. Questions that cross the minds of people such as "Is there any point to all of this?" or "Why is there something rather than nothing?" might seem of interest only to professional philosophers, but they are also questions that little children ask and questions that recur to nearly all individuals at life's turning points.

Nature supposedly locates us in the world of hard facts where questions have answers and disagreements can be resolved with more data. Man, it is said, has disrespected and wounded nature. The claim is made that the bounteous mother is in the process of disappearing and will soon be replaced by the evil stepmother who will teach man that he is subject to the laws that nature decided before the speck of matter called humanity began to strut its stuff on earth.

The eighteenth century was sure that the old-time religious meaning of life could be replaced by nature as the bounteous source of gifts. But now the scientific world has unwittingly raised religious questions about whether life on earth is worthwhile and why. Scientists are not accustomed to the role of apocalyptic doomsayer, which is a religious function. They are comfortable collecting data and connecting one dot with another. Scientists need a better story for their new mission. The claim that man should go back to being an obedient player in nature's game is a religious story that is hopelessly inadequate.

The connection that people have to the passage of time, to the lives of their children and grandchildren, and to their own deaths involve a religious sensibility. The story that traditional religions offer, which involves a creator god, a centrality of human life to existence, a meaning that connects each person to an overall purpose of the world, includes fanciful myths. The story is nonetheless more compelling than the story climatologists and evolutionary biologists tell when they keep insisting that everything they say is fact while in fact the facts are embedded in the myth of nature as mother of us all.

Ethics for Men, Women, and Their Kin

At its best, Christian tradition implies that human beings—men and women in their diverse roles—are at the center of the animal kingdom and at the center of a world of wondrous things. Only from the center can humans exercise their responsibility of respecting each thing. Respect by men and women means an appreciation of the beauty of each kind and each individual. Respect can sometimes entail acting to heal wounds that have been caused by past human actions. The same respect can extend to efforts by men and women to improve upon what is natural (what is given by birth). This use of human power to improve the world is dangerous and should be used with awareness that humans do not understand the entire web of life. There are unintended consequences when humans use the things in their environment and try to make novel contributions to the universe.

While the fabric of intra-human relations need not be prominent in every picturing of the universe, one thing that should never be forgotten is that human beings are holding the camera. To assume otherwise is to take the position of a godlike view of the universe from above the give and take of earthly existence. Apart from a divine mind, every view is an animal's view, and the human mind's eye, directly or through one of its instruments, provides the most far-reaching view. Every ethic is a human ethic; the issue is how well the humans see the world and respond to what surrounds them.

Peter Singer begins his *Practical Ethics* "with a conscious disavowal of any assumption that all members of our own species have, merely because they are members of our own species, any distinctive worth or value that puts them above members of other species."[16] No human rights are to be accorded to unique human beings. But human uniqueness does not put humans *above* other species; human uniqueness situates humans in the middle of all other species; the human superiority lies in their power to be responsible.

If one were to try to put into practice a belief that humans are equal to every other species and should not try to act otherwise, the absurdity of the claim would be apparent. Any distinctly human activity would have to be eliminated, except perhaps activity to end the human species.[17] If one looks at the humans as a species, there is no discontinuity between a human species and other species. But because of human uniqueness, the continuity includes fantastic differences in human history, including the invention of the idea of species.

In the seventeenth century, the conflict was between a moral and a mathematical approach to understanding the world. The term *laws of nature* was used for describing the universe empirically and mathematically. The term that was left to moralists was *natural law*, which included a mixture of ancient wisdom and ordinary experience. Natural law was a misleading term long before the seventeenth century. A *law of natures* would have been closer to the moral need for understanding how to treat each kind of being with care and respect.

Human morality depends upon guidance from the deepest inclinations of human-nature and from reflection on the experience of human beings. The thirteenth or the seventeenth centuries did not have all the answers to what is in accord with human-nature; neither does the twenty-first century. The law of natures can provide guidance on outlawing practices that are clearly destructive of a human's nature. Examples are murder, torture, slavery, and destroying the environmental conditions for life on earth. Moral judgments have to include these principles of human-nature and in addition empirical data and human testimony.

The humans' outlook on the whole universe has to be tested by how humans treat their closest kin. Those animals who can engage us as friends remind us that we have an untold number of friends who live beyond our perception. We cannot see the whole world because it is simply too big, and we do not even have a view of all the animals; the bear, giraffes, and elephants in the first row block our sight.

Just as the "chosen people" are a stand-in for all people, so the unique human being is a stand-in for all beings on earth. A claim that nature has rights has no practical meaning. Humans cannot provide the guarantee of a legal right to each individual of every species. While a chimp or a dolphin deserves to be thought of as having rights and to receive legal protection, millions of species depend on humans having a nonviolent attitude toward all their fellow travelers.

Trying to bring humans *down* to the level of other animals will not improve the lot of anyone. Instead, humans have to be encouraged to accept their place at the center of the earth, the animal that is responsible *to* the whole universe and responsible *for* actions that can affect the whole earth. As Wendell Berry wisely puts the case, "It is only by remaining human—that is, by the acceptance and proper use of the human powers—that they can understand, respect, and preserve the animals."[18]

Chapter 14

Missing in Action: Religious Education

ost of the topics discussed in the previous chapters point to the need for education. Few church officials would disagree with the proposition that education is a desirable good, something to be done as well as possible. Unfortunately, parish budgets or diocesan investments do not reflect such a belief. That is not surprising. There is frequently a gap between what the leaders of an institution profess to believe in (BP, General Motors) and where they put their money. The problem is more acute when the institution is not in the money-making business but professes to be concerned with the spiritual life of its members and the good of the human race. Still, if it were only a matter of getting a religious institution to shift items in its budget, the problem would be clear enough. The bigger problem is the question whether leaders of the Roman Catholic Church and those of other religious institutions have any sense of what a religious education would require in today's world.

When documents of the Roman Catholic Church refer to education, they are mostly concerned with having their members be regular churchgoers and followers of the official teachings of the bishops. That is an understandable aim for the church's education; there is nothing wrong with aiming to have members be regular practitioners. Throughout most of the church's history, education occurred through ordinary family life, sermons on Sundays, and schools for those members who wished to be conversant with the intricacies of church doctrine.

However, for more than a century it has been obvious to many people that for the health of the church and the lives of its members something wider and deeper is needed. In the United States, the main effort of the Roman Catholic Church to improve education was to construct an entire school system to parallel the state system. It was an extraordinary project. One could say that in the nineteenth century and the first half of the twentieth century the Catholic school system succeeded; the church not only survived, but it flourished. The system never had a chance of reaching all Catholic families, but the extent of the system was nevertheless astounding.

Since the middle of the twentieth century, the Roman Catholic Church, along with other religious groups, have been faced with a new landscape. Roman Catholics often think of Vatican II as bringing about the big changes in the church, but Vatican II was reacting to the big changes that had already become evident in the church and the world around the church. The council was a search for how to get a handle on this new environment. The council made a good start, but it could only begin the rethinking and reformulating of its positions in relation to other religious groups, to modern philosophy, to science and technology, and to the presence of worldwide communication media.

The overall task might be called education, but the meaning of education is itself in flux. Educational literature as a whole is still dragging around nineteenth-century language, but a new language cannot simply be invented. One of the areas where educational language is especially deficient is in anything pertaining to religion. The Roman Catholic Church shares in the deficiency and confusion about what would constitute a religious education. It does not have a model for how the world might speak of religious education. However, the Roman Catholic Church, simply by its size and its age, should be a major contributor in a worldwide evolution of the thinking and practice of religious education.

Religious Education Movement

Although the words *religious* and *education* occasionally were joined as early as the seventeenth century, the term *religious education* could not be said to exist until the second half of the nineteenth century. Not surprisingly, the term was first used in the United States by Unitarians. Although the United States was in some obvious ways a Protestant Christian country, it was a country with no establishment of religion, an arrangement that allowed into the public arena a crazy quilt of religious groups and religious movements. The term *religious education* was an acknowledgment both of a diversity of religions in the country and that such diversity needs an educational context.

It was fitting that Unitarians invented the term *religious education*. Throughout their history, they have thought of themselves as the forward edge of a unifying process of religion. Many of the nation's founding fathers were Unitarians who thought that history was moving in their direction. Thomas Jefferson wrote in 1822, "I can confidently expect that the present generation will see Unitarianism become the general religion of the United State." And in another letter, he added, "I trust that there is not a young man living in the United States who will not die a Unitarian."[1] Jefferson badly underestimated the staying power and revival of evangelical Protestantism. But Unitarians have continued to be a prod to other religious groups to find common ground for working together.

In 1903, the term *religious education* was stamped with a meaning by the founding of the Religious Education Association. The new organization stated its mission as providing a religious ideal to education and an educational ideal to religion. The main tasks for carrying out that mission were dialogue between religions, the professionalizing of church education, and the inclusion of religion in the curriculum of public (state) schools. Although the founders of the association wished to include all religious groups in this educational undertaking, their own views and language reflected the liberal Protestantism of the day. Not many Jews or Roman Catholics were attracted to an organization that they viewed as a successor to the Protestant Sunday school of the nineteenth century.[2]

Protestant seminaries at the turn of the twentieth century initiated a course called Christian Education, which tended to be a competitor with religious education. It represented a more traditional Protestant education. The role of the Christian educator in local congregations was thought to be especially suitable for a woman. The word *Christian* in Christian Education had an ecumenical meaning, insofar as it was open to all Protestants while it excluded Roman Catholics. In the early decades of the twentieth century, a religious education movement made some headway, but in the 1930s, it could not cope economically with the Great Depression and educationally with a conservative movement in Protestant theological circles. By the 1950s, *Christian Education* was the winner as the preferred term in Protestant denominations. Religious education became the name of an historical movement that had failed because it was too liberal for the practical needs of Protestant congregations.

The Roman Catholic Church was barely touched by this Protestant discussion of religious education and Christian education. *Catholic education* became identified with the parish school and with the smaller network of secondary schools. That usage unfortunately implied that most Catholics did not get a Catholic education. For youngsters who attended the state schools, the Roman Catholic Church imitated the Protestant Sunday school with parish Sunday schools but with less success than the Protestants.

Since it was not a part of Catholic education, parish education received little attention and practically no money. For adults, there was the Sunday sermon (by priests not usually trained for the task) and a yearly mission to revitalize the parish. The main source of Catholic education was the family, although parents were seldom included in the meaning of Catholic educator. Sunday school teaching was given the name Confraternity of Christian Doctrine. Generations of devoted Catholics worked in CCD, but it was difficult work without much organizational support or investment of resources.

The term *religious education* was not common in Catholic circles. However, since much of education for Catholics was outside *Catholic education* and *Christian education*, there was an opening for *religious education.* The term began to surface in the 1930s, often in contrast to *theology*, which was a clerical preserve. But unfortunately, the term *religious education* was spread mainly as the alternative to Catholic education; that is, religious education became equivalent to CCD.

By the early 1960s, the Catholic school system was no longer on the rise. There was need for a rethinking of what a Catholic education might mean. A controversy was sparked by Mary Perkins Ryan's book *Are Parochial Schools the Answer?* Ryan was one of a group of men and women who had worked tirelessly at liturgical reform, family education, and social justice. The title of the book asked a question, but many people did not bother to read the book before concluding that she was attacking Catholic education.

The chief defender of the schools was a young sociologist named Andrew Greeley, who dismissed Ryan's book as the work of a "housewife." In any debate on the question of Catholic education, Greeley could amass scientific data. His defense of the schools that were sponsored by the Roman Catholic Church was well articulated. The tragic part, however, was that Greeley regularly described the choice for the church as between "Catholic education" and "religious education." The contrast did not make any logical sense. His real question was whether a slightly upgraded CCD could duplicate the effects of a Catholic school. Not much sociological data was needed to conclude that it could not.[3]

Despite Greeley's insistence that most Roman Catholics supported Catholic schools and that the US episcopacy had not sufficiently tapped into their generosity, the system continued to shrink. *Religious education* expanded in meaning, as some parishes hired individuals for a job called director of religious education, and some dioceses created a diocesan job of overseeing religious education. Some Catholic universities began offering graduate programs in religious education. But *religious education* in the Roman Catholic Church of the United States still carries the scars of the 1960s as meaning an idealistic attempt to replace *Catholic education* with an expanded CCD and adult education programs.

For the present meaning of religious education and its future possibilities, a movement that began in England in the 1940s offers the best hope. *Religious education* in England and Wales was assigned a legally recognized meaning as composed of two elements: the practice of worship and instruction in religious matters.[4] At first, the actual school practice of Christian instruction and Christian worship did not change, but in the 1960s, the instruction part took on a new meaning with the development of curricula that included other religions besides Christianity. At the same time, an exercise of worship became more difficult to sustain in an increasingly diverse situation.

The result was a tendency to equate religious education with the religious instruction in the schools, even to the point that religious education became the name of the school subject. Despite that drawback, the British use of religious education did give a public place to the question of religious education, a usage of *religious education* found in English-speaking countries except the United States.[5] The United Nations in its 1966 Covenants on Human Rights surprisingly referred to religious education; unfortunately, it referred to it only in the context of a parental right.

The Roman Catholic interest in religious education that started in the 1960s gave a spark of life to the Religious Education Association and to an offshoot organization for professors of religious education (even though there were few professors so named). The bump in interest and membership did not last long. Religious education in the United States remains at the margin both in educational writing and in church writing. The future of the Religious Education Association probably lies with a still small but significant internationalization of the organization. Some Europeans, Australians, Africans, and Asians have joined the organization's Canadians and US Americans.

At present, Roman Catholics remain the main users of religious education in the United States. The Roman Catholic Church could be a leader in the United States finally facing up to the challenge of education in matters religious. But Roman Catholics would need to make a jump from an intramural meaning of religious education to a meaning in which the Roman Catholic Church would be tested by interaction with other religions and with secular society. A Roman Catholic Church in which members practice their religion intelligently and are knowledgeable about other religions would seem to be the direction for the church to move, but it is doubtful that church leaders are ready to accept the risk of taking that route. Education in religious matters can lead some people to leave the church.

The need for education in religion is of civic and political importance. After September 11, 2001, the United States and the European Union took opposite paths in the matter of religious education. The European Union took the lead in initiating a worldwide discussion of how religion and education are related within nation-states and internationally. The European Commission has funded research leading to a series of studies of religious education in European countries. That discussion continues. The thinking behind such a movement is that there cannot be peace without an educational approach to religion and serious attention to religion in educational institutions. The United States has been conspicuously absent from this discussion. Its reaction to the 2001 events has been to use military means to protect its population while it has neglected education in religious matters.

Ambiguity of *Education*

Most people have some awareness that the term *education* is ambiguous. Since the mid–nineteenth century, education has regularly been conflated with school. We may not be sure of what education is, but we know that school is the place to get it. Nonetheless, most (educated) people recognize that *education* can also describe a process or an achievement that does not belong exclusively to schools. Although this meaning of education may be vague on specifics, this older and wider meaning of education, as a lifelong and life-wide process, is still frequently used.

If one is going to distinguish effectively between education and school, one has to set out an institutional pattern of education from infancy to old age. For doing that, one has to name forms of education and how they interact.

The first educational form is the family. In many ways, the most important educational period in life is the first few years. A person's direction in life is largely set in infancy and early childhood. The most important teachers for most people are their parents. Even after childhood, family connections remain powerful educational influences. People participate in family education not only as a child but as a parent and then as a grandparent. The family in the context of other communal groups is the first great educational institution.

A second institutional form that education takes is the work that a person does. Work is the contribution that a person makes to society. Some people are fortunate enough to have their jobs be their work. Other people have to find their real work at times that are outside their jobs. There are few things as satisfying as work well done and the pleasure of knowing that one has made an important contribution to other lives. Educational reform needs to be concerned with the working conditions that shape human lives.

The third educational institution is the school, which should not be asked to carry the whole burden of education. Schools should be allowed to concentrate on what they are good at—namely, thoughtful reflection on life's great questions carried out with the aid of literature and science. In our current arrangement, too much of schooling is wasted on the young, while older adults who could appreciate the experience do not have the opportunity. Many young people would be better off experiencing the demands of a job for getting a sense of life's journey. They would subsequently have more material to later reflect upon in the classroom.

There is one more educational institution that is present throughout life but usually becomes most prominent in old age—namely, leisure. When a person retires from a job, he or she is then faced with finding a new form of work. Leisure is the name we give to a wide range of activities that can be enjoyed when there is no longer the pressure of parental work or the need of employment that is tied to making a living. For some older people, hours of leisure drag by and are filled with empty entertainment. For other people, leisure means the chance of a lifetime, the possibility of travel, learning, and experimenting with new ways of living. For some people, illness limits what they can do, but even illness can be a form of teaching others and a situation in which one learns about the human condition.

Education consists of the interaction of these several forms of learning. The four forms sometimes overlap; for example, work can be an element within the family, and a family atmosphere can influence the work site. While *job* and leisure are opposites, *work* can be an experience of leisure. The world of work can include school, and at some periods of life, school is a person's work. The process of education is not a neat set of boxes but a rich mixture of life's possibilities. Whatever else education means, it refers to directing human life toward greater productiveness and happiness.

The ambiguity of *education* is especially important to recognize in the area of religion. Religious education cannot thrive without the family, the religious community, and other venues besides the school. Religious education can challenge and clarify the contemporary meaning of education that places the entire burden of its accomplishment on the school and schoolteachers.

Two Meanings of *Religion*

The religious part of religious education has a more radical ambiguity than does *education*. *Religion* is ambiguous in a way that is seldom recognized even by scholars. Religion has an ancient and a modern meaning. The two meanings are not simply a narrow and a wide meaning. Rather, the two meanings are nearly opposites.

Religion is a term that was coined by Cicero to describe true worship of the gods.[6] The Christian Church took over the term from the Romans, along with many other religious terms, such as piety, virtue, devotion, and revelation. Until the late sixteenth century, the church retained the ancient meaning of religion as devotional practices. Augustine's treatise, *On True Religion*, is about the genuine devotion that, according to Augustine, existed from the beginning of the world and is now called Christian. Thomas Aquinas treats religion as an element within the virtue of justice.[7] John Calvin's *Institutes of Christian Religion* in 1536 is about true piety. A century later, *Christian religion* would have a quite different meaning.

The modern meaning of religion refers to a diversity of institutions. It originated as a reference to Catholic religion and Protestant religion in the late sixteenth century.[8] Within a few decades, these two religions were folded into "the Christian religion." But *religion* was now an available term to describe a diversity of institutions, including Jewish religion and Muslim religion. In the older meaning of religion, there could be only one religion or at least one true and genuine religion. In the modern meaning of religion, there is necessarily a diversity of religions, even when only one religion is being spoken about. With the new meaning of religion, the idea of religious tolerance became possible. The claim to be the one true religion simply does not apply. Catholic and Protestant religions each laid claim to *containing* true Christian religion, but neither Catholic nor Protestant religion could be the true religion.

There are endless conflicts over religion in US public life; the First Amendment of the Constitution is part of the confusion. The amendment's religion clause is a conceptual muddle. The authors tried to avoid European language by striking a balance about religion. But in one cryptic clause they implied two different meanings of religion. The first part of the clause says that Congress shall make no law respecting an "establishment of religion," a phrase that did not make much sense in the eighteenth century and means even less today. Presumably, the phrase was intended to mean that one religious group (for example, the Presbyterian denomination) would not be officially endorsed by the federal government. The second half of the clause allows for the "free exercise thereof." It presumably refers to religious practices of people, but the phrase has no antecedent. The amendment's clause states two things that the federal government should not do, but there is no guidance as to what the government should do about both *religions* and *religion*.

Thomas Jefferson in an 1804 letter to Baptists in Danbury, Connecticut, unwisely reintroduced the European language of "church and state."[9] That phrase had little usage in the United States until the late nineteenth century when it surfaced out of concern for the rising power of the Roman Catholic Church. The Supreme Court gave legal status to church-state language in the 1940s when there was little doubt that "the church" meant the Roman Catholic Church. The language of church and state took over discussion of religion in the country. There subsequently developed a cottage industry regarding issues of church-state relations in which lawyers and courts decide what the First Amendment supposedly means.

The language of church-state, which controls discussion of religion in public schools, is an obstacle to thinking about religion and education. In the 1960s, the US Supreme Court ruled that religious devotions such as state-mandated prayer and reading the Bible should have no place in the state schools. Evangelical Protestants were shocked by the court applying church-state language to their practices. They argued that reading from the Bible in a classroom or saying a prayer before a football game is not the action of a church. They had logic and history on their side. The Supreme Court was presumably trying to say that the United States was no longer a Protestant country. The "separation of church and state" was a clumsy way to do so.

The Two Parts of Religious Education

The ambiguity of both *religion* and *education* leads to a meaning of religious education as composed of two processes: 1) teaching people religion and 2) teaching people religious practice. The two processes are very different and can be in conflict in the life of an individual. The distinction within religious education draws upon the modern meaning of religions as institutions in need of study and the older meaning of religion as practices of worship. The distinction also reflects a meaning of education that is designed for school learning and a meaning of education that schools cannot effectively encompass.

There cannot be progress in relating religion and public schools so long as legal experts confuse religion as practices of devotion and religion as the name of diverse institutions that are in need of academic study. The Supreme Court has never addressed the question of religious education; it has never had a language to do so. The court is not a reliable source for educational distinctions. A contrast that was made by Justice Arthur Goldberg between "teach religion" and "teach about religion" immediately became educational orthodoxy but is not a clear or helpful contrast.[10] The teaching of religion is a proper function of state institutions; that is, religion(s) needs to be academically examined. The assumption that it is a bad thing to teach religion in state-supported institutions probably misunderstands the verb *teach* and certainly misunderstands the term *religion*.

Understanding Religion. Religion as an area of scholarly interest stands next to economics, mathematics, or psychology. It can be the name of a course in a church-related school or in a secular university. To understand religion is to step back and compare one religion with another, even if the comparison is between two versions of the same religion—for example, in a church history course. The term *religious studies*, which is of recent coinage, is, perhaps intentionally, ambiguous. It allowed Catholic colleges to introduce an alternative to *theology*, a term that had been driving away secular support of church-related colleges.

The process of teaching people religion has the aim of understanding. When one teaches religion, the educational concern is, "Do you understand?" Other physical and social activities are bracketed in a religion course while one asks, "What is going on here? Why do these people act this way? How have things changed over time? How does this activity compare to the activity of other religious groups?" The student of religion focuses on the examination of data, audio or visual records, books and essays. The underlying question is, can I grasp with some logic the human experiences grouped under the term *religion*?

For an understanding of religion, a person need not participate in any particular religious way of life. However, it is difficult to see how one can understand a phenomenon unless one has some feel for it. Many social scientists make pronouncements on religion while showing no sign that they grasp what a religious question is. In regard to religion, which includes the most inner of experiences, one at least has to know what it would be like to be a practitioner of a particular religious way of life.

Throughout most of history, most people attained only a limited understanding of their own religion and practically no understanding of other religions. Here is the crucial change in the modern world that presses the issue of understanding on increasing numbers of ordinary people. The Roman Catholic Church is one of the most interesting case studies of a religion because a constraint upon questioning was suddenly lifted as a result of Vatican II. The immediate effect has likely been a decrease in the devoutness of Catholics, together with an increase in skepticism, a development that was not at all what the fathers of the council intended. But to the extent that understanding is also on the increase, there is hope that the ground is being laid for a flowering of a healthier piety and greater devotion.

The great test for Roman Catholic Church leaders is whether they are ready to risk the spread of understanding of the Catholic religion, including its relation to other religions and to secular society. At this moment of history, it is not sufficient to provide an explanation of Catholic doctrine; there is a need to understand religion. When the context is the understanding of religion, then a whole barrage of questions arise that cannot be asked within Catholic theology. An individual's question may be not what is the meaning of a text in the gospel of Matthew but why is there a New Testament; not should the bishop be obeyed, but is *God* a meaningful term; not should women be ordained but whether religion is inherently sexist. These are not unusual questions; any educated person is likely to have such thoughts at the edge of his or her consciousness.

In trying to get an understanding of religion, a double conversation is needed: a dialogue between religions and a dialogue of religions with secular life. Each of these dialogues admits of a great range in the depth of the comparing. For example, understanding Christianity implies a background understanding of Judaism. The engagement with Judaism might be only some references to the Jewish meanings of faith, messiah, and kingdom. Alternatively, Jewish voices might be brought into the discussion of the logic and concepts of Christianity. In either case, a course on Christian religion has an inherent relation to Jewish religion. During the past half century in the United States, there has been progress in Catholic-Protestant-Jewish understanding. However, the issue is still often assumed to be a specialty for a few experts. A Roman Catholic who grows up in the United States today is not religiously educated without some knowledge of Protestantism and Judaism.

The dialogue between Christian and Jewish religions now needs the third member of Abraham's descendants. The entrance of Muslims in significant numbers is the test of an adequate religious education. Christian-Jewish-Muslim conversation is more complicated but also more realistic than Christian-Jewish dialogue. With its history of religious diversity, the United States should be a leader in conceptualizing and practicing this part of religious education as an understanding of religion(s).

Where does such understanding of religion(s) occur? It can happen anywhere, but the place that is deliberately established for this process is the classroom. A space and a time are set aside for a group of people who wish to understand some subject matter. A language that is disciplined and tolerant carries the inquiry to a deeper level than is usually possible outside the classroom. The classroom is a place to challenge every orthodoxy, whether political, economic, or religious.

In practice, schools do other things than sponsor academic learning. Particularly with younger children, schools cannot avoid socializing students to live in a particular way. But that function of the school should decrease as students mature; the intellectual work of the classroom should become dominant. As a zone of free inquiry, the work of the classroom stands in tension not only with society but even with the school that houses it.

The application of the principle of academic inquiry varies according to the age of students. Our society generally recognizes and accepts critical thinking in university classrooms. But every classroom has to have an atmosphere of respect for the play of the mind. No subject matter and no question can be proscribed. An honest classroom discussion—one that does not presume that there is an answer to be inculcated—can be dangerous. To search for the meaning of suicide, drugs, or sexual behaviors should be done with full awareness of the life-and-death importance of classrooms.

In the United States, teaching people religion is an activity thrown back almost entirely on religious institutions. That is too heavy a burden to carry, but church, synagogue, temple, or mosque has to do the best it can. The Roman Catholic Church supports schools where some excellent teaching of religion occurs. Many writers on secular education assume, without examining the evidence, that teachers of religion in Catholic schools merely proselytize and indoctrinate. In my experience, there is more indoctrinating going on in civics and social studies classes than in Catholic school religion courses.

Religious Practice. In the other process within religious education, the aim of teaching is "religious practice in a particular way." The aim, for example, is to produce observant Jew, devout Catholic, or practicing Muslim. The teacher (community and environment) teaches people to pray before explaining what prayer is. The individual Roman Catholic believes in the Holy Trinity, receives Holy Communion, and follows the gospel teaching on love. A person learns to perform these religious practices, having been taught to do so by example or instruction.

The teacher demands obedience to a moral path before ethical systems are explained. For a small child, it is simply too early to grasp theology, ethics, and the logic of religion. But even for an adult convert, the first step in learning religious practice is the impression conveyed by individual participants, the practices of the institution, and the public face of the group. Every student can begin to learn only if there is trust in the teacher.

The parish is the place that is supposed to teach people religious practices in a Catholic way. The religious education that is most appropriate for a parish is a liturgical life for its members and their moral engagement with the nonchurch world. From community worship and contemplative prayer flow the energies for protest in the name of justice. The parish does have to be aware of the other form of religious education—namely, the teaching-learning of religion. The parish's concern for teaching people religion might be channeled into providing books, sponsoring occasional discussions of religion, and working with other church groups to influence public policy.

The parish is not the sole agency for teaching people to be religious in a Catholic way. The family is the earliest and most powerful teacher of a religious way of life, but the parish is the most visible organizational form for Catholics. At its best, the parish extends the influence that mothers and fathers and other relatives have provided. Most parishes simply cannot be a community, although some parishes are umbrellas for several kinds of community and communal expressions. New forms of church organization ought to come from the needs of educational communities and not from bureaucratic convenience.

There is no age restriction in the experience of being religious. It starts in early childhood when the young child is filled with religious wonder. In the child's experience, everything in the world is a miracle. The religious sensibility of children lacks a high degree of particularity. The young child cannot grasp particular doctrines, but he or she can grasp that a Christian particularity is important for his or her parents and other trusted adults.

During a lengthy period, ranging between the ages of about five and twenty-one, understanding religion is likely to take precedence over religious practice. The modern world teaches, if not skepticism, at least a demand for empirical and logical evidence. For a while, it may seem that religious practice has been undermined. For some people, the quest for understanding religion seems permanently to triumph over the practices of a religious life.

For many other people, however, the religious attitude of childhood slowly returns in adulthood, now disciplined by the transition of adolescence and young adulthood. The question at this stage of life is once again a religious sensibility, but it is now possible to invest a religious way of life with greater intellectual understanding and free choice—greater particularity—than was possible in childhood. What most people need in order to sustain a religious life in adulthood are supportive friends, occasional discussions, and meaningful rituals at life's crucial moments of joy and sadness.

Those who appropriate the term *teacher* for religious education should know which of the two processes they are engaged in at a particular time and a particular place. The tragedy is that, for lack of clarity about this distinction, institutions may end up doing neither task: their academic inquiry is not challenging enough, and their formation is not particular enough. Endless talk about Catholic doctrines is not religious education. What deserves the title of a comprehensive religious education is teaching people religion with all the breadth and depth of intellectual excitement that one is capable of, and teaching people to be religious with all the particularity of the verbal and nonverbal symbols that shape a way of life.

Conclusion

When the Universal Declaration of Human Rights was being composed in 1948, religion was such a contentious issue that the chairperson of the committee, Eleanor Roosevelt, decided to exclude it.[11] Her decision may have been necessary to get approval of the document, but the United Nations has had to repeatedly come back to the issue. The UN's several surveys of religion and education indicate that no nation has worked out a consistent and effective religious education.[12] The most common pattern is that a nation has one dominant religion and may tolerate one or more other religions. The United Nations constantly confronts volatile situations where religion is part of the problem. The choice is usually between violent conflict and a tolerance based on some understanding of religion. The United Nations itself has to play the role of religious educator in trying to reach peaceful settlements.

Much of the world sees the greatest threat to peace in a clash between the United States as a Christian country and the world of Islam. President Barack Obama altered the picture by expressing a tolerance and an understanding of Islam. As a result, he has had to endure vitriolic attacks from "Christianists," those who hold a radical ideology that subsumes elements of Christian tradition within a chauvinistic nationalism. Without the development of religious education in the United States, starting with US participation in worldwide discussions of religion, the international field is left to potentially violent conflicts between Islamists and Christianists.

The hope of many leaders of the Western Enlightenment that religion would soon disappear has not been fulfilled. A movement in the 1960s that declared God to be dead has been outlasted by believers in God. In fact, the 1970s were a time of explosive religious growth around the world. When the Soviet empire dissolved, religion emerged from hiding and showed surprising vitality. To many secular thinkers, this turn of events was just further evidence of human delusions and superstitions. But even people skeptical of religion would do well to try to understand what religion is and why it does not go away.

In the world beyond the Abrahamic religions, *religion* is an imported word, but it can be used to include practices of Buddhists, Hindus, and other groups. That is, Hindus can be said to practice religion even if it may not be appropriate to call Hinduism a religion. In China, there is a long tradition that can be described as religious; by the end of the nineteenth century, there were one million temples in China. After the Communist movement tried to eliminate religious practice, religion has again flourished in China in wildly diverse ways. It is estimated that more people now go to church on Sunday in China than do so in Western Europe. That statistic says something about the stark decline of Christian churches in Western Europe, but the implications for China are nonetheless startling.[13] How do political leaders around the world deal with the popular power of religions?

The Roman Catholic Church in the United States could be a leader in helping the nation and the world come to grips with its religious problems. A church that is striving to be catholic or universal could be a major contributor to developing an effective religious education for peace in the world. Catholic tradition has a long and rich history of education that until modern times was not centered on the school. The development of the school has been invaluable in the modern world. But even the best of schools cannot carry the whole burden of education. Religious institutions, including the Roman Catholic Church, do need modern education in the form of schools. In turn, contemporary education needs the challenge that both parts of religious education offer: the religious practices of particular groups and the teaching-learning of religions.

Notes

Introduction

[1] In Pope John Paul II's 1994 encyclical *Veritatis Splendor*, the pope says in addressing the bishops that "this is the first time, in fact, that the Magisterium of the Church has set forth in detail the fundamentals of this teaching."

[2] The *New York Times* on March 5, 2014, reported that Pope Francis had said in an interview the previous day that "women must have a greater presence in the church hierarchy." That would mean either that the pope was changing the meaning of hierarchy or changing his view of women's ordination. Actually he had said that "women should play a larger role in decision making."

[3] Thomas Aquinas, *Summa Theologiae, IIa. IIae. Prologue*: "In moral matters, general statements are of minimal utility because actions are particular."

[4] Thomas Aquinas, *Summa Theologiae*, I. II. q. 94, art. 4, 5.

[5] What I say here and in the following chapters about natural law is inspired by Thomas Aquinas but with the attempt to translate his thirteenth-century thought into today's language. See Karl Rahner, "Faith of the Christian and the Doctrine of the Church," *Theological Investigations* vol. 14 (New York: Seabury Press, 1977), 330–56.

[6] I do not deny that political advocacy is needed to change public opinion and politicians on the state execution of prisoners. But the issue is one of getting people to recognize that the United States's actions are morally indefensible. There is a realistic hope that the practice can simply be stopped in the not too distant future. On the issue, see Vicki Schieber and others, *Where Justice and Mercy Meet: Catholic Opposition to the Death Penalty* (Collegeville: Liturgical Press, 2013).

[7] Passionate anti-abortionists might believe that the issue is similar to the execution of prisoners. I will argue that there are important differences. Throughout most of Catholic tradition, early abortions were not equated with homicide. There is no realistic hope to get rid of abortion. What is needed are policies that regulate abortion; the watchwords should be early, rare, safe, and available.

8 Cardinal Gerhard Müller, head of the congregation on doctrine, writes, "There is no sense in discussing the problem of same-sex partnership at the synod .... Fear of God and respect for revealed truth and for the family which is built on this truth."

9 The first document that the council proposed was entitled "Sources of Revelation." It was largely a repetition of what the Council of Trent had said in the sixteenth century. The document approved at the last session of the council, called *Dei Verbum* or the Constitution on Divine Revelation, was largely the work of biblical scholars. *Documents of Vatican II* (New York: America Press, 1966).

10 Quoted in Massimo Faggioli, "Off Script," *Commonweal*, Oct. 9, 2015, 12.

11 William Antonio, Michele Dillon, and Mary Gautier, *American Catholics in Transition* (Lanham: Rowman and Littlefield, 2013). The study also reveals what previous studies have shown that what still unites the generations are the doctrine of resurrection, devotion to the mother of Jesus, and a concern for the poor.

12 Clifford Longley, "The Church Ill at Ease with Itself," *The Tablet,* July 5, 2014, 4–5.

13 Final report of the 2015 synod, par. 84–86.

14 *The Tablet*, October 25, 2014.

Chapter 1

1 The statement by Cardinal George Pell is quoted in *The National Catholic Reporter*, December 7, 2014, 7.

2 Karl Rahner, "Basic Theological Interpretation of the Second Vatican Council," in *Theological Investigations* vol. 20 (New York: Crossroad, 1981), 77–89.

3 For a careful summary and interpretation of the Vatican II document on the church, see Paul Lakeland, *A Council That Will Never End* (Collegeville: Michael Glazier, 2013).

4 Prominent theologians at the time did recognize this problem. Karl Rahner in "Membership of the Church according to the Teaching of Pius XII's Encyclical '*Mystici Corporis*,'" *Theological Investigations* (Baltimore: Helicon Press, 1967), II: 83, uses "people of God for humanity." Yves Congar wrote that "the People of God is *de jure* coextensive with humanity .... However, it can only be truly a people if it has a certain structure." Yves Congar, "The People of God," in *Vatican II: An Interfaith Appraisal*, ed. John Miller (Notre Dame: University of Notre Dame Press, 1966), 199.

5 Jack Welch, *Jack: Straight from the Gut* (New York: Hachette, 2003), 433: "Hierarchy is dead. The organization of the future will be virtually layerless and increasingly boundaryless ...."

6 Dionysius, the Syrian monk who first used the term *hierarchy*, wrote that "A hierarchy is a sacred order, a state of understanding and an activity approximating as closely as possible to the divine....Thus, so far as I know, is the first rank of heavenly beings. It circles in immediate proximity to God." Dionysius the Areopagite, *The Celestial Hierarchy* (Whitefish: Kessinger Publishing, 2014), 164, 212.

7 "Bishops speak in the name of Christ and the faithful are to accept their teaching." *Lumen Gentium,* 25a.

8 John Henry Newman, *On Consulting the Faithful in Matters of Doctrine* (London: Collins, 1986).

9 Yves Congar, *Lay People in the Church,* 2nd ed. (Westminster: Newman Press, 1965), 25.

10 *The Tablet,* July 11, 2015, 29. The pope was speaking in St. Peter's Square to members of the Renewal in the Holy Spirit movement.

11 Gershom Scholem, "Revelation and Tradition as Religious Categories in Judaism," in *The Messianic Idea in Judaism* (New York: Schocken Books, 1971), 282–304.

12 Leo Baeck, as cited in Victor Seidler, *Jewish Philosophy and Western Culture: A Modern Introduction* (New York: Tauris, 2008), 71.

13 An interview published in the Buenos Aires newspaper, *Vangardia,* June 17, 2014.

14 Francis Oakley, *The Conciliarist Tradition: Constitutionalism in the Catholic Church 1300–1870.* (New York: Oxford University Press, 2008).

15 Austin Ivereigh, *The Great Reformer: Francis and the Making of a Radical Pope* (New York: Henry Holt, 2014). Epilogue.

Chapter 2

1 The standard collection of defined doctrines is Henry Denzinger, *The Sources of Catholic Dogma* (Fitzwilliam, NH: Loreto Press, 2002); or John Clarkson and others, *The Church Teaches* (Charlotte: Tan Books, 2009).

2 For example, John Dewey, the most famous philosopher of education in US history, failed to reflect at length on the act of teaching.

3 The only modern philosopher who takes seriously the way that a child learns is Ludwig Wittgenstein, *Philosophical Investigations* (New York: Macmillan, 1950). Wittgenstein contrasts his view with St. Augustine's *Confessions.* Although Wittgenstein does have his differences with Augustine, the fact that he debates Augustine is indicative of the fact that Augustine seems to be the first great thinker who reflected on how the child learns.

4 A good example is Alison Gopnik, *The Philosophical Baby: What Children's Minds Tell Us about Truth, Love and the Meaning of Life* (New York: Farrar, Straus and Giroux, 2009).

5 Maria Montessori, the great student of infants, described the newborn baby as all intelligence. *Education for a New World* (Madras: Kalakshetra, 1959), 31.

6 Jean-Jacques Rousseau, *Emile* (New York: Basic Books, 1979) is the one great educational classic that takes this principle seriously.

7 Augustine, *Confessions* (New York: Oxford University Press, 1998), Book One.

8 The philosopher who follows out this train of thought is Wittgenstein.

9 For a description of "executable advice," see Richard Burton and others, "Skiing as a Model of Instruction," in *Everyday Cognition,* ed. Barbara Rogoff and Jean Lave (Cambridge: Harvard University Press, 1984), 139–150.

10 In two of the best-known books on dying, Elisabeth Kübler-Ross, *On Death and Dying* (New York: Macmillan, 1969) and Sherwin Nuland, *How We Die* (New York; Knopf, 1994), the authors credit the dying patients as their main teachers.

11 For a lengthier discussion of the use of educational languages by the Roman Catholic Church, see my *Fashioning a People Today* (New London: Twenty-Third Publications, 2007), 54–147.

12 Austen Ivereigh, *The Great Reformer: Francis and the Making of a Radical Pope* (New York: Henry Holt, 2014).

13 *Constitution on the Sacred Liturgy,* Article 34.

14 It is all but universally assumed in secular educational writing that Catholic schools are places of indoctrination. The accusation is seldom based on a knowledge of existing schools and is insulting to the many teachers in Catholic schools who do not indoctrinate students. The system as a whole, however, does need variety in the staff, various teaching methods, and protection against defenders of orthodoxy to do its proper work of academic instruction.

Chapter 3

1 Pope Pius XI, *Casti Connubi,* issued on Dec. 31, 1930.

2 Pope Pius XII, "The Prolongation of Life," *The Pope Speaks* 4 (Spring, 1958), 395–96; Address to the International Congress of Hematology, Sept. 12, 1958.

3 Congregation for the Doctrine of the Faith, *Declaration on Euthanasia,* May 1980.

4 In chapter 8, I discuss the inherent ambiguity in the phrase "hastening death," which is where the line blurs between to kill and allow to die.

5 John Rock, *The Time Has Come: A Catholic Doctor's Proposal to End the Battle over Birth Control* (New York: Avon Books, 1963).

6 A detailed account of the work of the birth control commission can be found in Robert McClory, *Turning Point* (New York: Crossroad, 1997). The document produced by the commission, "Responsible Parenthood," is in the appendix, 171–187.

7 Pope Paul VI, *Humanae Vitae* (Rome: Vatican Publications, 1968).

8 Andrew Greeley was one of the first people to grasp that *Humanae Vitae* was the moment when the Roman Catholic Church split; see *Catholic Schools in a Declining Church* (Kansas City: Sheed and Ward, 1976), 152–53.

9 The Supreme Court decision was said to refer only to "closely held corporations" that are not traded publicly. But the decision did not just apply to small family businesses. Hobby Lobby is a corporation with 43,000 employees in forty-three states. There is widespread doubt that the decision will remain restricted to this one category of business corporation.

10 Interview in *Corriere della Serra,* March 4, 2014.

[11] United States Conference of Catholic Bishops, *Synod of Bishops on the Family* (Washington: US Catholic Conference, 2014), par. 54.

[12] Peter Steinfels, "Contraception and Honesty," *Commonweal*, June 1, 2015, 12–19 points out that a synod that "says nothing fresh about the spectacularly obvious rift between official teaching and actual behavior in Catholic married life is an invitation to cynicism."

[13] Pope Francis, *Laudato si* (Rome: Vatican, 2015), par. 50; in an appreciative reflection on *Laudato si*, Rowan Williams takes issue only with this paragraph on control of birth: "Embracing our Limits: The Language of *Laudato Si*," *Commonweal*, Oct. 9, 2015, 13–15.

Chapter 4

[1] Mary Ann Glendon, *Abortion and Divorce in Western Law* (Cambridge: Harvard University Press, 1987).

[2] *General Social Surveys 1972–1987, Cumulative Codebook* (Chicago: University of Chicago Press, 1987); Kristin Luker, *Abortion and the Politics of Motherhood* (Berkeley: University of California Press, 1984).

[3] David Leonhardt, "Why Abortion is not like other Issues," *New York Times*, July 14, 2013.

[4] Alasdair MacIntyre, *Three Rival Versions of Moral Inquiry: Encyclopedia, Genealogy and Tradition* (Notre Dame: University of Notre Dame Press, 1991), 44.

[5] Kristin Luker, *Abortion and the Politics of Motherhood* (Berkeley: University of California Press, 1985), 60.

[6] Helen Horowitz, *Rereading Sex: Battles over Sexual Knowledge and Suppression in Nineteenth-Century America* (New York: Knopf, 2002), 195–97.

[7] Robert Burt, *Death is that Man Taking Names: Intersections of American Medicine, Law and Culture* (Berkeley: University of California Press, 2004), 71.

[8] Burt, *Death*, 75–79.

[9] Kelefa Sanneh, "The Intensity Gap," *New Yorker*, October 27, 2014, 39.

[10] A helpful narrative on this period is Patricia Miller, *Good Catholics: The Battle over Abortion in the Catholic Church* (Berkeley: University of California Press, 2014).

[11] Congregation for the Doctrine of the Faith, *Declaration on Certain Questions concerning Sexual Ethics* (Rome: Vatican Press, 1975), sections IX and X.

[12] Edward O. Wilson, *The Meaning of Human Existence* (New York: Liveright, 2014) is an example of a leading biologist declaring what human existence means. Not surprisingly, religious questions for him are simply unintelligible.

[13] A key moment in this shift was a book by Oscar Cullman, *Resurrection or Immortality* (New York: Macmillan, 1968), which opposed the idea of soul. Catholics were not likely to go that far, but starting with F. X. Durwell, *The Resurrection* (New York: Sheed and Ward, 1963), the Catholic Church joined in emphasizing resurrection as the authentic Christian doctrine.

[14] Congregation for the Doctrine of the Faith, *Declaration on Procured Abortion* (Rome: Vatican Press, 1974), section 7.

[15] John Noonan, ed., *The Morality of Abortion: An Almost Absolute Value in History* (Cambridge: Harvard University Press), 1970.

[16] Jerome, *On Ecclesiastes,* 2:5; Augustine, *De Originae animae,* 4.4.

[17] John Noonan, *The Morality of Abortion*, 20.

[18] I refer here to church officials. There is also a small industry of conservative Roman Catholic philosophers and theologians dedicated to reconciling Thomas Aquinas with current church teaching on abortion. A good example is Germain Grisez, *Abortion: The Myths, the Realities and the Arguments* (Washington: Corpus Books, 1970). For a list of such works, see John Haldane and Patrick Lee, "Aquinas on Human Ensoulment, Abortion and the Value of Life," *Philosophy,* 78 (2003), footnote 5.

[19] For a careful study of Thomas Aquinas's texts, see Fabrizio Amerini, *Aquinas on the Beginning and End of Life* (Cambridge: Harvard University Press, 2013), especially chapter 5.

[20] Amerini, *Aquinas,* note 19.

[21] The statistics are from the Guttmacher Institute, which has done extensive study of the question.

[22] Paul Griffiths, "Legalize Same-Sex Marriage," *Commonweal,* June 28, 2004.

[23] Peter Steinfels, "Beyond the Stalemate: Forty years after 'Roe'," *Commonweal,* July 14, 2013, 12–18.

[24] *Summa Theologiae,* Ia, xxix. 2.

[25] The US Supreme Court has been ridiculed for saying that corporations are people. The court was not inventing the idea. The blind spot in the *Citizens United v. Federal Elections Commission* decision was not to recognize that the money of (artificial) persons can overwhelm the political process.

[26] Christopher Kaczor, *The Ethics of Abortion: Women's Rights, Human Life and the Question of Abortion* (New York: Routledge, 2010).

[27] Katha Pollitt, *Pro: Reclaiming Abortion Rights* (New York: Picador, 2014).

[28] Carol Gilligan, *In a Different Voice* (Cambridge: Harvard University Press, 1982); Ronald Dworkin, *Life's Dominion: An Argument about Abortion, Euthanasia and Individual Freedom* (New York: Vintage Books, 1994), 57: "Feminists do not hold that a fetus is a person with moral rights of its own, but they do insist that it is a creature of moral consequence. They emphasize not the woman's right suggested by the rhetoric of privacy, but a woman's responsibility to make a complex decision that she is best placed to make."

Chapter 5

[1] Sherwin Nuland, *How We Die* (New York: Morrow, 1994).

[2] Elisabeth Kübler-Ross. *Death and Dying* (New York: Macmillan, 1970).

3 M.D. Chenu, *Nature, Man and Society in the Twelfth Century: Essays in New Theological Perspectives in the Latin West* (Toronto: University of Toronto Press, 1997).

4 Aristotle, *Metaphysics*, 1014b.

5 Aristotle, *Metaphysics*, 1015a.

6 Aristotle, *Metaphysics*, 1103a 14.

7 Peter Coates, *Nature: Western Attitudes since Ancient Times* (Berkeley: University of California Press, 2004), 27.

8 R.W. Sharples, *Stoics: Epictetus and Skeptics* (New York: Routledge, 1996), 77.

9 Marcus Aurelius, *Meditations* (London: Penguin Books, 1964), II:12.

10 Epictetus, *The Handbook* (Indianapolis: Hackett Publishing, 1983), #13, 5, 27.

11 Chenu, *Nature, Man and Society in the Twelfth Century.*

12 Margaret Wertheim, *Pythagoras' Trousers: The Ascent of Mathematical Man* (New York: Random House, 1995), 83.

13 Thomas Aquinas's treatment of natural law is contained in the *Summa Theologiae*, I–II, q. 95. A helpful commentary can be found in Pamela Hall, *Narrative and Natural Law: An Interpretation of Thomistic Ethics* (Notre Dame: University of Notre Dame Press, 1994), 28–29.

14 Sharples, *Stoics,* 77.

15 Francis Bacon, *The Organon and Related Writings* (Indianapolis: Bobbs-Merrill, 1960), 118–19.

16 Bacon, *Organon*, 14.

17 Bacon, *Organon,* 273.

18 Sigmund Freud, *The Future of an Illusion* (New York: Norton, 1961), 36.

19 C. S. Lewis, *The Abolition of Man* (New York: Harper's, 1948), 80.

20 On matters of sex, Thomas Aquinas is, not surprisingly, a poor guide for today. He lacked the experience and knowledge that on his own principles were needed for developing a sexual ethic that would be adequate today. Perhaps his most helpful comment is that "nothing hinders the natural from being changed since many things for the benefit of human life have been added over and above the natural law, both by the divine law and by human laws." *Summa Theologiae,* I–II q. 95, art. 5.

Chapter 6

1 John Hardwig, "Is There a Duty to Die?" *Hastings Center Report*, 27(1997), 34–42. Hardwig asks many provocative questions about whether a person who reaches a certain age and physical condition should choose to die rather than overburden one's family, friends, and the medical system. However, the author undermines his argument in the essay's first paragraph by equating duty and responsibility. That collapses the meaning of responsibility. Humans have a responsibility *for* their decisions after being responsible *to* their situation. The best choice might be seen as accepting that life is now complete. An argument that starts from responsibility for one's decisions and to one's situation has a much better chance of succeeding than one that announces a duty to die.

2 For a penetrating analysis of what is wrong with autonomy as the basis of ethics, see Matthew Crawford, *The World Beyond Your Head: On Becoming an Individual in an Age of Distraction* (New York: Farrar, Straus and Giroux, 2015).

3 Robin Marantz Henig, "A Life or Death Situation," *New York Times* magazine, July 17, 2013.

4 For example, Joan Tronto, *A Political Argument for an Ethic of Care* (New York: Routledge 1993); Annette Baier, *Reflections on How We Live* (New York: Oxford University Press, 2010).

5 William May, *The Physician's Covenant: Images of the Healer in Medical Ethics* (Louisville: Westminster/Knox, 2000), 79.

6 Albert Camus, *The Plague* (New York: Vintage Books, 1972), 119.

7 The quotation is from geriatrician Bruce Ferrell, cited by Jane Brody in her *New York Times* column of March 4, 2014. She is also the source for the empirical studies of the number of people who are suffering from considerable pain in old age.

8 *Catechism of the Catholic Church,* 2nd ed. (New York: Random House, 2012), 608.

9 Karl Menninger, *Man Against Himself* (New York: Mariner, 1956).

10 Hans Küng has said that he contemplates assisted dying for himself. To the question of whether that is suicide his answer is, "Yes, it is suicide. But it is not murder." Interview in *The Tablet*, Feb. 1, 2014, 7. "Suicide" was coined precisely to distinguish self-killing from murder. I am doubtful that a positive meaning of *suicide* can be recovered from its connotations of the past several centuries.

11 Daniel Callahan, *The Troubled Dream of Life: In Search of a Peaceful Death* (Washington: Georgetown University Press, 2000), 78, responding to Rachels's denial of any difference between intended and unintended effects asks, "If I stop shoveling my driveway in a heavy snow storm because I cannot keep up with it, am I thereby intending a driveway full of snow?"

12 Modern ethicists come back to the principle of *double effect* but unfortunately continue using it with esoteric examples that are unlikely to ever confront anyone. David Edmonds, *Would You Kill the Fat Man: The Trolley Problem and What Your Answer Tells about Right and Wrong* (Princeton: Princeton University Press, 2014).

13 Stephen Carter, *The Culture of Disbelief* (New York: Anchor Books, 1994), 242–43, commenting on the case of Nancy Cruzan whose parents removed her from life support and allowed death to occur, writes, "The starvation that occurs when feeding and hydration cease—not the underlying injury that caused the coma—is the cause of the end of that precious human substance. And it is the family, the unit to which the state has delegated the decision, that has made the choice to cease the feeding and, thus, to destroy that precious substance."

14 Ronald Dworkin, *Life's Dominion: An Argument about Abortion, Euthanasia and Individual Freedom* (New York: Vintage, 1994), 195. Hans Küng, *Can We Save the Catholic Church* (New York: Harper Collins, 2013), 166–67, makes a puzzling

240

comment on Catholic moral teaching about the dying. Küng says that "the popes have increasingly come out in favor of postponing death at all costs, even if this means, prolonging a more vegetative state with no hope of restoring the person to conscious human life." He makes an off-hand reference to the Karen Quinlan and Terry Schiavo cases in the United States, which he says made "the official Catholic moral stance appear absurd and inhuman even in the eyes of many Catholics." Küng surely knows there is more to official teaching on the care of the dying than his one paragraph devoted to this issue.

15 James Rachels, "Active and Passive Euthanasia," *New England Journal of Medicine*, 292, January 9, 1975, 18–20.

Chapter 7

1 Phillipe Ariès, *Western Attitudes to Death* (Baltimore: Johns Hopkins University Press, 1975), 36.

2 Geoffrey Gorer, *Death, Grief and Mourning* (New York: Ayer, 1979).

3 Sigmund Freud, "Mourning and Melancholy," *Standard Edition of the Complete Psychological Works of Sigmund Freud* (London: W.W. Norton, 1953–74) vol. XIV.

4 Harold Kushner, *When Bad Things Happen to Good People* (New York: Avon Books, 1981), 89.

5 Samuel Heilman, *When a Jew Dies* (Berkeley: University of California Press, 2001).

6 Elisabeth Kübler-Ross, *Death and Dying* (New York: Macmillan, 1970).

7 Erich Lindemann, "Symptomatology and Management of Acute Grief," *American Journal of Psychiatry* 101(1944).

8 Although Jewish tradition warns against excessive weeping, the Talmud also says that anyone who cries at the death of a good person is forgiven all his sins; *Shabbat 105b*. See also *The Tibetan Book of the Dead*, ed. W. Evans-Wentz (New York: Oxford University Press, 1960), 87, 195.

9 C. S. Lewis, *A Grief Observed* (New York: Harper, 2009), 69: "Grief is like a long valley, a winding valley where any bend may reveal a totally new landscape …. Sometimes the surprise is the opposite one; you are presented with exactly the same sort of country you thought you had left behind miles ago. That is when you wonder whether the valley isn't a circular trench. But it isn't. There are partial recurrences but the sequence doesn't repeat."

Chapter 8

1 Christine Firer Hinze and J. Patrick Hornbeck, eds., *More than a Monologue: Sexual Diversity in the Catholic Church* (New York: Fordham University Press, 2013).

2 US Conference of Catholic Bishops, *Ministry to Persons with a Homosexual Inclination: Guidelines for Pastoral Care* (Washington: U.S. Conference of Catholic Bishops, 2006), 14.

[3] Seth Stephens Davidowitz, "How Many American Men Are Gay?" *New York Times,* Dec. 8, 2013, 5.

[4] For a more extensive commentary on these biblical texts, see Matthew Vines, *God and the Gay Christian: The Biblical Case in Support of Same-Sex Relationships* (New York: Convergent Books, 2014).

[5] *Declaration on Certain Questions Concerning Sexual Ethics* (Rome: Congregation for the Doctrine of the Faith, 1975).

[6] Masturbation is a nineteenth-century word. If there is any reference to masturbation in the New Testament or in the first few centuries of Christianity, it is certainly obscure.

[7] Congregation for the Doctrine of the Faith, *On the Pastoral Care of Homosexual Persons.* (Rome: Vatican Press, 1986).

[8] Thomas Gumbleton, "Pastoral and Theological Response to Gays and Lesbians," in Hinze and Hornbeck, *More than a Monologue,* chapter 5.

[9] US Conference of Catholic Bishops, *Ministry to Persons with a Homosexual Inclination,* 9.

[10] William Baude, "Is Polygamy Next?" *New York Times,* July 21, 2015, A27.

[11] Massimo Faggioli, "Off Script," *Commonweal,* Oct. 9, 2015, 12.

[12] Margaret Mead, "Marriage in Two Steps," in *The Family in Search of a Future,* ed. Herbert Otto (New York: Appleton-Century-Crofts, 1970), 75–84.

[13] "The Church Today," *Documents of Vatican II,* par. 50.

[14] Ryan Anderson, *Truth Overruled: The Future of Marriage and Religious Freedom* (Chicago: Regnery, 2015).

[15] Jeanine Gramick and Robert Nugent, *Building Bridges: Gay and Lesbian Reality and the Catholic Church* (W. Mystic: Twenty-Third Publications, 1992).

[16] Congregation for the Doctrine of the Faith, *Notification Regarding Sr. Gramick and Fr. Nugent* (Rome: Vatican Press, 1999).

[17] Interview in *America*, September 30, 2013.

[18] Editorial, *Commonweal*, October 28, 2014.

[19] Final Report of the Synod of 2015, par. 76.

[20] Margaret Farley, "Love Shaped and Grounded in Faith," *The Tablet*, September 27, 2014, 11–12.

Chapter 9

[1] John Howard Yoder, *The Politics of Jesus* (Grand Rapids: Eerdmans, 1972).

[2] Gerd Theissen, *Sociology of Early Palestinian Christianity* (Philadelphia: Fortress Press, 1964), 64.

[3] Max Weber, "Politics as a Vocation," in *Max Weber: Selections in Translation* (Cambridge: Cambridge University Press, 1978).

[4] Reinhold Niebuhr, *Moral Man and Immoral Society: A Study in Ethics and Politics* (New York: Charles Scribner's Sons, 1932).

5 George Packer, "Peace and War," *The New Yorker*, December, 2009, 46.

6 Hannah Arendt, *The Human Condition* (Chicago: University of Chicago Press, 1958), 241.

7 Martin Luther King Jr., *Why We Can't Wait* (New York: Harper and Row, 1964), 38.

8 Carrie Gustafson, *Religion and Human Rights* (Armonk: M.E. Sharpe, 1999), 101.

9 Origen, *Contra Celsus* (Cambridge: Cambridge University Press, 1980).

10 Garry Wills, *St. Augustine* (New York: Viking Press, 1999).

11 R. A. Marcus, *Saint Augustine's Views on the Just War* (Oxford: Blackwell, 1983).

12 Augustine, *Concerning the City of God* (Baltimore: Penguin Books, 1972), 1:21, 4:15, 19:7.

13 Thomas Aquinas, *Summa Theologiae* (New York: McGraw Hill, 1966), 1a, 2ae, 90–97.

14 Ernst Bloc, *The Principle of Hope* (Cambridge: MIT Press, 1986), 127.

15 Steven Ozment, *Mysticism and Dissent* (New Haven: Yale University Press), 1973.

16 Bernard McGinn, *Meister Eckhart: Teacher and Preacher* (New York: Paulist Press, 1986).

17 José Chapiro, *Erasmus and our Struggle for Peace* (Boston: Beacon Press, 1950).

18 Pope John XXIII, *Pacem in Terris* (New York: Macmillan, 1968), 127.

19 "Church in the Modern World," *Documents of Vatican II,* par. 80.

20 US Catholic Bishops, *Statement on Central America* (Washington: U.S. Catholic Conference, 1982).

21 US Catholic Bishops, *The Challenge of Peace* (Washington: U.S. Catholic Conference, 1983), 117.

22 *National Catholic Reporter,* February 11, 1972.

23 Peter Steinfels, *A People Adrift: The Crisis of the Roman Catholic Church in America* (New York: Simon and Schuster, 2003), 17–39.

24 Dorothy Day, *The Long Loneliness* (San Francisco: Harper, 1981).

25 Thomas Cornell and James Forest, *A Penny a Copy: Readings from the Catholic Worker* (New York: Macmillan, 1968).

26 William Miller, *Dorothy Day: A Biography* (New York: Harper and Row, 1982).

27 Patricia McNeal, *American Catholic Peace Movement* (Philadelphia: Temple University Press, 1974), 75–77.

28 Mel Piehl, *Breaking Bread: The Catholic Worker and the Origin of Catholic Radicalism in America* (Philadelphia: Temple University Press, 1982), 195–98.

29 George Gallup and Jim Castelli, *The American Catholic People* (New York: Doubleday, 1987), 82.

30 Gerard Twomey, *Thomas Merton: Prophet in the Belly of a Paradox* (New York: Paulist Press, 1978), 33.

31 Gordon Zahn, *Thomas Merton on Peace* (New York: McCall, 1971), 257.

32 Thomas Merton, *Seeds of Destruction* (New York: Farrar, Straus and Giroux, 1964), 151, 115.

33 Zahn, *Thomas Merton on Peace,* 75.

34 The same attitude toward success voiced about Merton was made of Dorothy Day by Andrew Bacevich. He quotes Day that "Success, as the world determines it, is not the criterion by which a movement should be judged …. We must be prepared and ready to face seeming failure." Bacevich criticizes Day for not attending to the present. He neglects her phrase "as the world determines it" and the word "seeming." He says that "whatever may await humanity at the end of time afflictions endured in the here-and-now matter a great deal." This accusation is even less appropriate for Day than Merton. Day spent her life trying to heal the wounds of violence and injustice in the here and now. Andrew Bacevich, "Peace Activism. What Is It Good For?" *Commonweal,* Sept. 27, 2013, 18–20.

35 Thomas Merton, *Faith and Violence* (Notre Dame: University of Notre Dame Press, 1968), 23.

36 Zahn, *Thomas Merton,* 231.

37 Robert Handy, "An Affidavit," *American Report,* April 7, 1973, 7.

38 *Washington Post,* April 23, 1971, 1.

Chapter 10

1 Giuseppe Alberigo and Joseph Komonchak, eds., *History of Vatican II: Toward a New Era in Catholicism,* vol. 2 (New York: Orbis Books, 1995), pp. 26–31.

2 David Schultenover, *Vatican II: Did Anything Happen* (New York: Continuum, 2007).

3 Gabriel Moran, *Scripture and Tradition: A Survey of the Controversy* (New York: Herder and Herder, 1963).

4 Josef Ratzinger, *Salt of the Earth* (San Francisco: Ignatius Press, 1997), 72; *The Theology of History in Saint Bonaventure* (Chicago: Franciscan Press, 1971).

5 The French edition was published in Bruges: Desclée de Brouwer, 1963; the English translation was published by Alba House in 1966.

6 Both books were published by Herder and Herder in 1966.

7 Jon Roberts, *Darwinism and the Divine in America: Protestant Intellectuals and Organic Evolution 1859–1900* (Notre Dame: University of Notre Dame Press, 2001), 159–162.

8 I invite the reader to survey any of a dozen books by Josef Ratzinger to test my claim of how he uses "Christian faith." See, for example, these books, which are all published by Ignatius Press: *Salt of the Earth* (2005), *Spirit of the Liturgy* (2000), *Called to Communion* (1996), *Introduction to Christianity* (2004).

9 John Noonan, *A Church that Can and Cannot Change* (Notre Dame: University of Notre Dame Press, 2005), 215.

10 Adela Yarbo Collins, *Crisis and Catharsis: The Power of the Apocalypse* (Philadelphia: Westminster Press, 1984), 172.

11 Karl Rahner, "Basic Theological Interpretation of the Second Vatican Council," in *Theological Investigations* vol. 20 (New York: Crossroad, 1981), 77–89.

12 Mark Lilla, *The Stillborn God* (New York: Knopf, 2007); Charles Taylor, *The Secular Age* (Cambridge: Harvard University Press, 2007).

13 Pope Francis, *Laudato si* (Rome: Vatican Publications, 2015), par. 85.

14 Victor Frankl, *Man's Search for Meaning* (New York: Washington Square Books, 1967), p. 71.

15 The phrase *lex credendi, lex orandi* is from Vincent of Lerins, *The Commonitory of Vincent of Lerins* (Ithaca: Cornell University Press, 1914).

16 Gabriel Marcel, *The Mystery of Being* (New City: St. Augustine Press, 2001) did much to reestablish the meaning of mystery as a category distinct from that of problem; this meaning of mystery has roots that go back to St. Paul and St. Augustine.

17 "Dogmatic Constitution on Divine Revelation," *Documents of Vatican II*, translated by Austin Flannery (Grand Rapids: Eerdmans, 1975), preface.

18 Soren Kierkegaard, *Fear and Trembling* and *The Sickness unto Death* (Princeton: Princeton University Press, 1954), 210.

19 "Dogmatic Constitution on the Church," *Documents of Vatican II*, par. 1.

20 Ormond Rush, *Still Interpreting Vatican II* (New York: Paulist Press, 2004), 29.

21 Aristotle, *Ethics* 1155a23.

Chapter 11

1 Vicki Hearne, *Adam's Task: Calling Animals by Name* (New York: Knopf, 1986).

2 Martin Buber, "Education," in *Between Man and Man* (New York: Macmillan, 1965), 92: "We practice responsibility for that realm of life allotted and entrusted to us for which we are able to respond, that is, for which we have a relation of deeds which may count—in all our inadequacy—as a proper response."

3 William Schweiker, *Responsibility and Christian Ethics* (Cambridge: Cambridge University Press, 1995), 146–147.

4 Gabriel Marcel, *Philosophy of Existentialism* (New York: Citadel, 1961), 99.

5 Dietrich Bonhoeffer, *Ethics* (New York: Macmillan, 1955), 259; Frank Kermode, *Genesis of Secrecy* (Cambridge: Harvard University Press, 1979), 38.

6 In his encyclical *Laudato si,* Pope Francis comments on the Cain and Able story about a proper relationship with our neighbor "for whose care and custody I am responsible." That seems to me to overstep the proper boundaries of a neighborly relation.

7 Ira Byock, *Dying Well* (New York: Riverhead, 1997); Daniel Callahan, *The Troubled Dream: Living with Mortality* (New York: Simon and Schuster, 1993).

8 Anthony Giddens, *The Transformation of Intimacy* (Stanford: Stanford University Press, 1992), 107–08.

9 Pope Francis, *Laudato si*, par. 67.

10 Elizabeth Wolgast, *Ethics of an Artificial Person* (Stanford: Stanford University Press, 1992), 9–10.

11 Hannah Arendt, *The Life of the Mind: Vol I: Thinking* (New York: Harcourt, Brace, Jovanovich, 1978), 5.

12 P. W. Duff, *Personality in Roman Private Law* (Cambridge: Cambridge University Press, 1938).

13 James Coleman, *The Asymmetrical Society* (Syracuse: Syracuse University Press, 1982), 84.

14 The most imaginative writing in this area has been done by Albert Hirschman, *Exit, Voice and Loyalty: Responses to Decline in Firms, Organizations and States* (Cambridge: Harvard University Press, 1970).

15 *New York Times*, April 12, 2014, A11.

16 Peter French, *Responsibility Matters* (Lawrenceville: University of Kansas Press, 1992), 145: "The endurance of corporate persons, a prospect that terrorized the Enlightenment liberals, insures the projection of moral and cultural responsibilities in both temporal directions."

Chapter 12

1 Diane Orentlicher, "Relativism and Religion" in Michael Ignatieff, *Human Rights as Politics and Idolatry* (Princeton: Princeton University Press, 2001), 141–58.

2 Gabriel Moran, *Uniquely Human: The Basis of Human Rights* (Bloomington: Xlibris, 2013), 197–231.

3 Frederick Douglass, "The Nature of Slavery," in *Autobiographies* (New York: Library of America, 1994), 427.

4 Francis Bacon, *The New Organon* (Cambridge: Cambridge University Press, 2008).

5 *Mishnah Abot* 1:1.

6 Ellis Rivkin, *The Shaping of Jewish History: A Radical New Interpretation* (New York: Charles Scribner's Sons, 1971), 77. Rivkin particularly emphasizes Christianity taking over the idea of God as a personal father and the doctrine of bodily resurrection.

7 Giorgio Agamben, *The Highest Poverty: Monastic Rules and Form of Life* (Stanford: Stanford University Press, 2013), 54.

8 Thomas Aquinas, *Summa Theologiae*, I. II., q. 90, a.4.

9 Thomas Aquinas, *Summa Contra Gentiles* III: 122; *Summa Theologiae*, I. 29. 2.

10 Thomas Aquinas, *Summa Theologiae*, 1a.1. ad 2.

[11] Gratian, *The Treaty on Laws with the Ordinary Gloss* (Washington: Catholic University Press, 1993).

[12] Brian Tierney, *The Idea of Natural Rights* (Grand Rapids: Eerdmans, 1990), chap. 2.

[13] John Locke, *The Second Treatise on Civil Government* (New York: Prometheus Books, 1986), chap. 9, par. 123, 124.

[14] Locke, *Second Treatise*, chap. 5, makes clear that he thought a man's "property" was "his own person" and what is needed for his life.

[15] The rights of man were said to be liberty, property, security, and resistance to oppression. Interestingly, the original Declaration of 1789 did not include "life" as a natural right.

[16] Karl Marx, "On the Jewish Question," in *Early Texts* (Oxford: Blackwell, 1971), 223.

Chapter 13

[1] Lynn White Jr., "The Historical Roots of Our Ecological Crisis," *Science* 155 (March 10, 1967, 1203–07); the essay has been reprinted numerous times. Pope Francis seems to draw on White's title for par. 101–114 of *Laudato si*: The Human Roots of the Ecological Crisis.

[2] A. D. Nock, *Conversion: The Old and the New in Religion from Alexander the Great to Augustine of Hippo* (New York: Oxford University Press, 1963), 210.

[3] Eric Freudenstein, "Ecology and Jewish Tradition" in *Judaism and Human Rights*, ed. Milton Konvitz (New Brunswick: Rutgers University Press, 2001), 273.

[4] Augustine's views are in his Commentary on Genesis or *On the City of God*, Book 13; for a summary of this literature of the church fathers, see George Ovitt, *The Restoration of Perfection: Labor and Technology in Medieval Culture* (New Brunswick: Rutgers University Press, 1988).

[5] White, "The Historical Roots of Our Ecological Crisis," 1207; Roderick Nash, *Rights of Nature* (Madison: University of Wisconsin Press, 1989), 94.

[6] G. K. Chesterton, *Saint Francis of Assisi* (Garden City: Image Books, 1959), 87.

[7] Frank Bruni, "The Sunny Side of Greed," *New York Times,* July 1, 2015, A29. The movie *Wall Street* has a famous line, "Greed is good." Some people seem to have adopted that meaning of greed in place of what had always been the name of a vice.

[8] Roger Sorrell, *Saint. Francis of Assisi and Nature* (New York: Oxford University Press, 1988), 8; Regis Armstrong, *Francis of Assisi: The Saint* (New York: New City Press, 1999), 7. For an accurate history of his life, see Augustine Thompson, *Francis of Assisi: The Life* (Ithaca: Cornell University Press, 2013).

[9] Sorrell, *Saint Francis*, 49.

[10] Peter Singer, "Individuals, Humans and Persons," *Unsanctifying Human Life: Essays on Ethics*, ed. Helga Kuhse (Oxford: Blackwell, 2002), 193.

[11] Quoted in Robert Sapolsky, "A Natural History of Peace," *Foreign Affairs,* 85 (Jan/Feb., 2006), 104.

[12] For Erigena, see John Macquarrie, *In Search of Deity* (London: SCM Press, 2012), 95: "Man is not inappropriately called the workshop of all creation, since in him the universal creature is contained. For he understands like an angel, reasons like a man, is sentient like an animal, has life like a plant and subsists in body and soul. There is no creature that he is without."

[13] Pope Francis, *Laudato si*, par. 115–119; Austen Ivereigh and Kathryn Jean Lopez, *How to Defend the Faith without Raising your Voice* (Huntington: Our Sunday Visitor, 2015), chap. 4.

[14] Elizabeth Kolbert, *The Sixth Extinction: An Unnatural History* (New York: Holt, 2014) has the bewildering sentence: "It doesn't much matter whether people care or don't care. What matters is that people change the world." The second sentence may be a more inclusive truth than the first sentence. But surely a care of the world is important. Otherwise, why care about writing or reading a book on the environment?

[15] C. S. Lewis, *The Abolition of Man* (New York: Harper One, 2009), 69.

[16] Peter Singer, *Practical Ethics* (Cambridge: Cambridge University Press, 1993), ix.

[17] This policy would seem to be implied in Paul Taylor, *Respect for Nature: A Theory of Environmental Ethics* (Princeton: Princeton University Press, 1986), 115: "Given the total, absolute, and final disappearance of *Homo Sapiens,* then, not only would the Earth's Community of Life continue to exist but in all probability its well-being would be enhanced."

[18] Wendell Berry, *Standing By Words* (San Francisco: North Point, 1983), 168.

Chapter 14

[1] Dickinson Adams, *Jefferson's Extracts from the Gospels* (Princeton: Princeton University Press, 1983), 405, 409.

[2] The first meeting of the Religious Education Association attracted college presidents and leading politicians. William Rainey Harper, "The Scope and Purpose of the New Organization," *Proceedings of the First Convention* (Chicago: Religious Education Association, 1903).

[3] Andrew Greeley, *Catholic Schools in a Declining Church* (Kansas City: Sheed and Ward, 1976).

[4] W. Roy Niblett, "The Religious Education Clauses of the 1944 Act: Aims, Hopes and Fulfillment," *Religious Education 1944–84*, ed. A. G. Wedderspoon (London: George, Allen and Unwin, 1964).

[5] Robert Jackson, *Religious Education in Europe* (Münster: Waxman, 2007).

[6] Cicero, *The Nature of the Gods*, II: 7–9: "If we compare ourselves with other peoples, in other respects we shall find that we are equal or even inferior; but in religion and the worship of the gods we are pre-eminent."

[7] Thomas Aquinas, *Summa Theologiae*, IIae, q. 81.

[8] Peter Harrison, *"Religion" and the Religions in the English Enlightenment* (Cambridge: Cambridge University, 1990), 37.

[9] Daniel Dreisbach, *Thomas Jefferson and the Wall of Separation between Church and State* (New York: New York University, 2002).

[10] Arthur Goldberg's distinction is found in *Abington School District v. Schemmp,* 374 U.S. 203, 1963. In contrast to Goldberg's comment, which is endlessly quoted, one seldom finds quoted a definitive statement by Chief Justice William Rehnquist: "The 'wall of separation between church and state' is a metaphor based on bad history, a metaphor which has proved useless as a guide to judging. It should be frankly and explicitly abandoned." *Wallace v. Jaffree,* 472 U.S. 38, 92, 106 (1985).

[11] Mary Ann Glendon, *A World Made New: Eleanor Roosevelt and the Universal Declaration of Human Rights* (New York: Random House, 2001), 87.

[12] For UN Surveys, see Nathan Lerner, *Religion, Beliefs and International Human Rights* (New York: Orbis Books, 2000), 11–32.

[13] Fenggang Yang, *Religion in China: Survival under Communist Rule* (New York: Oxford University, 2014.

Bibliography

Agamben, Giorgio. *The Highest Poverty: Monastic Rules and Forms of Life*. Stanford, CA: Stanford University Press, 2013.

Amerini, Fabrizio. *Aquinas on the Beginning and End of Human Life*. Cambridge, MA: Harvard University Press, 2013.

Anderson, Ryan. *Truth Overruled: The Future of Marriage and Religious Freedom*. Chicago, IL: Regnery, 2015.

Antonio, William, Michele Dillon and Mary Gautier. *American Catholics in Transition*. Lanham, MD: Rowman and Littlefield, 2013.

Armstrong, Roger. *Francis of Assisi: The Saint*. New York: New City, 1999.

Bacevich, Andrew. "Peace Activism: What Is It Good For?" *Commonweal*, September 27, 2013:18–20.

Baier, Annette. *Reflection on How We Live*. New York: Oxford University Press, 2010.

Bacon, Francis. *New Organon*. Cambridge: Cambridge University Press, 2008.

Baker, Sara Josephine. *Fighting for Life*. New York: New York Review of Books, 2013.

Beckwith, Francis. *Defending Life: A Moral and Legal Case against Abortion Choice*. Cambridge: Cambridge University Press, 2007.

Boswell, John. *Christianity, Social Tolerance and Homosexuality: Gay People in Western Europe from the Beginning of the Christian Era to the Fourteenth Century*. Chicago, IL: University of Chicago Press, 2009.

Bottum, Joseph. "The Things We Share: A Catholic's Case for Same-Sex Marriage." *Commonweal*, September 13, 2013: 14–25.

Bowers, Chet. *Elements of a Post-Liberal Theory of Education*. New York: Teachers College Press, 1987.

Brown, Theresa. *Critical Care*. New York: Harper, 2010.

Burt, Robert. *Death is that Man Taking Names: Intersections of American Medicine, Law, and Culture*. Berkeley, CA: University of California Press, 2004.

Bynum, Carol Walker. *Resurrection of the Body in Western Christianity 200–1336*. New York: Columbia University Press, 1995.

Callahan, Daniel. *The Troubled Dream of Life: In Search of a Peaceful Death.* Washington, DC: Georgetown University Press, 2000.

Catechism of the Catholic Church. 2nd ed. New York: Random House, 2012.

Chesterton, G. K. *Orthodoxy.* Garden City, NY: Image Books, 1959.

————. *Saint Francis of Assisi.* Garden City, NY: Image Books, 1959.

Chenu, M. D. *Nature, Man and Society in the Twelfth Century: Essays on New Theological Perspectives in the Latin West.* Toronto, ON: University of Toronto Press, 1997.

Clark, John, ed. *The Church Teaches.* Charlotte, NC: Tan Books, 2009.

Coates, Peter. *Nature: Western Attitudes since Ancient Times.* Berkeley, CA: University of California Press, 2004.

Commonweal editors. "The Truth about Marriage." *Commonweal,* August 5, 2013.

————. "Pope Frank: Open Debate at the Synod." *Commonweal,* October 28, 2014.

Congar, Yves. *Lay People in the Church.* 2nd ed. Long Prairie, MN: Newman Press, 1965.

Congregation for the Doctrine of the Faith, *Declaration on Procured Abortion.* Rome: Vatican Press, 1974.

————. *Declaration on Certain Questions concerning Sexual Ethics.* Rome: Vatican Press, 1975.

————. *Declaration on Euthanasia.* Rome: Vatican Press, 1980.

————. *On the Pastoral Care of Homosexual Persons.* Rome: Vatican Press, 1986.

————. "Notification regarding Sr. Gramick and Fr. Nugent." *Origins,* 29(July 2, 1999): 133–36.

————. *Constitutions regarding Proposals to Give Legal Recognition to Unions between Homosexual Persons.* Rome: Vatican Press, 2003.

Conway, Trudy, David Matzko McCarthy and Vicki Schieber. *Where Justice and Mercy Meet: Catholic Opposition to the Death Penalty.* Collegeville, MN: Liturgical Press, 2013.

Cooper, Kate. *Band of Angels: The Forgotten World of Early Christian Women.* New York: Atlantic Books, 2013.

Cousins, Norman. *Anatomy of an Illness.* New York: Bantam Books, 1981.

Cowdell, Scott. *René Girard and Secular Modernity.* Notre Dame, IN: University of Notre Dame Press, 2013.

Cozzens, Donald. *Notes from the Underground: The Spiritual Journey of a Secular Priest.* New York: Orbis Books, 2013.

Cullman, Oscar. *Immortality or Resurrection?* New York: Macmillan, 1968.

Cunningham, Lawrence, ed. *Intractable Disputes about the Natural Law.* Notre Dame, IN: University of Notre Dame Press, 2009.

Curran, Charles. *The Development of Moral Theology.* Washington, DC: Georgetown University Press, 2013.

D'Antonio, Michael. *Mortal Sins: Sex, Crime and the Era of Catholic Scandal.* New York: Thomas Dunne Books, 2013.

Denzinger, Henry, ed. *The Sources of Catholic Dogma.* Fitzwilliam, NH: Loreto Press, 2002.

Documents of Vatican II. New York: America Press, 1966.

Dolan, Timothy. "The Pope's Case for Virtuous Capitalism." *Wall Street Journal,* May 22, 2014.

Durwell, F. X. *Resurrection.* New York: Sheed and Ward, 1963.

Dworkin, Ronald. *Life's Dominion: An Argument about Abortion, Euthanasia and Individual Freedom.* New York: Vintage Books, 1994.

Edmondo, David. *Would You Kill the Fat Man: The Trolley Problem and What Your Answer Tells about Right and Wrong.* Princeton, NJ: Princeton University Press, 2014.

Eibl-Eibesfeldt, Irenaeus. *The Biology of Peace and War: Men, Animals and Aggression.* New York: Viking Press, 1979.

Faggioli, Massimo. "The Italian Job." *Commonweal,* June 5, 2014.

———. "Off Script." *Commonweal,* October 9, 2015: 10–12.

Farley, Margaret. *Just Love: A Framework for Christian Sexual Ethics.* New York: Continuum, 2006.

———. "Love Shaped and Grounded in Faith." *The Tablet,* September 27, 2014: 11–12.

Fawcett, Edmund. *Liberalism: The Life of an Idea.* Princeton, NJ: Princeton University Press, 2014.

Finnis, John. "Three Schemes of Regulation," in *The Morality of Abortion.* Edited by John Noonan. 172–207. Cambridge, MA: Harvard University Press, 1970.

———. *Natural Law and Natural Rights.* New York: Oxford University Press, 1980.

Freudenstein, Eric. "Ecology and Jewish Tradition." *Judaism and Human Rights.* Edited by Milton Konvitz. 265–274. New Brunswick, NJ: Rutgers University Press, 2001.

Gadamer, H. G. *Truth and Method.* New York: Continuum, 2004.

George, Robert and Christopher Tollefsen. *Embryo: A Defense of Human Life.* New York: Doubleday, 2008.

Glendon, Mary Ann. *Abortion and Divorce in Western Law.* Cambridge, MA: Harvard University Press, 1987.

Goffman, Erving. *Asylums: Essays on the Social Situation of Mental Patients and Other Inmates.* New York: Anchor Books, 1961.

Gramick, Jeanine and Robert Nugent, *Building Bridges: Gay and Lesbian Reality and the Catholic Church.* W. Mystic, CT: Twenty-Third Publications, 1992.

———. *Voices of Hope: A Collection of Positive Catholic Writings on Gay and Lesbian Issues.* New York: Center for Homophobia Education, 1995.

Griffiths, Paul. "Legalize Same-Sex Marriage." *Commonweal*, June 28, 2004.

Gritsch, Eric. *Martin, God's Jester: Luther in Retrospect.* Philadelphia, PA: Fortress Press, 1983.

Grisez, Germain. *Abortion: The Myths, the Realities, and the Arguments.* New York: Corpus Books, 1970.

Gumbleton, Thomas. "Pastoral and Theological Responses to Gays and Lesbians." In *More than a Monologue: Sexual Diversity and Catholicism.* Edited by Christine Firer Hornbeck and J. Patrick Hinze, chapter 5. New York: Fordham University Press, 2013.

Haldane, John and Patrick Lee. "Aquinas on Human Ensoulment, Abortion and the Value of Life." *Philosophy* 78(2003), 255–78.

Hall, Pamela. *Narrative and Natural Law.* Notre Dame, IN: University of Notre Dame Press, 1994.

Hardwig, John. "Is There a Duty to Die?" *Hastings Center Report*, 27(1997): 34–42.

Häring, Bernard. "A Theological Evaluation." in *The Morality of Abortion.* Edited by John Noonan, 123–45. Cambridge, MA: Harvard University Press, 1970.

Hedges, Chris. *War is a Force that Gives Us Meaning.* New York: Public Affairs, 2002.

Henig, Robin Marantz. "A Life or Death Situation." *New York Times Magazine*, July 7, 2013.

Hibbs, Thomas. "Divine Irony and the Natural Law: Speculation and Edification in Aquinas." *International Philosophical Quarterly* 30(1990), 419–29.

Hinze, Christine Hirer and J. Patrick Hinze, eds. *More than a Monologue: Sexual Diversity and the Catholic Church.* New York: Fordham University Press, 2013.

Hirschman, Albert. *The Rhetoric of Reaction.* Cambridge, MA: Harvard University Press, 1991.

Horowitz, Helen. *Re-reading Sex: Battles over Sexual Knowledge and Suppression in Nineteenth-Century America.* New York: Knopf, 2002.

Hume, David. "Of the First Principle of Government." in *Selected Essays.* Edited by Stephen Copley and Andrew Edgar, 24–28. New York: Oxford University Press, 1993.

Ivereigh, Austen. *The Great Reformer: Francis and the Making of a Radical Pope.* New York: Henry Holt, 2014.

————. and Kathryn Jean Lopez. *How to Defend the Faith without Raising your Voice.* Huntington, IN: Our Sunday Visitor, 2015.

Jenkins, Philip. *Jesus Wars.* New York: Harper Collins, 2010.

Johnson, Elizabeth. *Quest for the Living God: Mapping Frontiers in the Theology of God.* New York: Bloomsbury, 2011.

————. *Ask the Beasts: Darwin and the God of Love.* New York: Bloomsbury, 2014.

Kaczor, Christopher. *The Ethics of Abortion: Women's Rights, Human Life and the Question of Justice.* New York: Routledge, 2010.

Kasper, Walter. *Mercy: The Essence of the Gospel and the Key to Christian Life.* New York: Paulist Press, 2014.

Keenan, James. *A History of Catholic Moral Theology in the Twentieth Century: From Confessing Sins to Liberating Consciences.* New York: Continuum, 2010.

Keller, Bill. "How to Die." *New York Times*, October 1, 2012.

Kilby, Karen. *Balthasar: A (Very) Critical Introduction.* Grand Rapids, MI: Eerdmans, 2013.

King, Martin Luther, Jr. *I Have a Dream: Writings and Speeches that Changed the World.* New York: Harper One, 1992.

Kübler-Ross, Elisabeth. *On Death and Dying.* New York: Macmillan, 1970.

Kurlansky, Mark. *Nonviolence: The History of a Dangerous Idea.* New York: Modern Library, 2008.

Lash, Nicholas. "Teaching or Commanding?" *America*, December 13, 2010: 17–20.

Leonhardt, David. "Why Abortion is not like Other Issues." *New York Times,* July 14, 2013.

Leuba, James. *The Psychological Origin and the Nature of Religion.* London: Constable and Company, 1912.

Lewis, C. S. *The Abolition of Man.* New York: Harper, 2009.

Lindemann, Erich. "Symptomatology and Management of Acute Grief." In *Death and Identity.* Edited by Robert Fulton, 187–201. New York: John Wiley, 1965.

Longley, Clifford. "The Church Ill at Ease with Itself." *The Tablet*, July 5, 2014: 4–5.

Louisell, David and John Noonan, "Constitutional Balance." In *Morality of Abortion.* Edited by John Noonan, 220–260. Cambridge, MA: Harvard University Press, 1970.

Lovejoy, Arthur and George Boas. *Primitivism and Related Ideas in Antiquity.* Baltimore, MD: Johns Hopkins University Press, 1935.

Luker, Kristin. *Abortion and the Politics of Motherhood.* Berkeley, CA: University of California Press, 1985.

MacCulloch, Diarmaid. *Silence: A Christian History.* New York: Viking Press, 2014.

MacIntyre, Alasdair. *Three Rival Versions of Moral Inquiry: Encyclopedia, Genealogy and Tradition.* Notre Dame, IN: University of Notre Dame Press, 1991.

Macquarrie, John. *In Search of Deity.* London: SCM Press, 2012.

Matchar, Emily. "In Liberal Europe, Abortion Laws Come with their own Restrictions." *Atlantic Monthly*, August 5, 2013.

May, William. *The Physician's Covenant: Images of the Healer in Medical Ethics.* Louisville, KY: Westminster/John Knox Press, 2000.

McClory, Robert. *Turning Point.* New York: Crossroad, 1997.

Mead, Margaret. "Marriage in Two Steps." in *The Family in Search of a Future.* 75–84. Edited by Herbert Otto. New York: Appleton-Century Crofts, 1970.

Menninger, Karl. *Man Against Himself.* New York: Mariner, 1956.

Merton, Thomas. *Seeds of Destruction*. New York: Macmillan, 1964.

Miller, Patricia. *Good Catholics: The Battle over Abortion in the Catholic Church*. Berkeley, CA: University of California Press, 2014.

Moran, Gabriel. *Scripture and Tradition*. New York: Herder and Herder, 1963.

————. *Theology of Revelation*. New York: Herder and Herder, 1966.

Morwood, Michael. *It's Time: Challenges to the Doctrine of the Faith*. New York: Barnes and Noble, 2013.

Murray, Charles. *Losing Ground: America's Social Policy 1950–1980*. New York: Basic Books, 1984.

Nash, Roderick. *The Rights of Nature: A History of Environmental Ethics*. Madison, WI: University of Wisconsin Press, 1989.

National Conference of Catholic Bishops, Committee on Pastoral Research and Principles, *Principles to Guide Confessors in Questions of Homosexuality*. Washington, DC: U.S. Conference of Catholic Bishops, 1973.

————. *Human Sexuality: A Catholic Perspective for Education and Lifelong Learning*. Washington, DC: U.S. Conference of Catholic Bishops, 1991.

————. *Always Our Children*. Washington, DC: U.S. Conference of Catholic Bishops, 1997.

Niebuhr, Reinhold. *Moral Man and Immoral Society: A Study in Ethics and Politics*. New York: Charles Scribner's Sons, 1932.

Nock, A. D. *Conversion: The Old and the New in Religion from Alexander the Great to Augustine of Hippo*. New York: Oxford University Press, 1963.

Noonan, John. *Contraception: A History of its Treatment by Catholic Theologians and Canonists*. Cambridge, MA: Harvard University Press, 1966.

————. ed. *The Morality of Abortion: An Almost Absolute Value in History*. Cambridge, MA: Harvard University Press, 1970.

————. *A Church that Can Change and Cannot Change*. Notre Dame, IN: University of Notre Dame Press, 1993.

Nuland, Sherwin. *How We Die*. New York: Morrow, 1994.

Oakley, Francis. *The Conciliarist Tradition: Constitutionalism in the Catholic Church 1300–1870*. New York: Oxford University Press, 2008.

O'Brien, George Dennis. *The Church and Abortion: A Catholic Dissent*. Lanham, MD: Rowman and Littlefield, 2010.

Ovitt, George. *The Restoration of Perfection: Labor and Technology in Medieval Culture*. New Brunswick, NJ: Rutgers University Press, 1986.

Pitkin, Hanna. *Wittgenstein and Justice*. Berkeley CA: University of California Press, 1993.

Pope Francis, *Joy of the Gospel*. Rome: Vatican Press, 2013.

————. "Interview." *America*, September 30, 2013.

————. "Interview,. Corriere della Serra, March 4, 2014.

Pope Pius XII. *Casti Connubi*. Rome: Vatican Press, 1930.

————. "The Prolongation of Life." *The Pope Speaks* 4 (Spring, 1958): 315–316.

————. *Address to the International Congress of Hematology*, September 12, 1958.

Porter, Jean. "Does the Natural Law Provide a Universally Valid Morality?" in *Intractable Disputes about Natural Law*. Edited by Lawrence Cunningham, 54–96. Notre Dame, IN: University of Notre Dame Press, 2009.

Prusak, Bernard. "A Riskier Discourse." *Commonweal*," November 23, 2012.

Rachels, James. "Active and Passive Euthanasia," *New England Journal of Medicine*, 292(January 9, 1975): 78–80.

Rahner, Karl. "Faith of the Christian and the Doctrine of the Church," *Theological Investigations* Volume 14: 330–56. New York: Seabury Press.

————. "Basic Theological Interpretation of the Second Vatican Council." *Theological Investigation* Volume 20. New York: Crossroad, 1981: 77–89.

————. "Art against the Horizon of Theology and Piety." *Theological Investigations* Volume 23. New York: Crossroad, 1982.

Rivkin, Ellis. *The Shaping of Jewish History: A Radical New Interpretation*. New York: Charles Scribner's Sons, 1991.

Roberts, Jon. *Darwinism and the Divine in America: Protestant Intellectuals and Organic Revolution 1859–1900*. Notre Dame, IN: University of Notre Dame Press, 2001.

Rock, John. *The Time Has Come: A Catholic Doctor's Proposal to End the Battle over Birth Control*. New York: Avon Books, 1963.

Sharp, Gene. *From Dictatorship to Democracy: A Conceptual Framework for Liberation*. London: Merlin Press, 1993.

Singer, Peter. *Practical Ethics*. Cambridge: Cambridge University Press, 1993.

Smith, Christian and others. *Young Catholic America: Emerging Adults, In, Out of, and Gone from the Church*. New York: Oxford University Press, 2014.

Sorrell, Roger. *Saint Francis of Assisi and Nature*. New York: Oxford University Press, 1988.

Steinfels, Peter. *A People Adrift: The Crisis of the Roman Catholic Church in America*. New York: Simon and Schuster, 2004.

————. "Beyond the Stalemate: Forty Years after Roe." *Commonweal*, June 14, 2013: 12–18.

————. "Contraception and Honesty." *Commonweal*, June 1, 2015: 10–12.

Sullivan, Francis. *Magisterium*. Eugene, OR: Wipf and Stock, 1983.

Taylor, Frederick Winslow. *The Principles of Scientific Management*. Charlestown, SC: Create Space, 2013.

Temple, William. *Nature, Man and God: Being the Gifford Lectures*. New York: Macmillan, 1951.

Thompson, Augustine. *Francis of Assisi*. Ithaca, NY: Cornell University Press, 2013.

Tronto, Joan. *A Political Argument for an Ethic of Care*. New York: Routledge, 1993.

Turner, Denys. *Thomas Aquinas*. New Haven, CT: Yale University Press, 2013.

United Nations. *Universal Declaration of Human Rights*. New York, United Nations, 1948.

————. *Convention on the Elimination of all Forms of Discrimination against Women*. New York: United Nations, 1979.

————. *Convention on the Rights of the Child*. New York: United Nations, 1989.

————. *Declaration on the Elimination of Violence against Women*. New York: United Nations, 1993.

United States Conference of Catholic Bishops, *Human Sexuality: A Catholic Perspective for Education and Lifelong Learning*. Washington, DC: US Catholic Conference, 1990.

————. *Between Man and Woman: Questions and Answers about Marriage and Same-Sex Unions*. Washington, DC: US Catholic Conference, 2003.

————. *Ministry to Persons with a Homosexual Inclination: Guidelines for Pastoral Care*. Washington, DC: US Catholic Conference, 2006.

Vines, Matthew. *God and the Gay Christian: The Biblical Case in Support of Same Sex Relationships*. New York: Random House, 2014.

White, Lynn, Jr. "The Historical Roots of our Ecological Crisis," *Science* 155(March 10, 1967): 1203–07.

Williams, Rowan. "Embracing Our Limits: The Language of *Laudato Si.*" *Commonweal*, October 9, 2015: 13–15.

Wilson, Edward. *The Meaning of Human Existence*. New York: Liveright, 2014.

Zahn, Gordon. *Thomas Merton on Peace*. New York: McCall's, 1971.

About the Author

Gabriel Moran has worked in education and religious education for more than fifty years.

He has published twenty-five books and several hundred essays on issues of community, education, and religion. He has been an academic instructor since 1958 in high school, adult education, undergraduate colleges, and graduate schools. For the past thirty-five years he has taught at New York University, where he has chaired the program of religious education and also taught courses in the philosophy and history of education. In recent years, he has taught international ethics and in 2013 published *Uniquely Human: The Basis of Human Rights.*

Gabriel Moran has been especially interested in the Roman Catholic Church and the need for reforms in educational programs and some official teachings on moral issues. *Missed Opportunities: Rethinking Catholic Tradition* is his most comprehensive and compelling book on reform of the structure, language, and teaching of the Roman Catholic Church. He headed a large graduate program of religious education at Manhattan College and taught courses at two dozen Catholic universities. He often team-taught and coauthored books with his wife, Maria Harris, who was a prominent speaker and author on issues of spirituality, feminism, and the arts. Harris and Moran spoke at many venues in the United States and around the world in an effort to improve religious education. They worked together for forty years until her death in 2005.

Moran's contribution to rethinking Catholic tradition began with *Scripture and Tradition, Theology of Revelation,* and *Catechesis of*

Revelation, published at the time of the Second Vatican Council. He has continued to rethink those themes over the years, while broadening his concerns to the nature of teaching, the meaning of responsibility, and an ecumenical approach to religion. The hallmark of his writing has been an attentiveness to a careful use of language that opens new vistas on old questions. He lives in Manhattan and currently holds the title of Professor Emeritus of Educational Philosophy at New York University.

Index

A

abortion
changing context of practice of/
discussion of, 59–62
church's line of defense around, 53
and church's use of phrase right to
life, 8
invoking of natural law regarding
policies about, 9
as national problem, 54
need for national conversation
about, 57
possibility of compromise? 68–71
public discussions of as tangled in
confusion of language, 46
as representing moral failure, 54
Roman Catholic Church and,
63–68
survey of church members on topic
of, 14
abortion rights, use of phrase, 72
academic criticism, as language of
teaching, 38, 43
academic inquiry, 227, 229
adoption of children, church's attitude
toward gay couples adopting
children, 132
Africa, control of birth in, 50–51, 56

Akin, Todd, 72
alienable rights, 90
An Almost Absolute Value in History
(Noonan), 67
ALS (Lou Gehrig's disease), 98, 99
Always Our Children, 127
Amos 4:11, 123
Amour (movie), 98
Anderson, Ryan, 133
anima, 66
animal nature, 86, 207
animals
compared to humans regarding
engagement in art, religion,
science, and technology, 74
Hebrew Bible on, 78
human control of, 204
as open to world around them, 207
responsibility of, 171–172, 213
suffering of, 92, 207
teaching of, 33, 34
animatus, 66
annulment, 15
anthropocentrism, 208
anti-abortion laws, 60
anti-abortion movement, 63, 67, 69, 70
anti-Jewish outlook, of early church, 11
antislavery movement, 187, 191
apocalypse, 160

Are Parochial Schools the Answer?
    (Ryan), 218
Arendt, Hannah, 139, 180
Ariès, Philippe, 109
Aristotelian philosophy/
    Aristotelianism, 83
Aristotle, 67, 70, 78, 79–80, 168
artifice, use of, 45
artificial birth control, as redundant
    phrase, 47
artificial contraception, 54
artificial persons, 180–181, 183, 184
arts
    church's production of, 39, 43
    humans' use of, 45, 74
    role of, 42, 47, 86
assisted suicide, 88–89
Athenagoras, 66
Augustine of Hippo, 19, 66, 91, 140,
    147, 150, 157, 194, 222
autonomy, 90, 91

B

Bacevich, Andrew, 244n34
Bacon, Francis, 84, 192
baptism, 20, 23, 82
Barth, Karl, 10
Battin, Margaret Pabst, 90–91
Baude, William, 129
believe in, 157–158
believe that, 157–158
Bellow, Saul, 111
bereavement
    as necessity, 105
    process of, 111–112
    use of term, 105, 106
Bernard of Clairvaux, 194
Bernardin, Joseph, 63, 144
Berrigan, Daniel, 143, 144, 148, 149, 151
Berrigan, Philip, 148
Berry, Wendell, 213

Bible
    as attempt to use human words to
        convey both divine speaking
        and human responses, 164
    as book, 164
    as early stage of revelation/
        enlightenment, 156
    on environment, 203
    metaphor of speaking-answering
        in, 163
    and nonviolence, 136–139
    as not recognizing multiplicity of
        faiths, 157
    as one of two bases of church's
        official teaching on
        homosexuality, 119, 121–124
    as revelation of God, 161
    US Supreme Court ruling
        on reading of in state
        schools, 224
Bill of Rights (US), 89–90
biologist(s)
    Aristotle as, 79
    on meaning of life, 65
    view of humans by, 86
birth
    control of, 44, 47, 50–55
    as in need of artifice, 45
birth control
    artificial birth control, 47
    church as acknowledging need for
        but refusing to encourage more
        effective means to, 50, 51
    church theologians tying of to
        abortion, 53
    Laudato si as sidestepping issue of, 56
    Pope Paul VI's appointment
        of committee to advise on
        (1963), 52
    public discussions of as tangled in
        confusion of language, 46
birth control pill, 48, 51–52, 60

bishops
  as judges, 14
  birth control and, 53–55
  college of, 29
  called the hierarchy, 6, 21
  gap with priests, 27, with pope, 27
  on religious education, 214
  U.S. Conference of on
    homosexuality, 125–129, on
    peace, 143–144
  at Vatican II, 17–18
Blackmun, Henry, 62
Bloch, Ernst, 141
Burwell v. Hobby Lobby, 55, 180
Bush, George W., 137

C

cafeteria Catholics, 53
Cain and Able story, 245n6
Calvin, John, 222
Camus, Albert, 93
Canticle of Creatures (Francis of
  Assisi), 205
capital punishment, 8
care
  as central to development of ethics,
    91–92
  key moral principle in support of, 92
casuistry, 67
Catechesis of Revelation (Moran),
  155, 156
Catechism of the Catholic Church, on
  use of pain killers, 95
Catholic, use of term, 1
catholic, use of term, 2
Catholic education, 217, 218
Catholic school system, 215, 218
Catholic tradition
  on abortion, 67
  central role of in evolution of
    natural rights, 186, 192–196

on control of dying, 48
double effect as principle of, 99–100
as endlessly fascinating storehouse
    for intelligence, imagination,
    and playful possibilities,
    162, 169
good as mixed with bad, 104
as having good record of concern
    for vulnerable human
    beings, 72
human rights and, 186–198
on humans acting in accord with
    their nature, 120
as including last five centuries of
    Roman Catholic Church and
    Christian centuries before
    then, 1
Jewish influence on, 11
long and rich history of education
    in, 231
on mourning, 115–116
nature and, 76–77
and passive resistance, 136–151
as on side of protecting human
    beings against intrusions of
    technology that are violent, 55
tension between condemnation
    of and grappling with reality
    of force, violence, and war
    in, 136
tension between human and
    nature in, 45
Catholic Worker, 145
Catholic Worker movement, 144–145
catholicity, 1, 2
Catholic-Protestant-Jewish
    understanding, 226
CCD (Confraternity of Christian
    Doctrine), 217, 218
The Challenge of Peace (US bishops),
    143–144

change
    occurrence of in big
       institutions, 28
    pace of and opportunity for, 14
Chenu, M. D., 26
children
    adoption of by gay couples, 132
    impact of parent's suicide on when
       children not told truth, 115
    as promise of the future, 185
    teaching of, 32–35
China, religion in, 190, 231
Christ. *See also* Jesus
    as both Word of God and word of
       man, 166
    Christian movement as beginning
       from belief in death-
       resurrection of, 81
    as freeing Christians from law, 193
    good news about, 41
    as liberating believer from burden
       of law, 193
    paradox of, 166
    person of Jesus as, 11, 163
    Word of God as taking human
       form through, 165
Christian Education, 217
Christian faith, use of term, 157
Christian love, 139
Christian movement
    as attempt to deal with death by
       accepting it and going beyond
       it, 103
    beginning of, 11, 81
    as central to human awareness of
       its distinctiveness, 201
    depending on Old Testament of, 193
    influence of pagan on, 76
    as in large part responsible for
       invention of the book, 164
    life-death-resurrection of Jesus as
       central narrative of, 19, 103,
       136–137

Christian religion, 160, 164, 201,
    222–223, 226
Christian revelation, 9, 159–160, 161, 162
Christianists, 230
Christianity
    as developing language of
       supernatural, 76, 83
    great tragedy of, 11
Christian-Jewish relations/dialogue, 12,
    166, 226–227
Christian-Jewish-Muslim relations/
    conversations, 166, 226
chronic suicide, 97
church communities, 168
church doctrines, sources of, 7–12
church history, purpose of course on,
    43, 225
church reform
    conservative-liberal reform of
       Roman Catholic Church,
       25–30
    reforming tradition, 23–25
    Second Vatican Council as step in,
       17–18
    unfinished work of Vatican II,
       18–23
church teaching, definition, 38
*A Church that Can Change and Cannot
    Change* (Noonan), 159
church-state language, 223–224
Cicero, 78, 192, 222
*Citizens United v. Federal Elections
    Commission*, 180
classrooms, 32, 38, 43, 221, 224, 227.
    See also schools
Clement of Alexandria, 140
clerical sex scandal, impact of, 169
Code of Canon Law, 66
comfort. *See* mourn/comfort
Commonweal, 135
community, use of term, 168

community of speaking and listening, as form of the church, 153, 167–169

conception, definition, 64

condoms, use of, 51

confessing/forgiving, as language of teaching, 37, 40

Confraternity of Christian Doctrine (CCD), 217, 218

Confucius, 111

Congar, Yves, 22, 26

Congregation for the Doctrine of the Faith, 124–125, 135, 158

conscience, 82, 147, 172

conservative/conservatism, use of term, 25

consistent ethic of life, 63, 144

Consistent Life, 63

Constitution on Divine Revelation, 160, 161

continuing revelation, 156

contra naturam (contradiction of nature), 120

contraception
    abortion as fallback position on, 63–64
    improvements in devices for, 61
    public discussions of as tangled in confusion of language, 46
    Santorum speaking of, 54
    survey of church members on topic of, 14

Convention on the Rights of the Child (1989) (UN), 132

conversational, as one of three families of teaching languages, 37–38, 42–43

corporation
    as connection to future, 184
    definition, 180
    as legal person, 71, 180
    religious liberty of, 55, 180

Coughlin, Father, 145

Council of Florence, 29

Council of Trent, 18, 130, 152, 154, 167

Covenants on Human Rights (1966) (UN), 219

Crowley, Patricia, 52

Cruzan, Nancy, 240n13

Cyprian, 140

D

Daniélou, Jean, 26

Day, Dorothy, 143, 144–146, 147, 149, 151

De Lubac, Henri, 26

death and dying movement, 74

death penalty, 8

death/dying
    allowing to occur, 97–102
    of a child, 112
    control of, 44, 48–50
    education about, 107–108
    hastening of, 95–97
    as natural, 74
    as in need of artifice, 45
    public discussions of as shrouded in bad arguments and secret practices, 46
    role of church in discussion of, 89
    spiritual suffering as playing central in experiences of, 93
    stages of, 113, 114
    unnatural prolongation of, 49

debate, as language of teaching, 38

Declaration of Independence (US), 89, 90, 191

Declaration of Sentiments (Seneca Falls women's convention 1848), 188

Declaration of the Rights of Man and of the Citizen (France), 90, 191

Declaration on Procured Abortion, 66, 67

Dei Verbum, 155, 156

dementia, 97, 98, 99, 114
denial
    child's death as denial of what we
        assume are ways of God or
        nature, 112
    of death/dying, 96, 115
    in grieving, 115
Dewey, John, 235n2
dialogue
    Christian-Jewish relations/
        dialogue, 12, 166, 226–227
    Christian-Jewish-Muslim relations/
        conversations, 166, 226
    divine-human dialogue, 166
    interfaith dialogue, 157
    interreligious dialogue, 157,
        162, 226
    intra-church dialogue, 12
    use of term, 166
Didache, 66
"Dies Irae" (hymn), 104
Dionysius, 234n6
disaster relief, as sacramental
    practice, 169
disproportionate means (in use of
    medical interventions), 48
divine revelation
    conception of, 9–10
    finding the question, 153–156
    overview, 152–169
divine speaking, human answering,
    164–167
divine-human dialogue, 166
divine-human relation, 153, 158, 162
divorce
    church's coming to grips with, 15
    survey of church members on topic
        of, 14
do violence to no one, 45, 56, 92,
    97–98, 197, 207
Dobzhansky, Theodosius, 207

doctrine
    equating of teaching with, 31
    gap between doctrine and
        practice, 27
    sources of church doctrines, 7–12
"Dogmatic Constitution on Divine
    Revelation" (Dei Verbum), 156
"The Dogmatic Constitution on the
    Church" (Lumen Gentium), 18
Dolan, Timothy, 7
double effect, 100
Douglas, William, 62
Douglass, Frederick, 187
dramatic performance, as language of
    teaching, 37–38, 42–43
Duprey, Pierre, 13
dying. *See* death/dying
dying with dignity, use of phrase, 101

E

Eckhart, Meister, 141
education. *See also* Catholic education;
    Christian Education; parish
    education; religious education
    ambiguity of term, 220–222
    as distinct from school, 220
    meaning of as in flux, 215
educational forms/institutions
    family, 217, 220–221, 228
    leisure, 221, 222
    school, 221, 222
    work, 221, 222
end of the world, 160. *See also*
    apocalypse
end-of-life issues/decisions, 48, 88, 91,
    101, 103
enlightenment
    as subordinate to metaphor
        of speaking-answering in
        Bible, 163
    as work of sciences, 162

Enovid, 48
ensoulment, 67
environment, humans and their
environment, 208–211
environmental movement, 199, 200,
202–206
environmentalism
Catholicism and, 199–213
ethics for men, women, and their
kin, 211–213
humanly unique, 206–208
humans and their environment,
208–211
Laudato si as placing church on
side of, 200
Epicetus, 81
equality
economic inequality, 56
gender equality, 204
of human rights, 188
lack of for women, 4, 132
marriage equality, use of term,
129, 131
racial equality, 202
of species, 207
Erasmus, Desiderius, 141
Erigena, 207
ethics
care as central to development of,
91–92
for men, women, and their kin,
211–213
Eucharist, 39, 82
eulogy, 113
European Commission, on religious
education, 220
euthanasia, 50, 99, 101–102, 198
Evangelical Protestants
as opposing abortion, 62
reaction of to US Supreme Court
ruling on prayer and reading
the Bible, 224

execution of prisoners, by state, 8
extramarital sex, survey of church
members on topic of, 14

F

faith
as one of two categories shaping
church's life and its authority
pattern, 153
revelation and, 156–163
use of term, 157
the faithful, use of term, 6, 21–22
family. *See also* Synod on the Family
as educational form/institution,
217, 220–221, 228
government support of, 132
importance of in religious
education, 222
natural family planning, 56
family marriage, 132
Federal Drug Administration, 51
feeding tube, removal of, 101
fertilization, definition, 64
final judgment/last judgment, 65, 94, 158
First Amendment (US
Constitution), 223
First Letter to the Thessalonians, 41
First Vatican Council, 152, 167. *See also*
Vatican I
flat hierarchy, use of term, 20–21, 30
force-feeding, 101
forgiveness, 37, 40, 139, 180, 182
Francis of Assisi, 163, 194, 197, 204–206
Franciscan movement, 194
Frankl, Victor, 164
freedom
as consisting in ability to say
no, 177
as dependent on attentiveness and
reflection, 173
personal freedom, 106
religious freedom, 13

Freud, Sigmund, 84, 103, 106
funeral industry, 107
funeral liturgy, 40, 104
funeral rites/rituals, 104, 112, 113
funeral service, 111
funerals, on television, 108

G

Gandhi, Mahatma, 137, 139
gay marriage, 7, 133, 135
gay rights movement, 119, 124, 126, 202
gay sex, 133
gay unions, 69
gay(s)
    adoption of children by, 132
    author's puzzlement on eagerness
      of to marry, 131
    compassion for, 127, 128
    emergence of, 117, 119, 120
    Pope Francis's answer to question
      about gay people, 14, 134
    testimony of, 119, 120, 190
    use of term, 118
Genesis, 163, 190, 204
Genesis 1:28, 203
Genesis 19, 123
Genesis II, 178
Geneva Conventions, 150
glasnost, moves of Pope Francis as
    compared to, 12
God speaks, as central metaphor
    of biblical and Qur'anic
    traditions, 164
God Still Speaks (Moran), 156
Goldberg, Arthur, 224
good news as basic story, 41
Good Samaritan
    law, 176
    parable of, 174
Gorbachev, Mikhail, 12
Gorer, Geoffrey, 105, 107

Gramick, Jeanine, 133–134
grandparents, as teachers, 35
Gratian, 195
Greeley, Andrew, 218
grief
    healthy attitude toward, 103–116
    morbid grief, 115
    use of term, 105
grief industry, 107
Griffiths, Paul, 69
Guardini, Romano, 26
Gumbleton, Thomas, 127, 143

H

Handy, Robert, 149
Hardwig, John, 239–240n1
Häring, Bernard, 52
Hebrew Bible, 78–79, 174. *See also* Old
    Testament
hierarchical structure, 20, 21
hierarchy
    flat hierarchy, use of term, 20–21, 30
    the hierarchy, use of term, 6, 21, 27
"The Historical Roots of our Ecological
    Crisis" (White), 200
Holocaust museum (Washington, DC),
    109–110
Holy Communion, for divorced and
    remarried Catholics, 15
homosexual
    as adjective, 118
    as noun, 117, 134
    origin of term, 118
homosexual acts, Vatican's 1975
    condemnation of, 64
homosexual behavior, use of term, 121
homosexual inclination, 127
homosexual orientation, 117–135
homosexuality
    bases of church's official teaching
      on, 119–124

Bible as having nothing to say
about, 122
as example of assumptions about
human-nature that needed to
be reconsidered based on new
information, 120
lack of language to address
question of, 118
as part of human-nature, 190
Roman Catholic Church
documents on, 124–128
survey of church members on topic
of, 14
Synod on the Family's discussion
of, 15
Synod on the Family's impact on
church's attitude on, 134
homosexually oriented
Kinsey's findings on, 121
origin of term, 118
Hoover, J. Edgar, 149
hospice movement, 49, 101
How We Die (Nuland), 74
human beings
artificial as help to, 45
Catholic tradition as having
good record of concern for
vulnerable human beings, 72
Catholic tradition as on side
of protecting of against
intrusions of technology that
are violent, 55
Christian tradition as implying of
as center of animal kingdom/
world of wondrous things, 211
coming into existence of, 64–65,
67, 68, 69
description of, 207
forgiveness as starting with, 139
as grieving animals, 103
as having rights, 190, 192, 195

as making distinctions between
different kinds of life, 46
nature as foundation of, 77
as not autonomous, 171
not having free will as usually
imagined, 173
as outsider to natural world of
other living beings, 79
Pope Francis's referral to as
unique, 206
recognition of women as, 188
as responsible for their actions, 82,
170, 171, 172
slaves as, 70–71
specialness of, 71
suffering of, 92
teaching/learning as fundamental
act of, 31, 33, 34, 36
human birth, control of, 44. *See also*
birth, control of; birth control;
birth control pill
human community, concept of, 190
human death
control of, 44
as historical, social, artistic,
religious, and artificial, 49
as not natural, 74, 86–87
human rights
and Catholic tradition, 186–198
definition, 192
interest of international lawyers in,
189–190
literature on as heavily
sermonic, 189
movement for, 188
origin of term, 187–188
relation of to environmental
concerns, 199
as transnational, 190
use of term, 188
human rights movement, 199

human sexuality
    church's view of, 47
    as historical, imaginative, artistic, ethical, and religious, 51
    as integral to power relations, 117
Human Sexuality: A Catholic Perspective for Education and Lifelong Learning, 127
human uniqueness, 207, 211, 212
Humanae Vitae, 53, 56, 63
humanity, concept of, 190
humanly unique, 206–208
human-nature, 45, 74, 79, 80, 82, 86, 87, 120, 192, 201, 212
humans, and their environment, 208–211
The Human Condition (Arendt), 139

I

inalienable rights, 90, 195, 196, 197
individual, definition, 179
individual rights, 197
indoctrination, 43
infants, teaching of, 32–35
Institutes of Christian Religion (Calvin), 222
institutional church, use of phrase, 5
interfaith dialogue, 157
Internet, effect of on way death is publicly acknowledged and dead are remembered, 41
interreligious dialogue, 157, 162, 226
intra-church dialogue, 12
inventions, possible drawbacks of, 45–46
Ireland, legalization of same-sex marriage, 118, 128
"Is Polygamy Next?" (Baude), 129
Islamists/Islam, 12, 230. *See also* Muslims

J

Jefferson, Thomas, 90, 191, 196, 216, 223
Jerome, 66
Jesus. *See also* Christ
    church as trying to reset center of morality around life and teaching of, 121
    as discoverer of role of forgiveness, 139
    Francis of Assisi as attempting to live according to example of, 205–206
    Jewish scholars as helpful in explaining core teachings of, 137
    on peace and nonviolence, 137–138, 150
    relation of to God, 71, 166
    resurrection of, 19, 81
    suffering of, 94, 104
Jewish religion. *See* Judaism
Jewish-Christian conversation, 12
Judaism
    Christianity's Jewish roots, 11
    Christianity's repudiation of Jewish tradition, 11
    on environment, 204
    on God speaking, 174
    influence of on Catholic tradition, 11
    on resurrection, 103–104
    rituals of around death, 105, 110
    scholars of as helpful in explaining core teachings of Jesus, 137
    sense of what a human being is, 170
    understanding Christianity as implying a background understanding of, 226
Judeo-Christian, use of term, 203

Judeo-Christian tradition, as seen
    as enemy for environmental
    movement, 202–203
judgment
    church's acceptance of judgment of
        science, 65
    final judgment/last judgment, 65,
        94, 158
    of moral guilt, 172
    sense of as necessary element for
        responsibility, 170
Jungmann, Josef, 26
just war theory, 140, 141, 142, 143, 147
Justin Martyr, 140

K

Kant, Immanuel, 190
Kasper, Walter, 14
Kennedy, Anthony, 130
Kennedy, John, national mourning
    for, 108
Kennedy, Robert, national mourning
    for, 108
Kierkegaard, Soren, 166
King, Martin Luther, Jr., 108, 137, 139,
    143, 147
Kinsey, Alfred, 120–121
Kohut, Andrew, 57
Kübler-Ross, Elisabeth, 74, 75, 87, 112–114
Küng, Hans, 240n10
Kushner, Harold, 110

L

the laity, use of term, 21, 22, 27
language
    public discussions about
        contraception, abortion, and
        birth control as entangled in
        confusion of, 46
    of Roman Catholic Church, 4–7,
        23, 28

of teaching, 35–38
    in which practice called abortion is
        discussed, 58–59
Latourelle, René, 154
Laudato si, 56, 163, 178, 200, 204, 205
laws. *See also* natural law
    allowing suicide, 101
    anti-abortion laws, 60
    Code of Canon Law, 66
    Good Samaritan law, 176
    of nature, use of term, 82, 212
    revealed law/revealed truths, 9
lay ecclesial ministry, use of term, 6
lecturing, as language of teaching,
    36, 43
lesbian marriage, 135
lesbians
    adoption of children by, 132
    compassion for, 127, 128
    emergence of, 117–118
    testimony of, 119, 120, 190
Leviticus 18:22, 122
Leviticus 19:18, 139
Leviticus 19:20, 122
Leviticus 20:13, 122
Lewis, C. S., 85
LGBT community, 118
liberal/liberalism, use of term, 25
life. *See also* end-of-life issues/decisions
    beginning of human life, 46
    consistent ethic of life, 63, 144
    Consistent Life, 63
    right to, 8
    rule of, 194
Lin, Maya, 109
Lindemann, Erich, 115
liturgical assemblies, 39
liturgical community, 30, 168
liturgy
    description of, 165
    funeral liturgy, 40, 104
    as teacher, 42

living will, 75
Locke, John, 196
Lou Gehrig's disease (ALS), 98, 99
love
    Christian love, 139
    same-sex love, 120, 122, 124, 128
Luther, Martin, 158

M

magisterium, use of term, 5–6
the Magisterium, use of term, 6
Man's Search for Meaning (Frankl), 164
Marcus Aurelius, 81
marriage
    as about a man's property, 129
    Catholic ideal of mutual
        covenant, 130
    church's view on two ends of, 52,
        130, 132
    family marriage, 132
    gay marriage, 7, 133, 135
    idea of church rethinking of, 15
    kinds of, 130, 132
    lesbian marriage, 135
    partnership marriage, 132
    same-sex marriage. *See* same-sex
        marriage
    use of term, 131
marriage equality, use of term, 129, 131
Marx, Karl, 196
Marx, Reinhard, 14
mass shootings, and public
    mourning, 108
masturbation, church's view of, 64, 124
Matthew 25, 94
Matthew 25:31–46, 158
Maurin, Peter, 144
Maximos IV Saigh, 52
Mead, Margaret, 130
The Meaning of Human Existence
    (Wilson), 210

medical interventions, 48
medicine, modern era of, 88
memorials
    after September 11, 2001, 109
    Vietnam memorial (Washington,
        DC), 109
Menninger, Karl, 97
mercy killing, 101
Merton, Thomas, 144, 146–148, 149, 151
military policies, United States
    Catholic Conference on, 143
ministerial priesthood, use of term, 6
*Ministry to Persons with a Homosexual
    Inclination: Guidelines for Pastoral
    Care*, 127
Mitchell, John, 149
monasticism, 193–194
Montessori, Maria, 235n5
moral guilt, judgment of, 172
moral instruction, 41
Moral Man and Immoral Society
    (Niebuhr), 138
moral responsibility, 171–172, 185
Moran, Gabriel
    Catechesis of Revelation, 155, 156
    God Still Speaks, 156
    Theology of Revelation, 155, 156
morbid grief, 115
morphine, 76
Moses, 24
mourn/comfort
    as one of three families of teaching
        languages, 37, 40–41
    as reciprocal actions, 110
mourning
    healthy attitude toward, 103–116
    personal/communal mourning, 110
    public mourning, 106–110
    stages of, 112–116
    use of term, 105–106
Müller, Gerhard, 234n8

Muslims, 10, 40, 137, 157, 162, 164, 166, 223, 226, 228. *See also* Islamists/Islam

mystery
    human problems referred to as in Christian tradition, 165
    use of term to describe the church, 19, 21

mysticism, 141

N

natural death, 75–76

Natural Death Act (California, 1976), 75

natural family planning, 56

natural law
    Christian view of, 195
    description of, 83
    no agreement on, 86
    as one of two bases of church's official teaching on homosexuality, 120
    as source of church doctrines, 7–9
    as support for Catholic moral teachings, 76
    Thomas's treatment of, 8
    use of term, 76, 193, 197, 198, 212

natural persons, 71, 180, 181, 184

natural revelation, as work of sciences, 162

natural rights
    central role of Catholic tradition in evolution of, 186, 192–196
    concept of, 191–192
    seventeenth to twenty-first centuries' perspective on, 196–198

natural world, Christian attitude toward, 81–85

nature
    according to Christianity, 201
    call for man to conquer, 202, 209
    and Catholic tradition, 76–77
    as contrasted with artifice, 45, 46, 47
    history of, 77–81
    meaning of, 45, 46
    use of term, 77, 178, 193

neighbor, love of, 121, 122, 139, 174

Neoplatonism, 82, 83

Netherlands, laws allowing suicide in, 101

New England Journal of Medicine, 99

New Testament
    on end of the world, 160
    final judgment, 94, 158
    Roman Catholic protest as rooted in teaching of, 136
    as written in spoken Greek of the time, 164

New Ways Ministry, 133

New York Times, 132–133

Newman, John Henry, 22

Niebuhr, Reinhold, 138, 151

Nietzsche, Friedrich, 139

nonviolence
    Bible and, 136–139
    individual leaders and, 144–151
    postbiblical tradition and, 139–141
    in the twentieth century, 142–144

Noonan, John, 67, 159

nuclear weapons, 142, 143

Nugent, Robert, 133–134

Nuland, Sherwin, 74

nursing homes, 88, 90, 95, 97, 102, 114

O

Obama, Barack, 138, 230

Obama administration, insurance coverage for contraceptives, 54–55

Old Testament, 193. *See also* Hebrew Bible; *specific books of*

On Death and Dying (Kübler-Ross), 75, 112

On the Pastoral Care of Homosexual Persons, 125–126

On True Religion (Augustine), 222
1 Corinthians 6:9, 123
1 Corinthians 11:14, 123
1 Timothy 1:10, 123
ordinary means, contrasted with
    extraordinary means (in service of
    life), 48
ordination of women, 4
Orentlicher, Diane, 186
Origen, 140
Orthodox Jews, handling of mourning
    by, 105
orthodoxy, 10, 43, 53, 72, 158, 200,
    202, 224, 227
ortho-praxis, 158
Ottaviani, Alfredo, 53

P

Pacem in Terris (*Peace on Earth*), 142
pacifists/pacifism, 142, 147, 149
pain
    as inevitable, 94
    life as unfair in doling out of,
        94–95
    suffering as distinct from, 92
    treatment for, 95
    as useful, 93
Paneloux (fictional character in *The
    Plague*), 93
paradox, of Son of God, Son of
    Man, 166
parents, 220
    mourning of, 112
    as preaching, 36
    as providing example of mourning
        to their children, 108, 112
    as relinquishing responsibility for
        child's actions as child gets
        older, 184
    on responsible parenting, 56
    as teachers, 32, 34
parish education, 217

partnership marriage, 132
passive resistance, Catholic tradition
    and, 136–151. *See also* nonviolence
Paul, Saint, 79, 122–123, 137, 193
Pax Christi USA, 149–150
peace, Jesus on, 137–138, 150
peace activists, 143, 146, 148. *See also*
    Berrigan, Daniel; Day, Dorothy;
    Merton, Thomas
peace movement, 146, 148, 149, 202
Peace Protests (Erasmus), 141
people of God, use of phrase, 19–20, 21
personal-communal existence, 65
personhood amendments, 71
persons
    artificial persons, 180–181, 183, 184
    natural persons, 71, 180, 181, 184
Pew Research Poll, 118
Pharisees, 24
the pill, 48. *See also* birth control pill
The Plague (Camus), 93
Plato, 79, 103, 190
politics, church as involved in, 9
Pollitt, Katha, 72
pope. *See also specific popes*
    as needing to be both liberal and
        conservative in approach to
        reform, 26
    as occupying outsized role in
        governing of the church, 28
Pope Benedict XVI, on church's two
    proofs, 39
Pope Francis
    on abortion, 63
    address of to US Congress, 8,
        132, 144
    as advocate of world peace, 150
    answer of to question about gay
        people, 14, 134
    appointment of body of cardinals
        to aid him in governance, 29

as changing tone of language
spoken at the top, 13
on church teaching, 39
on church's obsession with
abortion, 73
on clerical abuse scandal, 182
first major document of, 3
kinship of with Francis of
Assisi, 205
Laudato si, 56, 163, 178, 200,
204, 205
moves of as compared to
glasnost, 12
reference of to human being as
unique, 206
references of to homosexuality, 134
slip of the tongue, 55
use of term "Judeo-Christian
tradition," 203
Pope Innocent III, agreement of that
abortion is not homicide until
fetus is formed, 66
Pope John Paul II
Pope Francis's quotation from, 163
Veritatis Splendor, 233n1
Pope John XXIII
ecumenical council 1959, 152
plea for peace, 142
Pope Paul VI, 53
appointment of committee to
advise on issue of birth
control, 52
Humanae Vitae, 53, 56, 63
intervention of regarding *The
Sources of Revelation*, 154
on issues not resolved by Second
Vatican Council, 167
Pope Pius XII
approval of use of Enovid in 1958, 48
on preventing death in instances
where there is no hope of
recovery, 49–50

publication of documents
published in 1958 by, 47–48
Potvin, Colette, 52
Practical Ethics (Singer), 211
practice, gap between doctrine and, 27
preaching, as language of teaching, 36,
42, 43
pregnancy
church's insistence on respect
for, 69
control of, 47
Prejean, Helen, 63
priests
confession and, 40
gap with laity, 27, with bishop, 27
humans as of creation, 208
place of, 4
responsibility for scandals, 182
sermons by, 217
temporary, 23
valid marriage before, 130
women as, 4
prisoners, state execution of, 8
Pro: Reclaiming Abortion Rights (Pollitt), 72
progressive, 1, 24
pro-life, versus pro-choice, 46, 57, 59
property
ambiguities in meaning of, 195–196
debate over as right of human-
nature or result of sin, 195
Francis of Assisi as renouncing
ownership of, 194
French declaration as including of
as natural right, 196
individual rights as concerned with
acquisition of, 197
marriage as about a man's
property, 129
as natural right of man according
to Locke, 196
need to limit individual's
ownership of, 196

proportionate means (in use of medical interventions), 48

Protestant
    and Catholic discussion of relation between scripture and tradition, 153–154
    Catholic-Protestant-Jewish understanding, 226
    Christian Education course, 217
    Evangelical Protestants, 62, 224
    split between Protestant and Roman Catholic Churches, 12

Q

Questiones Disputatae, 154
Quinlan, Karen, 240–241n14
Qur'an, 157, 164

R

Rachels, James, 99
Rahner, Karl, 10, 26, 161
Ratzinger, Joseph, 154, 157
Rehnquist, William, 249n10
religion. *See also* Christian religion; Christianity; Islamists/Islam; Judaism; Muslims; Protestant; Roman Catholic Church; Unitarians
    in China, 190, 231
    origin of term, 222
    two meanings of, 222–224
    understanding of, as one of two parts of religious education, 224–227
religious community, forms of, 30
religious education
    as academic field, 11
    Catholic school system, 215, 218
    deficiency and confusion about what constitutes, 215
    in England and Wales, 218–219

in European Union, 220
    origin of term, 216, 218
    religious education movement, 216–220
    two parts of, 224–229
Religious Education Association, 216, 219
religious freedom, 13
religious liberty, 54, 55
religious practice, as one of two parts of religious education, 227–229
religious studies, 10, 225
religious tolerance, 223
reproductive rights, use of phrase, 72
respect
    among religions, 40
    church's insistence on respect for pregnancy, 69
    description of, 211
    for dignity of persons with homosexual tendency, 128
    for gay people, 131
    for life, 73
    for nature, 202
    for outsiders to liturgical assemblies, 39
    of the past, 26, 129, 132
    for patient's wishes, 92, 95
    for the person, 197, 198, 207, 208
    for the play of the mind, 227
    for world of physical beings and power of human intelligence, 201
respirator, use of with dying person, 100–101
responsibility
    connections of to future, 184
    idea of, 170
    moral responsibility, 171–172
    as personal/corporate, 179–182
    and time, 182–185
    use of term, 170–171, 178
responsible, origin of term, 170

responsible for, 82, 140, 170, 171, 172–179, 181, 182, 183, 184, 185, 213
"Responsible Parenthood," 52
responsible to, 172–179, 183, 184, 213
resurrection
    Christian movement and, 19, 103, 136–137
    church idea of, 103–104
    of Jesus, 19, 81
    Judaism on, 103–104
retirement, of bishops and popes, 29
revealed law/revealed truths, as source of church doctrines, 9
revelation
    Christian revelation, 9, 159–160, 161, 162
    continuing revelation, 156
    divine revelation, 9–10, 152–169
    and faith, 156–163
    guidelines for religious use of, 158
    natural revelation, 162
    as not a prominent term in the Bible, 160
    as one of two categories shaping church's life and its authority pattern, 153
    as present activity of God, 161
    as source of church doctrines, 7, 9
    special revelation, 162
    as subordinate to metaphor of speaking-answering in Bible, 163
    use of term, 10, 153, 157, 158–159, 163, 165
Revelation, book of, 160
rhetorical, as one of three families of teaching languages, 36, 39, 41–42, 43
rhythm method, 50, 51
Rieux (fictional character in *The Plague*), 93

rights. *See also* human rights
    abortion rights, 72
    alienable rights, 90
    definition, 188–189
    gay rights movement, 124
    of humanity, 190
    inalienable rights, 90, 195, 196, 197
    individual rights, 197
    medieval discussion of, 90
    natural rights, 186, 191–198
    reproductive rights, 72
    right to die, 89–92
    right to life, 8
ritual
    of accepting responsibility, 177–178
    of community life, 107
    of confessing-forgiving, 37, 40
    of death, burial, and bereavement, 40, 103, 104, 106, 110, 112, 115
    denying value of, 41
    formulas of religious rituals, 110
    getting rid of dead rituals, 42
    importance of, 229
    on television and of television, 108
Rivkin, Ellis, 193
Rock, John, 51
Roe v. Wade, 53, 61–62
Roman Catholic Church
    danger in obsession with narrow range of moral issues, 12
    great strength of, 13
    language of, 4–7, 23, 28
    mission of, 2
    as not a democracy, 4
    split between Protestant and Roman Catholic Churches, 12
    structure of, 4
Romans 1:26–27, 122
Romans 11:24, 123

Roosevelt, Eleanor, 230
rule, use of term in monastic
   history, 194
rule of life, as basic rule, 194
Ryan, Mary Perkins, 218

S

sacraments, 11, 16, 26, 40, 81–82, 148,
   155, 167, 169, 192, 193
sacrifice, metaphor of, 94
Samaritan's Gift for Females, 60
same-sex love, 120, 122, 124, 128
same-sex marriage
   attitudes toward, 118
   church's attitude toward, 131, 135
   Griffiths's advocating for church
      acceptance of, 69
   legalization of, 118, 128–129, 131
   as option for gay and lesbian
      people, 128
Santorum, Rick, 54
Schiavo, Terry, 240–241n14
schools. See also classrooms; education;
   educational forms/institutions;
   religious education; teachers
   Catholic school system, 215, 218
   Sunday school teaching, 217
science
   acceptance of judgment of, 65
   beginning of modern science, 83, 201
   church should not try to compete
      with in enlightenment or
      revelation, 165
   enlightenment and natural
      revelation as work of, 162
   opponents of abortion as calling
      upon, 64
   role of, 165
   on sexual orientation, 120
   use of for supporting the
      beginning of human life, 44

Second Amendment (US
   Constitution), 90
Second Vatican Council. See also
   Vatican II
   condemnation of total war by,
      143, 147
   document on revelation by, 10
   on ethics of war, 142–143
   issues that could not be resolved
      by, 167
   preparation for, 152
   promise of, 2–3
   shift in tone of funeral liturgy, 104
   as start of long period of church
      upheaval, 153
   as step in church reform, 17
   struggle of with how to balance
      papal and episcopal
      authority, 29
Seneca Falls women's convention
   (1848), 187–188
September 11, 2001, national mourning
   for, 109
Sermon on the Mount, 137–138, 150
sexual activity. See also human sexuality
   church's view of, 53
   Roman Catholic Church as
      falling short in assimilating
      knowledge of and accepting
      diversity of practices, 86
sexual orientation, use of term, 126–
   127, 135
sexual pleasure
   church's view of, 47
   as important part of life, 51
sexual revolution, 130
sickness, role of church in discussion
   of, 89
Singer, Peter, 206, 211
slavery, 70, 159, 183, 190, 191, 212. See
   also antislavery movement

Socrates, 79
sodomy, origin and use of term, 123
soul
    according to Socrates, 79
    anima, 66
    anti-abortion literature as not
        saying much about, 65
    infusion of, 66–67
    protection of from disorderly
        inclinations of the body, 82
    shift of emphasis from, 65
The Sources of Revelation/"Sources of
    Revelation," 18, 154
special revelation, 162
spiritual suffering, 92–93, 97
stages
    of dying, 113, 114
    of mourning, 112–116
state execution of prisoners, 8, 44
Statement on Central America (US
    bishops), 143
Steinfels, Peter, 69–70
Stoics/Stoicism, 80–81, 82, 84, 192,
    193, 200–201
storytelling, as language of teaching,
    36, 41, 43
structural gap, 27–28
structural reform, 24
Suenens, Leo Joseph, 52
suffering
    of animals, 92, 207
    as distinct from pain, 92
    of human beings, 92
    of Jesus, 94, 104
    spiritual suffering, 92–93, 97
suicide
    assisted suicide, 88–89
    chronic suicide, 97
    impact of parent's suicide on
        children who have been lied to
        about parent's death, 115
    laws allowing, 101

Sunday school teaching, 217
supernatural
    language of, 76
    as work of Christian churches, 162
Synod on the Family (2014), 14–16, 27,
    56, 132, 134–135

T

teachers
    anything as potential teacher, 33
    congregations as, 39
    grandparents as, 35
    of how to die, 35, 37
    liturgy as, 42
    parents as, 32, 34, 220
    as preachers, 36
    of religious practice, 228–229
    schoolteachers, 32, 64, 222
teaching
    equating of with doctrine, 31
    how the Roman Catholic Church
        teaches, 38–43
    of infants/children, 32–35
    languages of, 35–38
    paucity of writing on meaning of
        verb to teach, 32
    use of term, 31
technology, protections against
    intrusions of, 55
temporary priesthood, 23
Tertullian, 66
Théologie de la Révélation
    (Latourelle), 154
theology
    church doctrine as protected by, 10
    use of term, 225
Theology of Revelation (Moran), 155, 156
therapeutic, as one of three families
    of teaching languages, 36–37,
    39–41, 43
Third Vatican Council, 3

Thomas Aquinas, 5, 8, 66–67, 71, 83, 140, 160, 194–195, 197, 198, 222
time
    image of, 3, 184
    responsibility and, 182–185
Torah, 193
total war, Second Vatican Council condemnation of, 147
tradition. *See also* Catholic tradition
    concept of, 1, 24–25
    idea of as invention of Pharisees, 24
    image of, 3, 24
    reform of, 23–25
Truth Overruled: The Future of Marriage and Religious Freedom (Anderson), 133

U

uniquely human, 206
uniqueness
    human uniqueness, 207, 211, 212
    use of term, 206
Unitarians, 216
United Nations
    convention on human rights of women, 72
    Convention on the Rights of the Child (1989), 132
    Covenants on Human Rights (1966), 219
    Universal Declaration of Human Rights (1948), 189, 230
United States Conference of Catholic Bishops, 124, 126–128
United States, legalization of same-sex marriage, 128–129
Universal Declaration of Human Rights (1948) (UN), 189, 230
unnatural
    church's concern for what is natural and what is unnatural, 120

Paul's use of term, 79, 122–123
    use of term, 46, 86, 120
unnatural acts, 86
unnatural birth control, 47
unnatural causes, 75
unnatural death, 75, 76
unnatural intrusions (into sexual life of people), 51
unnatural prolongation of dying, 49
US Constitution
    citizens' view of, 89
    First Amendment, 223
    Second Amendment, 90
US Supreme Court
    Burwell v. Hobby Lobby, 55, 180
    on church-state language, 223, 224
    Citizens United v. Federal Elections Commission, 180
    on legal acceptance of abortion, 68, 70
    Roe v. Wade, 53, 61–62
    on same-sex marriage, 129
Uterine Regulator, 60

V

Vatican I, 18, 19. *See also* First Vatican Council
Vatican II. *See also* Second Vatican Council
    Constitution on Divine Revelation, 160, 161
    as an event, 153
    language of reforms that started at, 28
    as lifting constraint upon questioning, 225
    limitations of, 215
    on marriage, 130
    preparation for, 152
    Rahner's influence on, 161
Veritatis Splendor, 233n1
Vietnam memorial (Washington, DC), 109

Vietnam War, Catholics on US part
in, 146
violence
abortion and, 62, 144
bishops' concern with, 144
in care of the dying, 98
Catholic tradition's tension
between condemnation of and
grappling with reality of force,
violence, and war, 136
church's checkered history of, 150
do violence to no one, 45, 56, 92,
97–98, 197, 207
Pax Christi USA's opposition
to, 149
protests by church against, 12,
63, 136
what to do if violence is
unavoidable, 46, 92, 138, 140

W

wakes, 110
war
just way theory, 140, 141, 142,
143, 147
opposition to, 141, 145, 146, 149,
150, 187. *See also* Berrigan,
Daniel; Day, Dorothy;
Merton, Thomas
Second Vatican Council
condemnation of total war,
143, 147

Weber, Max, 138, 181
welcome/thank, as language of
teaching, 37, 39
*When Bad Things Happen to Good
People* (Kushner), 110
White, Lynn, Jr., 200, 201, 203,
205, 208
Wilson, Edward O., 209–210
Wittgenstein, Ludwig, 235n3, 235n8
women
attitude to abortion, 61
birth control pill and, 48
on birth control commission, 52–53
care, writing on, 91
environmental movement and, 209
equality, 4, 132
human rights of, 189, 192
marriage and, 130
ordination of, 4, 234
professional, 61
religious, use of term, 6
suffrage movement, 144
U.N. Convention on, 72
voices of, 79
World War II, Catholics on US part
in, 145

Z

Zahn, Gordon, 147

CPSIA information can be obtained
at www.ICGtesting.com
Printed in the USA
LVHW022337280822
727058LV00021B/252

9 781491 784419